Learn OpenCV with Python by Examples

Second Edition

Implement Computer Vision Algorithms Provided by OpenCV with Python for Image Processing, Object Detection and Machine Learning

James Chen

Preface

In recent years, the field of Computer Vision has experienced a rapid growth and has become an essential part of many industries. The ability to extract meaningful information from images and videos has led to the development of innovative applications in various fields, including robotics, autonomous vehicles, medical imaging, security, and many others.

Computer Vision is a field of study that aims to enable machines to interpret and understand the visual world around us. It has become increasingly relevant in recent years, as we continue to develop more intelligent systems that can analyze and make sense of the vast amounts of visual data that we generate every day.

OpenCV is one of the most popular open-source libraries for Computer Vision and Image Processing, providing a wide range of algorithms for tasks such as image and video processing, object detection and recognition, feature extraction, and more.

Python, on the other hand, is a high-level programming language that has become one of the most popular languages for data science and machine learning communities, making it a perfect match for OpenCV.

This book is a practical guide that will help you learn the basics of computer vision using OpenCV and Python. The book is designed for anyone who wants to learn computer vision from scratch or for those who have some experience with OpenCV and want to expand their knowledge further. The book covers the fundamental concepts of image processing and computer vision and introduces the key algorithms and techniques provided by OpenCV to implement them.

Through step-by-step tutorials and hands-on examples, you will learn how to use OpenCV to perform tasks such as image filtering, feature detection, segmentation, object detection, and more. In addition, the book also covers the basics of Machine Learning algorithms, such as SVM, KNN, K-means, ANN, and CNN, and demonstrates how they can be applied in image processing tasks.

The book consists of seven chapters, each of which focuses on a specific computer vision task. The chapters are organized in a logical order, starting with the basics of image processing and working up to more advanced topics such as object detection, recognition, machine learning algorithms as well as deep learning neural networks. Each chapter contains multiple examples, each of which demonstrates a particular computer vision algorithm in a step-by-step manner. The examples are written in Python, and the code is explained in detail, so even beginners can follow along easily. All codes in this book are available at Github.

By the end of this book, you will have a solid foundation in computer vision and OpenCV, and you will be able to apply these skills to a wide range of real-world problems. Whether you want to develop your own computer vision applications, work with existing computer vision systems, or simply understand how these systems work, this book is an excellent resource.

Whether you are a student, a hobbyist, or a professional in the field, this book will help you gain a comprehensive understanding of OpenCV with Python and provide you with the necessary skills to implement advanced computer vision applications. I hope that this book will be a useful resource for you and that you will enjoy learning OpenCV with Python through practical examples.

Table of Contents

1. Introduction

1.1 What Is Computer Vision and OpenCV

Computer vision is an interdisciplinary field that focuses on enabling machines to interpret and understand visual data from the world around us. It involves the development of algorithms, techniques, and technologies that can analyze images and videos, recognize patterns, and extract useful information from visual data.

Computer vision has a wide range of applications, including autonomous vehicles, robotics, medical imaging, security and surveillance, and even entertainment. For example, computer vision algorithms can be used to detect objects in real-time video streams, recognize faces in images, and even help doctors diagnose medical conditions from medical imaging data.

To achieve these tasks, computer vision algorithms use a combination of techniques from various fields, such as image processing, machine learning, deep learning and artificial intelligence. Image processing techniques involve operations such as filtering, edge detection, and segmentation and so on, which help to preprocess and enhance visual data. Machine learning techniques, on the other hand, allow computer vision systems to learn patterns from large datasets and make predictions based on those patterns.

5

Overall, computer vision is a rapidly evolving field that holds great promise for the development of intelligent systems that can perceive and understand the world around us.

OpenCV, on the other hand, is a popular open-source computer vision library that provides a vast range of tools and algorithms for image and video processing. It is originally written in C++, but has interfaces for various programming languages, including Python, Java and so on, it's a cross-platform library, although this book will focus only on Python. OpenCV is designed to be fast and efficient, making it an ideal choice for real-time computer vision applications, and it has become a standard tool for many computer vision projects.

OpenCV is used for image and video processing, object detection, as well as machine learning. The library comes with many built-in mathematical algorithms and is fast enough for real-time video processing. Today it's widely used for resolving the related problems. Reference the official document for more information at below link,

https://docs.opencv.org/4.7.0/d1/dfb/intro.html

OpenCV's versatility and powerful set of tools make it a popular choice for a wide range of computer vision applications in various industries, including healthcare, automotive, security, entertainment, and more. It has a wide range of applications in today's world, which include but not limited to:

- Object detection and recognition: OpenCV can be used to detect and recognize objects in images and videos, allowing for applications such as security and surveillance systems.
- Facial recognition: OpenCV has powerful facial recognition capabilities, which can be used in applications such as biometric authentication and identity verification.
- Optical character recognition (OCR): OpenCV can be used to recognize text in images, making it a useful tool for applications such as document scanning and image-to-text conversion.
- Video processing: OpenCV can be used for real-time video processing applications, such as video stabilization and object tracking.

- Medical imaging: OpenCV can be used to process and analyze medical images, allowing for applications such as diagnosis and treatment planning.
- Robotics: OpenCV can be used in robotics applications for tasks such as object detection and tracking, as well as navigation and mapping.
- Augmented reality: OpenCV can be used to create augmented reality applications, such as virtual try-on applications for fashion and beauty products.

Python is a high-level programming language that has gained immense popularity in recent years, particularly in the data science and machine learning communities. It has a simple and easy-to-learn syntax, making it an ideal language for beginners, while also being a powerful tool for experienced developers. Python's popularity has led to the development of a vast range of libraries and frameworks, making it an excellent choice for a wide range of applications.

Python and OpenCV together form a powerful combination for computer vision projects. Python provides an easy-to-learn language that is great for prototyping and experimenting with ideas, while OpenCV provides a comprehensive set of tools for image and video processing. Python's integration with OpenCV makes it easy to write computer vision applications in a high-level language, allowing developers to quickly build and test their ideas.

Python and OpenCV are two essential tools for anyone interested in computer vision. Python's ease-of-use and flexibility, combined with OpenCV's powerful set of tools and algorithms, make it a go-to choice for many computer vision projects.

Then what you will learn from this book with OpenCV combined with Python?

- Read, show and save images.
- Read and show videos or webcam videos with the specific libraries.
- User interaction such as keyboard or mouse operations.
- Draw texts and shapes such as circles, rectangles, triangles, etc.

- Detection of colors and shapes from images, such as circles, rectangles, triangles, etc.
- Detection of faces, eyes and human from images or videos.
- Text recognition in images.
- Modify image quality or colors, e.g. blur, warp transform, blend, resize, adjust colors, etc.
- Machine learning methods, including K-Means, K-Nearest Neighbors, Support Vector Machines, Artificial Neural Networks and Convolutional Neural Networks.

The benefits of using OpenCV,

- Open source and free, easy and simple to learn.
- Fast for processing, especially used for video processing, for example detect objects from videos.
- Offers over 2,500 mathematical algorithms, they are efficient enough not only for image but also for video and real-time processing.
- The algorithms and functions are designed to take advantage of hardware acceleration and multi-core systems.

1.2   Target Audients of This Book

This book is written for anyone interested in learning computer vision using the Python programming language. The book is suitable for readers with any level of programming skills, from those with very limited knowledge of computer vision to the experienced ones, as it covers the basics of both Python programming and OpenCV from the ground up.

For beginners, the book begins with the step-by-step instructions for installation and setup of OpenCV, so readers can get started quickly and easily. It introduces Python from simplest statements to object-oriented classes, and begins with a hello world example. It also covers the fundamentals of computer vision, including basic image processing techniques such as pixels, color spaces with BGR and HSV, and conversion between them. It's a plus if the readers have some basic level of programming skills with any languages, but don't need to have previous experiences of Python and/or OpenCV.

For more experienced readers, the book covers more advanced topics such as object detection, facial recognition, as well as machine learning and deep learning with neural networks. The book includes numerous examples with practical and hands-on projects to help readers understand the concepts and techniques of OpenCV.

The book is also suitable for researchers, students, and professionals who want to expand their knowledge and skills in computer vision using OpenCV with Python. It provides a comprehensive guide for those who want to master the OpenCV library and use it for real-world applications.

In summary, this book is a valuable resource for anyone interested in computer vision and OpenCV, regardless of their programming skill level. The book covers a wide range of topics, from basic image processing techniques to advanced deep learning applications, making it an excellent choice for anyone looking to learn and apply OpenCV with Python.

1.3   Source Codes for This Book

All source codes used in this book are tested and working as of the release of this edition. The source codes are available from Github at the below link: *https://github.com/jchen8000/OpenCV*

It's suggested to use *git* to clone the source code, alternatively, you can also simply download the zip file from the above URL, and then extract the zip file to your local machine.

If you are not familiar with *git*, here is the quick get-started guide. Feel free to skip and go to the next section if you are familiar with it.

- Download *Git for Windows* at *https://git-scm.com/downloads*

- It has download links for Windows, macOS and Linux/Unix, simply click the one for your machine, and then download the latest version.
- Launch the downloaded installer and follow the on-screen instructions to install it.
- *Git* is a command line tool, open a cmd window, create a folder/directory say `OpenCV`, and clone the Github repository to the local machine by running the following command,

```
mkdir opencv
cd opencv
git clone https://github.com/jchen8000/OpenCV.git
```

- The source code will be downloaded to the folder/directory.

Now the source codes are downloaded to the local machine, after the installations of Python and OpenCV are completed as described in Chapter 2, you will be able to use the PyCharm (an integrated development environment for Python) to open the source codes from this folder.

1.4   Hardware Requirements and Software Versions

Below table shows the versions of OpenCV and Python as well as the libraries used in this book:

Software or Libraries	Version
Python	3.10
OpenCV	4.7.0
PyCharm	2022.3.2 (Community Edition)
numpy	1.24.2
keras & tensorflow	2.11.0
scikit-learn	1.2.2
matplotlib	3.7.1

The hardware requirements for PyCharm to run Python and OpenCV:

Hardware	Minimum	Recommended
RAM	4 GB of free RAM	8 GB of total RAM
CPU	Any modern CPU	Multi-core CPU
Disk space	3.5 GB free space	5 GB of free space
Monitor resolution	1024 x 768	1920 × 1080
Operating system	Microsoft Windows 8 or later macOS 10.13 or later Any Linux distribution that supports Gnome, KDE, or Unity DE.	Latest 64-bit version of Windows, macOS, or Linux (for example, Debian, Ubuntu, or RHEL)

Reference the PyCharm document for the details of system requirements at the below link:

https://www.jetbrains.com/help/pycharm/installation-guide.html#requirements

1.5   How This Book Is Organized

In order for beginners to get started, this book begins with some basics such as step-by-step installation and setup, if you have experiences and already known how to do it, please feel free to skip the chapters or sections.

Chapter 2 is to go through the installation process for Python and OpenCV, it also has instructions on how to install Python libraries. PyCharm, an integrated development environment, is used throughout this book. In the later chapters, we will need to install some other libraries to perform actions such as machine learning and neural networks.

Chapter 3 introduces OpenCV basics such as loading and displaying images, videos and webcams, drawing text and shapes like lines, circles and rectangles, etc. The image fundamentals will also be introduced in this chapter, like pixels and color spaces of BGR and HSV.

Chapter 4 is to explain the user interactions like keyboard and mouse operations.

Chapter 5 introduces some common methods for image processing, such as color modification, blur, blend and warp images. The concept of the histogram is also introduced in this chapter, and how to use the histograms in image processing.

Chapter 6 is to introduce object detection, shape (circle, rectangle, etc.) detection, color detection, text recognition, human detection, face and eye detection etc. We also explain two common image processing practices by examples, removing and blurring the backgrounds.

Chapter 7 is to introduce the machine learning features provided by OpenCV, including several widely used machine learning methods like K-Means Clustering, K-Nearest Neighbors, Support Vector Machines, Artificial Neural Networks as well as Convolutional Neural Networks.

There are mathematical algorithms behind the scenes for image processing and machine learning, this book will not focus on those mathematical stuffs, instead we will focus on how to use them via OpenCV with Python, although sometimes we explain some algorithms in very simple terms, but not deep-dive into details.

It's highly recommended to set up an environment on your PC to practice and execute the example source codes. There are many images throughout this book, which are the results of the execution of the codes. However, the images in this book are for reference only. You will be able to see the color images from the execution of the source codes on the environments of your PC.

All right, enjoy the wonderful world of Computer Vision!

2. Installation

This chapter will prepare for using OpenCV and Python. The first thing is to install Python and an Integrated Development Environment (IDE) if you do not have them already. After the installation is completed, need to install the OpenCV and other required packages on the IDE environment, and then we will create our first projects.

Python version 3.10 is used throughout this book, and PyCharm community edition is used as the Integrated Development Environment (IDE). Section 2.1 explains the details of installing Python and PyCharm.

For users who prefer Linux operating systems, the details of installation on Ubuntu will be explained in section 2.2.

Section 2.3 explains the installation of OpenCV and configuration of PyCharm, and a Hello OpenCV code to verify that the installation is successful.

Enjoy the installation of OpenCV and Python.

2.1   Install on Windows

2.1.1   Install Python on Windows 10

This section explains the installation of Python on Windows. Go to the Python website at *https://www.python.org/downloads/*, there is a list of available Python versions for download, look something like Figure 2-1, this is the available Python versions as of this writing, it could be different in the future when more are released.

Release Version	Release date	Download	Click for more
Python 3.10.10	Feb. 8, 2023	Download	Release Notes
Python 3.11.2	Feb. 8, 2023	Download	Release Notes
Python 3.11.1	Dec. 6, 2022	Download	Release Notes
Python 3.10.9	Dec. 6, 2022	Download	Release Notes
Python 3.9.16	Dec. 6, 2022	Download	Release Notes
Python 3.8.16	Dec. 6, 2022	Download	Release Notes
Python 3.7.16	Dec. 6, 2022	Download	Release Notes
Python 3.11.0	Oct. 24, 2022	Download	Release Notes
Python 3.9.15	Oct. 11, 2022	Download	Release Notes
Python 3.8.15	Oct. 11, 2022	Download	Release Notes
...	...	...	...

Figure 2-1 List of Python Versions for Download

It's not recommended to install the latest version, because a number of Python packages are used in this book, each package supports up to a specific Python version, some of them are not yet available to support the latest Python version. Here we use Python 3.10.x for this book.

Click *Download* from the webpage above and go to the next page, there is a list of available download files for different Operation Systems, which looks something like similar to Figure 2-2:

Version	Operating System	Description	MD5 Sum	File Size
Gzipped source tarball	Source release		25eb3686...	26044345
XZ compressed source tarball	Source release		dc8c0f27...	19612112
macOS 64-bit universal2 installer	macOS	macOS 10.9 and later	616554b1...	40930111

Windows embeddable package (32-bit)	Windows		8afb62c3...	7629980
Windows embeddable package (64-bit)	Windows		c02aded2...	8601296
Windows help file	Windows		e3edf06b...	9384836
Windows installer (32-bit)	Windows		1a9f5825...	27827240
Windows installer (64-bit)	Windows	Recommended	dce578fe...	28980224

Figure 2-2 List of Operation Systems for Python Installer

Download the one for your operation system, save and run the file. If you are using Windows and Mac OS, the installer files can be downloaded from here. If you are using Linux, we will explain how to install it on Ubuntu in the next section.

Run the downloaded installer file, it's pretty much straightforward although it will take several minutes. After installation is completed successfully, verify the Python on your system. Start a cmd command by clicking on Start icon of Windows and type "cmd" and hit return.

Type the following command in the cmd window:

```
python --version
```

The result should be shown something as below,

```
C:\>python --version
Python 3.10.5
```

The displayed is the version just installed, this indicates that the Python is correctly installed.

Please note, as long as the version is 3.10.x, it should be OK, it doesn't have to match the last number after the second dot.

2.1.2   PyCharm, the Integrated Development Environment

The next is to install PyCharm -- the Integrated Development Environment (IDE) for Python, which is used to write, edit, run and debug the Python codes. PyCharm is a very popular cross-platform Python IDE, it comes with rich features like integrated unit testing and Python debugger, error highlighting, code analysis and so on.

PyCharm has two versions: Community and Professional, the former is open-source and free for Python developers; the latter is paid edition and comes with more features. The free community version is good for this book.

Go to *https://www.jetbrains.com/pycharm/download* and click the *Download* button under Community. After the installer file is downloaded, run it and follow the on-screen instructions to install it.

It's straightforward to execute the installation process until completion. After the installation is completed, the PyCharm is available on your Windows system.

2.2   Install Python on Ubuntu

2.2.1   Install Python on Ubuntu

This section explains the installation of Python on a Linux system, specifically Ubuntu 22.04. As a prerequisite to installing Python, a root user or a user with sudo access is required.

Installing Python on Ubuntu with the *apt* tool is a simple and straightforward process, *apt* (Advanced Packaging Tool) is a command-line tool used in Ubuntu and other Debian-based Linux to manage packages, which are pre-compiled software packages that can be easily installed, updated, and removed on a Linux system. It provides a simple and easy-to-use interface for searching, installing, and removing packages. It also allows users to update the package list, upgrade the system to the latest, and manage software repositories.

Here is the step-by-step guide:

1.   Start Ubuntu 22.04, login as a root user or a user with sudo privilege, and open a new Terminal window, run the following command to update and upgrade the system to ensure it's up-to-date:

```
$ sudo apt update && sudo apt upgrade
```

2. Install the prerequisites for Python by executing the following command:

    ```
    $ sudo apt install software-properties-common
    ```

3. Next, it's recommended to install the *deadsnakes PPA* to the sources list, which makes it possible to install multiple Python versions side by side on the Ubuntu system. So instead of only having Python 3.10 on the system, Python 3.9, 3.8, or 3.7 can also be installed on the same system simultaneously. See more details about *deadsnakes PPA* at *https://tooling.bennuttall.com/ deadsnakes/*. Execute the following command to install it,

    ```
    $ sudo add-apt-repository ppa:deadsnakes/ppa
    ```

    When prompted press Enter to continue:

    ```
    Press [ENTER] to continue or Ctrl-c to cancel
    adding it.
    ```

4. When completed, run the following command to update again to refresh the newly installed PPA, and then install Python 3.10:

    ```
    $ sudo apt update
    $ sudo apt install python3.10
    ```

5. After the above execution is completed successfully, Python 3.10 should be installed on the Ubuntu system and ready to use. Now verify it by typing the following command to show the version of installed Python:

    ```
    $ python3.10 –version
    ```

    The output is displayed below,

    ```
    Python 3.10.5
    ```

It indicates the Python is successfully installed on the system.

2.2.2 Install PyCharm on Ubuntu

PyCharm is a cross-platform tool and is also available on Linux. This section describes how to install it on the Ubuntu system.

It's very simple and straightforward to install it by Ubuntu command line:

```
$ sudo snap install pycharm-community –classic
```

All done. After the installation process is completed, the PyCharm can be launched by the following command:

```
$ pycharm-community
```

2.3   Configure PyCharm and Install OpenCV

2.3.1   Create a New Python Project

Start PyCharm and Create a New Project.

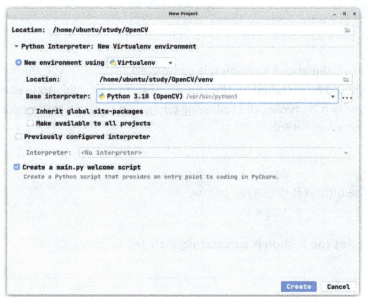

Figure 2-3 PyCharm -- Create a New Project

Explanations:

Location	Specify a local folder for the new project. All the project files will be stored in this folder.
New environment using	Leave it as default -- Virtualenv
Location	This will be automatically changed based on the Location above, it specifies the location for Python environment settings.
Base interpreter	Make sure it is using Python 3.10 which is installed in previous sections. This version will be used throughout this book.
Create a main.py welcome script	It doesn't matter if it's selected or not. If it's selected a main.py file will be automatically created together with the creation of the project.

After the parameters are set correctly, click *Create* button at the bottom to create the project.

2.3.2   Install and Upgrade OpenCV and Libraries

All libraries including OpenCV can be installed from within PyCharm after a project is created.

Select File -> Settings, the Settings screen is displayed,

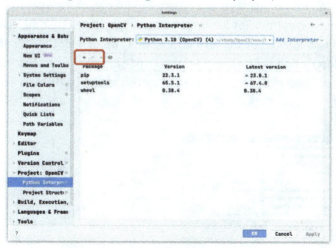

Figure 2-4 PyCharm -- Project Settings

19

The project name *OpenCV* is the one we just created in the last step, so in the left-side navigation panel it shows *Project: OpenCV* as Figure 2-4. If you name the project differently, it will show *"Project: [your project name]"*. Then select *"Python Interpreter"* under it.

In the right-side panel, the *Python Interpreter* should show the Python version we have installed in the previous section. If there are multiple Python versions on the system, they will appear in the dropdown list.

In the middle of the right-side panel in Figure 2-4, all packages are listed and available to this environment. If select different interpreters, if any, from dropdown list, a different set of available packages will appear in the package list area. The required packages can be installed from here.

There are +, − and triangle icons are shown at the top of the package list, as highlighted in Figure 2-4, + icon is to install new packages, − icon is to remove packages from the list, triangle icon is to upgrade existing packages.

In the package list in Figure 2-4, *pip* is an existing package, it's current version is 22.3.1, but the latest version is 23.0.1, so there is a triangle in front of the latest version number meaning a upgrade is available. To upgrade it, simply select the *pip* row and click the triangle icons at the top, it will upgrade it.

In order to install OpenCV, click the + icon at the top, the *Available Packages* screen is displayed as Figure 2-5 below, in the search bar enter *"opencv-python"* as keyword, a list of packages that included the keyword is displayed at the left-side. Select *"opencv-python"* from the list, its description is displayed on the right-side of the screen, including its version. Then click *Install Package* button at the bottom to install it.

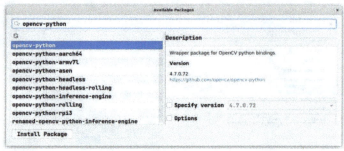

Figure 2-5 PyCharm -- Available Packages

Waiting for the message showing *"Package 'opencv-python' installed successfully"*. Then go back to the Settings window, *opencv-python* is shown in the list which indicates that it is installed, at the same time another package called *numpy* is also installed, as shown in Figure 2-6 below.

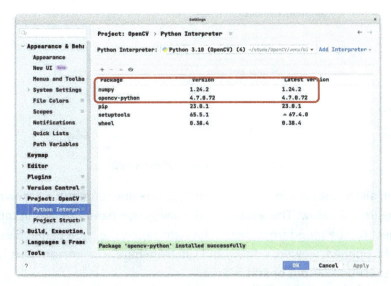

Figure 2-6 Pycharm -- Packages Installed and Upgraded

In the highlighted area in Figure 2-6 both *numpy* and *opencv-python* are installed. And *pip* is also upgraded to the latest version.

If for some reason *numpy* is not installed, you will need to do the same as above to install it, because it will be used in this book.

Then, close the Settings window by clicking OK button. An empty project is successfully created and required packages are installed.

2.3.3   Load the Project Files

Alternatively, instead of creating a brand-new project with PyCharm, you can download or clone the Git repository as described in section 1.3. After the source codes are available in the local machine, use PyCharm to open the project.

Launch PyCharm, in the *"Welcome to PyCharm"* screen, click *"Open"* button, select the folder of the source codes you have downloaded or cloned, then click *"OK"* to open the project files, as shown in Figure 2-7.

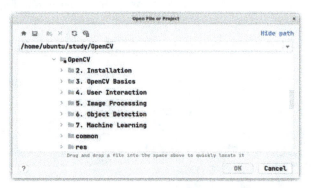

Figure 2-7 Pycharm -- Open a Project

Then, all the files are loaded into the PyCharm environment, as shown in Figure 2-8 below. The left side is the navigation panel, all files in this project can be found from there. The right side is the code panel, files can be opened, viewed, edited, and run from here. The bottom part is the execution output or status area.

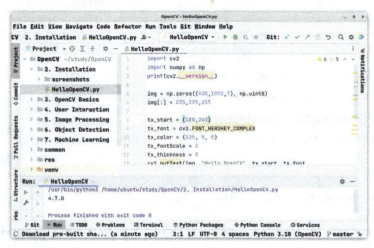

Figure 2-8 Pycharm IDE Screen

Before running the codes, make sure the correct *Python Interpreter* is selected and the required packages are available and upgraded to the latest versions, as described in the previous section 2.3.2.

Please reference the Pycharm Get-Started Guide at *https://www.jetbrains.com/help/pycharm/quick-start-guide.html* if you want to be more familiar with the IDE.

The source codes are organized in a way that corresponds to the chapters of this book; all the files are grouped by chapters. For example, all the source codes for chapter 3 are under the folder called "*3. OpenCV Basics*"; the source codes for chapter 4 are in the folder called "*4. User Interaction*", and so on.

All resource files like image or video files are in the *res* folder, and all common files are in the *common* folder.

2.3.4   Hello OpenCV

```
Source:        HelloOpenCV.py
```

Now let's try a very simple program to make sure the installation is appropriately completed. The source code file is called *HelloOpenCV.py* in "2. Installation" folder. From the left navigation panel, browse the files for this project, navigate to "*2. Installation*" and find "*HelloOpenCV.py*", double click it. It is opened in the right-side panel.

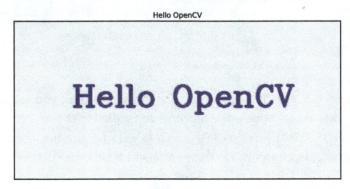

Figure 2-9 Hello OpenCV

To run the code, either click on the green arrow in the top right-hand corner of the PyCharm window or right-click on the Python file panel, in the popup menu, select *Run 'HelloOpenCV'* to execute the codes. The result is shown as Figure 2-9,

With this result displayed, you have everything needed for OpenCV and Python. Press any key to close it and finish the execution.

Alternatively, if you want to practice it on your own without using our source codes from Github repository, then you can start with a new project as described in previous sections 2.3.1 and 2.3.2.

Then create a new Python file by selecting File -> New... -> Python File, and give a new file name, e.g. *HelloOpenCV.py*. Then copy and paste the below codes into the right panel coding area, to run the code, either click on the green arrow in the top right-hand corner of the PyCharm window or right-click on the Python file and select "Run."

```python
1   import cv2
2   import numpy as np
3   img = np.zeros((320,640,3), np.uint8)
4   img[:] = 125,125,125
5
6   tx_start = (80,160)
7   tx_font = cv2.FONT_HERSHEY_COMPLEX
8   tx_color = (255, 255, 0)
9   tx_fontScale = 2
10  tx_thickness = 2
11  cv2.putText(img, "Hello OpenCV", tx_start, tx_font,
12              tx_fontScale, tx_color, tx_thickness)
13  cv2.imshow("Hello", img)
14  cv2.waitKey(0)
15  cv2.destroyAllWindows()
```

If you have not already configured a Python interpreter, you will be prompted to do so. Follow the prompts to configure an interpreter, and make sure the right version of Python is selected. Once the interpreter is configured, PyCharm will run the code and display the output, which is the same result in Figure 2-9. Then Press any key to close it and finish the execution. Congratulations, you are ready to go!

3. OpenCV Basics

This chapter will introduce some basic operations supported by OpenCV, such as opening image or video files and displaying them, converting color images to grayscale, or black-white images, connecting to a webcam of a laptop and showing the videos captured by it. This chapter will also introduce the fundamentals of digital images, like pixels, and color spaces.

Section 3.1 is to load and display a color image and a grayscale image.

Section 3.2 is to load and display videos. Section 3.3 to connect a webcam of the laptop and show it.

Section 3.4 is to explain the fundamentals of images including the pixels and color spaces.

Section 3.5 is to draw shapes including lines, rectangles, circles, ellipses and polylines. And section 3.6 to draw texts.

In section 3.7, we will apply the knowledge learned in this chapter to draw a graph that is similar to the OpenCV icon.

Enjoy the OpenCV basics.

3.1 Load and Display Images

> Source: ShowImage.py

After the PyCharm IDE is successfully installed and configured to use Python with OpenCV, now we are going to load an image and display it.

3.1.1 Load Color Images

In PyCharm, if you have the Github project loaded, then click on the *ShowImage.py* file, the image file is located in the *res* folder called *flower004.jpg*.

Alternatively, if you do not use the source files in the Github repository, create a new Python file called *ShowImage.py*, or whatever you like, copy and paste the following codes, and make sure you have your image file in your PyCharm project folder and correctly point to it.

```python
1  import cv2
2  img = cv2.imread("../res/flower004.jpg")
3  cv2.imshow("Image", img)
4  cv2.waitKey(0)
5  cv2.destroyAllWindows()
```

Explanations:

Line 1	`import cv2` *tells the Python to include the* `cv2` *(OpenCV) library. Every time when using OpenCV, must import the* `cv2` *package. This is typically always the first statement in the code file.*
Line 2	`cv2.imread()` *is the function to load an image, the image file path is specified in the argument.*
Line 3	`cv2.imshow()` *is the function to show the image. The first argument is the title of the window that displays the image, the second argument is the image that returned from* `cv2.imread()` *function.*
Line 4	*Wait for a keystroke. If do not wait for a keystroke, the* `cv2.imshow()` *will display the window and go to the next*

	immediately, the execution will complete and the window will disappear, this happens very quickly so you can hardly see the result. So `cv2.waitKey()` *is typically added here to wait for a user to press a key.*
Line 5	*Destroy all windows before the execution completes.*

Run the code, the loaded image is displayed, as shown in Figure 3-1:

Figure 3-1 Show Color Image

Please note, all images included in this book are for reference only, they might not be the same as the results of executing the codes, it's highly recommended to set up the working environment on your PC. You will be able to see the actual images on the screen by executing the codes.

`cv2.imread()` is an OpenCV function used to load the image from a file, here is its syntax:

Syntax	*cv2.imread(path, flag)*
Parameters	**path:** *The path of the image to be read.* **flag:** *Specifies how to read the image, the default value is cv2.IMREAD_COLOR.*

	cv2.IMREAD_COLOR: *Load a color image. Any transparency of the image will be neglected. It is the default flag. You can also use 1 for this flag.* **cv2.IMREAD_GRAYSCALE:** *Load an image in grayscale mode. You can also use **0** for this flag.* **cv2.IMREAD_UNCHANGED:** *Load an image as such including alpha channel. You can use **-1** for this flag.*
Return Value	*The image that is loaded from the image file specified in the* `path` *parameter*

3.1.2   Load Grayscale Images

Now let's load this image file in grayscale mode and display it.

Figure 3-2 Show Grayscale Image

Just simply replace the line 2 in above codes with the following, it tells the `cv2.imread()` to load image in grayscale mode.

```
2   img = cv2.imread("../res/flower004.jpg",
                    cv2.IMREAD_GRAYSCALE)
```

Execute the code and the grayscale image is shown as Figure 3-2.

3.1.3 Convert Color Image to Grayscale

An alternative way to have a grayscale image is to load the original image first, then use `cv2.cvtColor()` function to convert it to a grayscale image, this way we will have both original and grayscale images available for further processing. This is useful because in the future when we do the image processing, we want to process the image in grayscale mode while displaying the original color image.

Now replace the code line 2 and 3 in section 3.1.1 with the following:

```
1   img = cv2.imread("../res/flower004.jpg")
2   gray = cv2.cvtColor(img, cv2.COLOR_BGR2GRAY)
3   cv2.imshow("Image", img)
4   cv2.imshow("Image Gray", gray)
```

`cv2.cvtColor()` is an OpenCV function used to convert an image from one color space to another, here is its syntax:

Syntax	cv2.cvtColor(src, code[, dst[, dstCn]])
Parameters	src: source image to be converted. code: color space conversion code. dst: optional, the output image of the same size and depth as *src* image. dstCn: optional, the number of channels in the destination image. If the parameter is 0 then the number of the channels is derived automatically from *src* image. **cv2.COLOR_BGR2HSV/COLOR_HSV2BGR:** *Convert between BGR color image and HSV space.* **cv2.COLOR_BGR2GRAY/COLOR_GRAY2RGB:** *Convert between BGR color image and grayscale image* *Other conversion codes are not listed here, please reference OpenCV documents.*
Return Value	*The image that is converted from the source image*

Execute the codes, the color image and grayscale image are displayed side by side, as shown below.

Color Image   *Grayscale Image*

Figure 3-3 Convert a Color Image to Grayscale Image

3.2   Load and Display Videos

Source: ShowVideo.py

We were able to load and display an image, now we are going to work with videos, and see how OpenCV can process videos.

Open the *ShowVideo.py* file in PyCharm. If you are not using the Github project, then create a new Python file, and make sure you have a video file available. There is an mp4 video file called *"Sample Videos from Windows.mp4"* in the Github project, it will be loaded and displayed in this example. Below is the code,

```
1   #
2   # Show a video from local file
3   #
4   import cv2
5
```

```
6    cap = cv2.VideoCapture("../res/Sample Videos from
     Windows.mp4")

7

8    success, img = cap.read()
9    while success:
10        cv2.imshow("Video", img)
11        # Press ESC key to break the loop
12        if cv2.waitKey(15) & 0xFF == 27:
13            break
14        success, img = cap.read()
15   cap.release()
16   cv2.destroyWindow("Video")
```

Explanations:

Line 6	*Use `cv2.VideoCapture()` to load a video stream, the function returns a video capture object.*
Line 8	*Read the first frame from the video capture object, the frame image is stored in `img` variable, and the result is stored in `success` variable indicating True or False.*
Line 9-14	*Loop frame by frame until all frames in the video object are read, within the loop the image frames are processed one by one throughout the video.*
Line 10	*Use `cv2.imshow()` to display a frame. Each frame is an image.*
Line 12-13	*Wait for 15 milliseconds and accept a keystroke, if ESC key (keycode is 27) is pressed then break the loop. Changing the `cv2.waitKey()` parameter will change the speed of playing the video.*
Line 14	*Same as Line 8, load subsequent frames from the video capture object.*
Line 15	*Release the video capture object to release the memory.*
Line 16	*Close the Video window*

Execute the codes, it will load the video and play it in a window called `Video`. It will play until either the end of the video or ESC key is pressed.

The video is a sample from Windows Vista, it's located at: *https://github.com/jchen8000/OpenCV/raw/master/res/Sample%20Vid eos%20from%20Windows.mp4*.

The original video is from *https://www.youtube.com/watch?v=K1ShYerq6lg*

In Line 12 the `cv2.waitKey(15)` will wait for 15 milliseconds between each frame, changing the parameter value will change the speed of playing the video. If the parameter value is smaller then the play speed is faster, larger then slower.

Inside the loop from Line 9 to 14 you can process each image before showing it, for example you can convert each image to grayscale and display it, you will play the video in grayscale.

Replace the above Line 10 and 11 with the following two lines, it will convert the image from color to grayscale for every image frame inside the video, as a result, the video will be played in grayscale.

```
10      gray = cv2.cvtColor(img, cv2.COLOR_BGR2GRAY)
11      cv2.imshow("Video", gray)
```

Similarly, you can do other image processing inside the loop, for example recognize the people or faces and highlight them in the video. These will be explained in later this book.

3.3   Display Webcam

> Source: ShowWebcam.py

Like displaying videos, a similar technique is used to display webcam. Replace the above Line 6 with `cap = cv2.VideoCapture(0)`, it will load the laptop/desktop's default webcam and display it.

In the above section the parameter of `cv2.VideoCapture()` function was the path of the video file, now pass the index of the webcam device as parameter, here 0 is used as the default webcam, it will connect to the default webcam.

Some video properties can also be set here, as below,

```
1   import cv2
2
3   cap = cv2.VideoCapture(0)
    # read from default webcam
4
5   # Set video properties
6   cap.set(cv2.CAP_PROP_FRAME_WIDTH, 640)
    # set width
7   cap.set(cv2.CAP_PROP_FRAME_HEIGHT, 480)
    # set height
8   cap.set(cv2.CAP_PROP_BRIGHTNESS, 180)
    # set brightness
9   cap.set(cv2.CAP_PROP_CONTRAST, 50)
    # set contrast
10
11  success, img = cap.read()
12  while success:
13      cv2.imshow("Webcam", img)
14
15      # Press ESC key to break the loop
16      if cv2.waitKey(10) & 0xFF == 27:
17          break
18      success, img = cap.read()
19
20  cap.release()
21  cv2.destroyWindow("Webcam")
```

Explanation

Line 3	Load video from default Webcam.
Line 6	Set width of the camera video.
Line 7	Set height of the camera video.
Line 8	Set brightness of the camera video.
Line 9	Set contrast of the camera video.

For references, this is the list that can be used as parameter for `cap.set()`:

0	CAP_PROP_POS_MSEC	Current position of the video file in milliseconds.
1	CAP_PROP_POS_FRAMES	0-based index of the frame to be decoded/captured next.
2	CAP_PROP_POS_AVI_RATIO	Relative position of the video file
3	CAP_PROP_FRAME_WIDTH	Width of the frames in the video stream.
4	CAP_PROP_FRAME_HEIGHT	Height of the frames in the video stream.
5	CAP_PROP_FPS	Frame rate.
6	CAP_PROP_FOURCC	4-character code of codec.
7	CAP_PROP_FRAME_COUNT	Number of frames in the video file.
8	CAP_PROP_FORMAT	Format of the Mat objects returned by retrieve() .
9	CAP_PROP_MODE	Backend-specific value indicating the current capture mode.
10	CAP_PROP_BRIGHTNESS	Brightness of the image (only for cameras).
11	CAP_PROP_CONTRAST	Contrast of the image (only for cameras).
12	CAP_PROP_SATURATION	Saturation of the image (only for cameras).
13	CAP_PROP_HUE	Hue of the image (only for cameras).
14	CAP_PROP_GAIN	Gain of the image (only for cameras).
15	CAP_PROP_EXPOSURE	Exposure (only for cameras).
16	CAP_PROP_CONVERT_RGB	Boolean flags indicating whether images should be converted to RGB.
17	CAP_PROP_WHITE_BALANCE	Currently unsupported
18	CAP_PROP_RECTIFICATION	Rectification flag for stereo cameras (note: only supported by DC1394 v 2.x backend currently)

Make sure a webcam is attached to the laptop/desktop computer and enabled, execute the code you will see a window displaying whatever the webcam captures. Press ESC key to terminate.

3.4 Image Fundamentals

Source: ImageFundamental.py

3.4.1 Pixels

Pixels (short for "picture elements") are the smallest units of a digital image. Each pixel represents a tiny point of color that, when combined with other pixels, forms the complete image.

Pixels are typically arranged in a grid within a rectangle or square, with each pixel having a specific location within the image. The color of each pixel is represented by a combination of numerical values that represent the intensity of the three primary colors of blue, green, and red (BGR).

The resolution refers to the number of pixels in the image, usually expressed in terms of the width and height of the image in pixels. The higher the resolution, the more detail the image can contain, as there are more pixels available to represent the image. However, higher resolution images also require more storage space and processing power.

Typically, a digital image is made of thousands or millions of pixels, which are organized in rows and columns. For example, for an image of 640 x 480, there are a total of 307,200 pixels, and they are located in 480 rows and 640 columns. The coordinates of a pixel specify the location of the pixel, say a pixel with coordinates of (100, 100) means it is in column number of 100 and row number of 100.

Unlike a mathematics coordinate system, the digital image's coordinate of the origin (0,0) is located at the top left corner of the image. x-axis represents the columns and y-axis represents the rows.

As a color image shown in Figure 3-4, x-axis is the horizontal arrow at the top facing right, and y-axis is the vertical arrow at the very left and facing down. A pixel can be identified by a pair of integers specifying a x value (in column number) and a y value (in row number). In below Figure 3-4, the pixel at (100, 100) is identified and highlighted.

Color Image

(100, 100)
B: 151
G: 82
R:234

Figure 3-4 Pixels in a Color Image

For a 24-bit image, each pixel has 24 bits, it is made of blue, green and red values, each has 8 bits, which value is from 0 to 255. For example, the pixel at (100, 100) in above Figure 3-4 has blue value of 151, green of 82 and red of 234. The color of this pixel, shown as pink, is determined by these three values.

3.4.2 BGR Color Space and Channels

A digital image is represented in different color spaces, the color space refers to a specific way of representing colors in an image. It is a three-dimensional model that describes the range of colors that can be displayed or printed. There are several color spaces used in digital imaging, and each has a different range of colors and is used for specific purposes. Here we will introduce the BGR and HSV color spaces in this section and the next, both are commonly and widely used in image processing.

BGR stands for Blue, Green, and Red. It is a color space used to represent colors on electronic screens, like computer monitors, TVs, and smartphones. In this space, colors are represented by three primary colors: Red, Green, and Blue. Each primary color has a range of 0 to 255, meaning each color can have 256 possible values, which makes a total of 16.7 million (= $256 \times 256 \times 256$) possible colors.

Each primary color is called a channel, a channel has the same size as the original image. Therefore, an image in BGR color space has three channels, blue, green and red. Figure 3-5 shows the idea of how the three channels compose a color image.

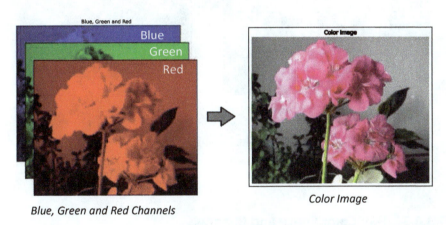

Blue, Green and Red Channels

Color Image

Figure 3-5 Blue, Green and Red Channels to Produce an Image

A single channel does not have any colors, it's a grayscale image. Because the three primary colors can build up a color, a single channel only has one value, which can only represent a grayscale, not a color.

Therefore, the above Figure 3-5 explains the concept, but not quite correct, because the blue, green and red channels are all in grayscale without colors. The above red channel is shown in red, looks like it is red, but that is not the case, it should be in grayscale. Similarly, the green and blue channels should be also in grayscale.

Figure 3-6 is the correct one, the blue, green and red channels are all in grayscale, they are mixed together to produce the color image.

Each channel is represented by an 8-bit value ranging from 0 to 255, the combination of the three primary colors at their maximum intensity (255, 255, 255) results in white, while (0, 0, 0) results in black, anything in between results in different colors. The same value in three channels, such as (125, 125, 125), represents a gray color.

Blue, Green and Red Channels   *Color Image*

Figure 3-6 Blue, Green and Red Channels to Produce an Image

3.4.3   HSV Color Space and Channels

In addition to the BGR color space, an image can also be represented by HSV (Hue, Saturation, Value) color space, also known as HSB (Hue, Saturation, Brightness), which is a cylindrical color space that describes colors based on three attributes: hue, saturation, and value/brightness, as shown in Figure 3-7. The three attributes are also represented in channels.

In the HSV color space, colors are represented as a point in a cylindrical coordinate system. The *hue* is represented by the angle on the horizontal axis, the *saturation* is represented by the radius or distance from the center, and the *value/brightness* is represented by the vertical axis.

The HSV is often used in graphics software for color selection and manipulation because it allows users to easily adjust the hue, saturation, and value/brightness of color separately. For example, changing the hue will change the color family, while changing the saturation or brightness will alter the intensity or lightness/darkness of the color.

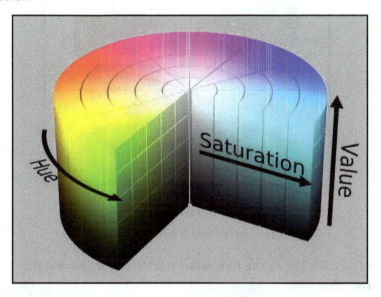

Figure 3-7 HSV Color Space

SharkD, CC BY-SA 3.0 via Wikimedia Commons
https://en.wikipedia.org/wiki/HSL_and_HSV#/media/
File:HSV_color_solid_cylinder_saturation_gray.png

Hue represents the color portion of the image, which is described as an angle on a color wheel ranging from 0 to 359 degrees. Figure 3-8 shows the color wheel, different colors are distributed around a circle with red at 0 degree, green at 120 degrees, and blue at 240 degrees. Hue value at different angles represent different colors.

Normally the hue value is from 0 to 359 representing an angle of the circle, however in OpenCV the values of hue are different, since the values are stored in an 8-bit datatype with the range of [0, 255], which can not store the entire hue value of [0, 359]. OpenCV is using a trick to resolve it, the hue value is divided by 2 and stored in the 8-bit datatype. Therefore, the hue in OpenCV is [0, 179].

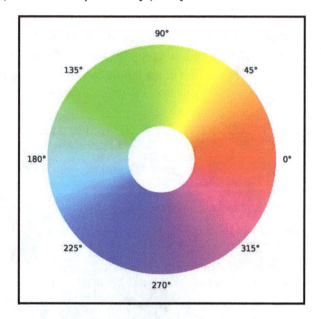

Figure 3-8 Color Wheel

Generated by source codes at common/color_wheel.py

The below table shows the Hue value at different angles and the corresponding color name and code:

Hue	Color Code	Color Name
0°	#FF0000	red
15°	#FF4000	vermilion
30°	#FF8000	orange
45°	#FFBF00	golden yellow
60°	#FFFF00	yellow
75°	#BFFF00	yellowish green
90°	#80FF00	chartreuse
105°	#40FF00	leaf green
120°	#00FF00	green
135°	#00FF40	cobalt green

150°	#00FF80	emerald green
165°	#00FFBF	bluish green
180°	#00FFFF	cyan
195°	#00BFFF	cerulean blue
210°	#0080FF	azure
225°	#0040FF	blue, cobalt blue
240°	#0000FF	blue
255°	#4000FF	hyacinth
270°	#8000FF	violet
285°	#BF00FF	purple
300°	#FF00FF	magenta
315°	#FF00BF	reddish purple
330°	#FF0080	ruby red, crimson
345°	#FF0040	carmine

The above table is from https://en.wikipedia.org/wiki/Hue

Saturation represents the intensity or purity of the color, the value is defined from 0 to 100 percent, where 0 is gray and 100 percent is the pure color. As the saturation increases the color appears to be purer, a highly saturated image is more vivid and colorful. As the saturation decreases the color appears to be faded out, a less saturated image appears towards a grayscale one.

In OpenCV, however, its value range is extended to [0, 255] instead of [0, 100].

Value/Brightness represents the overall brightness of the color, the value is defined from 0 to 100 percent, where 0 is black and 100 is the brightest level of the color. Similar to saturation, in OpenCV the range for Value/Brightness is [0, 255], instead of [0, 100].

Same as BGR channels, the HSV is also separated into three channels as well, each in grayscale. Figure 3-9 illustrates how the Hue, Saturation and Value/Brightness channels can compose a color image.

Hue, Saturation and Value Channels

Color Image

Figure 3-9 Hue, Saturation and Value Channels to Compose an Image

In summary, the HSV color space is a cylindrical color model that describes colors based on their hue, saturation, and value/brightness. It's widely used in various applications that involve color selection, manipulation, and analysis.

3.5 Draw Shapes

```
Source:     DrawShapes.py
Library:    common/Draw.py
```

In this section we will use OpenCV functions to draw the following shapes on an empty canvas,

- Lines
- Rectangles
- Circles
- Ellipses
- Polylines

3.5.1 Create an Empty Canvas

So far, the images we have used are coming from the image files, now we are going to create an empty canvas from numpy library for drawing. Remember when we installed OpenCV in section 2.3.2, *numpy* is also installed together with *opencv_python*, so it's already available to our project. If for some reason it is not installed, install it following the descriptions in section 2.3.2.

numpy is a popular Python library for numerical computing that provides a powerful multi-dimensional array object and various functions for performing mathematical operations on the arrays. It provides efficient storage and manipulation of arrays and allows for fast mathematical operations on the entire array without the need for loops. It is one of the fundamental libraries for scientific computing in Python and is widely used in fields such as data science, image processing, machine learning, and engineering.

As we know an image is made of pixels in rows and columns and channels, in another word 3-dimensional array. Therefore, numpy is good for supporting this type of operation.

Now import numpy in the beginning of the code.

```
1   import cv2
2   import numpy as np
```

Then create a canvas with the size of 480 in width and 380 in height, a canvas is an empty image. Remember a color image has three channels representing BGR color space, so the array we are going to create using *numpy* should have three dimensions – 380, 480, and 3. The datatype of the array is *uint8*, it contains 8-bit values ranging from 0 to 255.

```
3   canvas = np.zeros((380, 480, 3), np.uint8)
4
5   cv2.imshow("Canvas", canvas)
6   cv2.waitKey(0)
7   cv2.destroyAllWindows()
```

Explanation

43

| Line 3 | np.zeros () create an array that has 380 rows, 480 columns, and 3 channels corresponding to blue, green and red. np.zeros () will fill the array with all 0, as we explained earlier all 0 means a black color. |

Execute the above code, the result is a window with the black canvas with the size of 480 x 380.

Now we want to paint the canvas with some color. See line 4 in the below codes, it will set values of (235, 235, 235) to the array, which means to set a color to the canvas image, this color code is blue = 235, green = 235 and red = 235, it represents light gray.

```
4   canvas[:] = 235,235,235
```

The canvas is painted in light gray, as Figure 3-10, we will draw shapes on it. If you want to paint it with different color, simply change the values in line 4.

Canvas

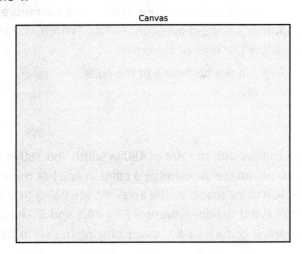

Figure 3-10 Canvas in Light Gray

3.5.2   Draw a Line

cv2.line() function is used to draw a line segment between start point and end point,

Syntax	cv.line(img, pt1, pt2, color, thickness, line_type)	
Parameters	img	The canvas image.
	pt1	Start point of the line segment.
	pt2	End point of the line segment.
	color	Line color.
	thickness	Line thickness.
	line_type	Type of the line, below are the values for line types:
		cv2.FILLED
	cv2.LINE_4	4-connected line algorithm
	cv2LINE_8	8-connected line algorithm
	cv2.LINE_AA	antialiased line algorithm

Create a function `draw_line()` to wrap the `cv2.line()` function, and set default values for `color`, `thickness` and `line_type`, when this function is invoked later don't have to specify these parameters because these default values will be used.

```
1  def draw_line(image, start, end,
2                 color=(255,255,255),
3                 thickness=1,
4                 line_type=cv2.LINE_AA):
5      cv2.line(image, start, end, color, thickness,
                 line_type)
```

Call this function to draw a line,

```
7   # Draw a line
8   draw_line(canvas,
9             start=(100, 100),
10            end=(canvas.shape[1]-100,
                  canvas.shape[0]-100),
11            color=(10, 10, 10),
```

```
12          thickness=10)
```

The result looks like Figure 3-11:

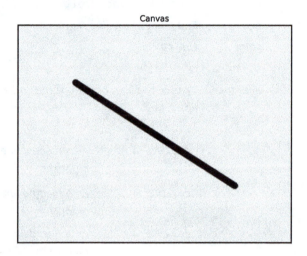

Figure 3-11 Draw a Line on the Canvas

3.5.3   Draw Rectangles, Circles, Ellipses and Polylines

Similarly draw other shapes, now begin with defining our wrapper functions for drawing shapes, like the above `draw_line()` function.

```
1   def draw_rectangle(image, top_left,
                       bottom_right,
2                      color=(255,255,255),
3                      thickness=1,
4                      line_type=cv2.LINE_AA):
5       cv2.rectangle(image, top_left,
                      bottom_right,
6                     color, thickness, line_type)
7
8   def draw_circle(image, center, radius,
9                   color=(255,255,255),
10                  thickness=1,
```

```
11                     line_type=cv2.LINE_AA):
12        cv2.circle(image, center, radius, color,
                     thickness, line_type)
13
14   def draw_ellipse(image, center, axes, angle,
                     start_angle, end_angle,
15                    color=(255,255,255),
16                    thickness=1,
17                    line_type=cv2.LINE_AA):
18        cv2.ellipse(image, center, axes, angle,
                     start_angle, end_angle,
19                    color, thickness, line_type)
20
21   def draw_polylines(image, points,
                       is_closed=True,
22                      color=(255,255,255),
23                      thickness=1,
24                      line_type=cv2.LINE_AA ):
25        cv2.polylines(image, points, is_closed,
                        color, thickness, line_type)
```

The results look like Figure 3-12:

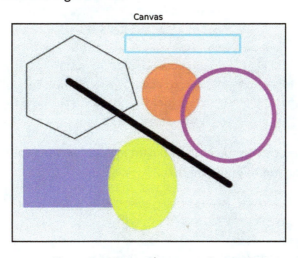

Figure 3-12 Draw Shapes on Canvas

Open *DrawShapes.py* file from the Github repository, it has all the codes to draw the shapes, execute it and the results look like Figure 3-12 above.

We don't explain the functions in the above codes one by one; they are straightforward and similar to the above `cv2.line()` function.

For details, please reference OpenCV documents for drawing functions at *https://docs.opencv.org/4.7.0/d6/d6e/group__imgproc__draw.html*

3.6   Draw Texts

> Source: DrawTexts.py
> Library: common/Draw.py

OpenCV provides functions not only for drawing shapes, but also for texts. `cv2.putText()` function is used for drawing texts.

Similarly, define a wrapper function `draw_text()`:

```
1   def draw_text(image, text, org,
2                   font_face=cv2.FONT_HERSHEY_COMPLEX,
3                   font_scale=1,
4                   color=(255,255,255),
5                   thickness=1,
6                   line_type=cv2.LINE_AA):
7       cv2.putText(image, text, org, font_face,
8                   font_scale, color, thickness,
                    line_type )
```

Then create a canvas, paint it with light gray color, then call `draw_text()` function to draw the texts.

```
10  canvas = np.zeros((380, 480, 3), np.uint8)
11  canvas[:] = 235,235,235
12  #Draw a text
13  draw_text(canvas, "Hello OpenCV", (50, 100),
14              color=(125, 0, 0),
```

```
15                  font_scale=1.5,
16                  thickness=2)
17   cv2.imshow("Hello OpenCV", canvas)
18   cv2.waitKey(0)
19   cv2.destroyAllWindows()
```

The result is shown as Figure 3-13:

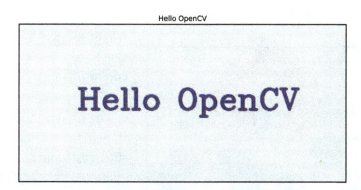

Figure 3-13 Draw Texts on Canvas

This version of OpenCV supports a limited set of fonts, below table shows the supported fonts.

Font Code	Description
FONT_HERSHEY_SIMPLEX	normal size sans-serif font
FONT_HERSHEY_PLAIN	small size sans-serif font
FONT_HERSHEY_DUPLEX	normal size sans-serif font (more complex than FONT_HERSHEY_SIMPLEX)
FONT_HERSHEY_COMPLEX	normal size serif font
FONT_HERSHEY_TRIPLEX	normal size serif font (more complex than FONT_HERSHEY_COMPLEX)
FONT_HERSHEY_COMPLEX_SMALL	smaller version of FONT_HERSHEY_COMPLEX
FONT_HERSHEY_SCRIPT_SIMPLEX	hand-writing style font
FONT_HERSHEY_SCRIPT_COMPLEX	more complex variant of FONT_HERSHEY_SCRIPT_SIMPLEX
FONT_ITALIC	flag for italic font

Reference OpenCV documents for more details at
https://docs.opencv.org/4.7.0/d6/d6e/group__imgproc__draw.html.

3.7 Draw an OpenCV-like Icon

```
Source:      DrawTexts.py
Library:     common/Draw.py
```

Now let's use our wrapper functions to draw a complicated image, not exactly the same but similar to the OpenCV Icon, like Figure 3-14.

Canvas

Figure 3-14 OpenCV-like Icon

A light-gray colored empty canvas of size 360 x 320 is created, same as above.

`cv2.ellipse()` function will be used to draw the three non-closed circles, a start angle and an end angle can be specified for the ellipse.

`cv2.putText()` function will be used to draw the texts at the bottom.

Below are the code snippets, the axes of the ellipse are defined as (50, 50) so it appears as a circle instead of an ellipse. The center of the three circles and the start and end angles of each are defined based on the position of the OpenCV-like icon.

```
1  def draw_opencv_icon(image):
2      axes = (50, 50)
3      center_top_circle = (160, 70)
4      center_lowerleft_circle = (
            center_top_circle[0]-80,
5            center_top_circle[1]+120 )
6      center_lowerright_circle = (
            center_top_circle[0]+80,
7            center_top_circle[1]+120 )
```

```
8          angle_top_circle = 90
9          angle_lowerleft_circle = -45
10         angle_lowerright_circle = -90
11         start_angle = 40
12         end_angle = 320
13         draw_ellipse(image,center_top_circle,
                       axes,
14                     angle_top_circle,
                       start_angle, end_angle,
15                     color=(0, 0, 255),
16                     thickness=40)
17         draw_ellipse(image,
                       center_lowerleft_circle,
                       axes,
18                     angle_lowerleft_circle,
                       start_angle, end_angle,
19                     color=(0, 255, 0),
20                     thickness=40)
21         draw_ellipse(image,
                       center_lowerright_circle,
                       axes,
22                     angle_lowerright_circle,
                       start_angle, end_angle,
23                     color=(255, 0, 0),
24                     thickness=40)
25         draw_text(image, "OpenCV", (10,330),
                     color=(0,0,0),
26                   font_scale=2.4, thickness=5)
27
28 if __name__ == '__main__':
29     canvas = np.zeros((360,320,3), np.uint8)
30     canvas[:] = 235,235,235
31     draw_opencv_icon(canvas)
32     cv2.imshow("Canvas", canvas)
33     cv2.waitKey(0)
34     cv2.destroyAllWindows()
```

Execute the code, the result is shown in Figure 3-14.

4. User Interaction

O penCV provides functions that allow users to interact with images and videos in various ways. In previous sections `cv2.waitKey()` function has been used to accept user input from the keyboard and the ESC key can be detected by checking the key code returned by the function. And `cv2.destroy AllWindows()` function closes all the windows that were created using the `cv2.imshow()`. These are very simple user interaction functions.

In addition, OpenCV provides several other functions for user interaction, this chapter will introduce some commonly used ones.

Section 4.1 introduces the mouse operations, and how to use the callback function to capture the mouse events.

Section 4.2 uses the mouse to draw circles, and section 4.3 to draw polygons. Section 4.4 uses the mouse to specify a rectangle to crop the image.

Section 4.5 introduces the trackbars, or sliders, for users to input values.

The important thing for user interaction is the *callback* functions, they are used by almost all user operation events. This chapter explains how the callback functions are defined and used with Python.

Enjoy the User Interaction with OpenCV and Python.

4.1 Mouse Operations

```
Source:     Mouse.py
Library:    common/Draw.py
```

OpenCV provides a facility to control and manage a variety of mouse events, and it provides the flexibility for programmers to manipulate user interactions. It can capture the events generated by mouse operations, such as left-button-down, right-button-down, mouse-move and double-click etc. The callback functions can be used to capture these mouse events.

Below code snippets will print out the list of all mouse events that OpenCV supports:

```
1   import cv2
2
3   for event in dir(cv2):
4   if "EVENT" in event:
5           print(event)
```

It displays a list of mouse events which is outlined in below table:

EVENT_FLAG_ALTKEY	When the ALT key is pressed.
EVENT_FLAG_CTRLKEY	When the CTRL key is pressed.
EVENT_FLAG_LBUTTON	When the left mouse button is down.
EVENT_FLAG_MBUTTON	When the middle mouse button is down.
EVENT_FLAG_RBUTTON	When the right mouse button is down.
EVENT_FLAG_SHIFTKEY	When the SHIFT key is pressed.
EVENT_LBUTTONDBLCLK	When the left button is double-clicked.
EVENT_LBUTTONDOWN	When the left button is clicked.
EVENT_LBUTTONUP	When the left button is released.
EVENT_MBUTTONDBLCLK	When the middle button is double-clicked.

EVENT_MBUTTONDOWN	When the middle button is clicked.
EVENT_MBUTTONUP	When the middle button is released.
EVENT_MOUSEHWHEEL	When a horizontal scroll is executed with the mouse wheel.
EVENT_MOUSEMOVE	When the mouse is moving.
EVENT_MOUSEWHEEL	When a vertical scroll is executed with the mouse wheel.
EVENT_RBUTTONDBLCLK	When the right button is double-clicked.
EVENT_RBUTTONDOWN	When the right button is clicked.
EVENT_RBUTTONUP	When the right button is released.

This example will show how to use the callback function to capture the mouse events. Load and show an image, when a mouse click happens on the image, the x, y coordinates of the pixel and the blue, green and red values will be printed on a separate window.

```
1   def mouse_event(event, x, y, flags, param):
2       if event == cv2.EVENT_LBUTTONDOWN:
3           blue = img[y, x, 0]
4           green = img[y, x, 1]
5           red = img[y, x, 2]
6           mycolorImage = np.zeros((100, 280, 3),
                                    np.uint8)
7           mycolorImage[:] = [blue, green, red]
8           strBGR = "(B,G,R) =
                    (" + str(blue) + ", "+str(green)+",
                    " + str(red) + ")"
9           strXY = "(X,Y) = ("+str(x)+", "+str(y)+")"
10          txtFont = cv2.FONT_HERSHEY_COMPLEX
11          txtColor = (255, 255, 255)
12          cv2.putText(mycolorImage,strXY, (10,30),
                    txtFont, .6, txtColor,1)
13          cv2.putText(mycolorImage,strBGR, (10,50),
                    txtFont,.6,  txtColor,1)
14          cv2.imshow("color", mycolorImage)
```

```
15
16   if __name__ == '__main__':
17       img = cv2.imread("../res/flower003.jpg")
18       cv2.imshow("image", img)
19       cv2.setMouseCallback("image", mouse_event)
20       cv2.waitKey(0)
21       cv2.destroyAllWindows()
```

Explanations:

Line 1	Define the mouse callback function. The event type and coordinates (x, y) are in the parameter of the callback function.
Line 2	Check if the event is left mouse button down.
Line 3 - 5	Retrieve the BGR color values at the coordinates of x, y.
Line 6	Create a canvas that is used to display the coordinates and color values.
Line 7	Paint the canvas with the color at the point of the mouse click.
Line 8 - 9	Create the texts that will be displayed – the coordinates and color value.
Line 10, 11	Specify the font and color of the texts to be displayed.
Line 12, 13	Display the texts using `cv2.putText()` function.
Line 14	Show the canvas in a separate window.
Line 16	The main entrance for code execution.
Line 17, 18	Load and show an image.
Line 19	Set a callback function for capturing mouse events.

Execute the code, the image is loaded and displayed, whenever a mouse click happens on the image, the pixel's coordinates (*x, y*) and color values (B, G, R) are displayed in a separate window, and the background color is filled with the color of the pixel, as shown in Figure 4-1.

Color Image

Pixel Color

(X,Y) = (243, 109)
(B,G,R) = (218, 129, 255)

Figure 4-1 Mouse Click on an Image

4.2   Draw Circles with Mouse

```
Source:        DrawCircleWithMouse.py
Library:       common/Draw.py
```

This example will use mouse to draw circles with `cv2.circle()` function provided by OpenCV. Here's the basic syntax of the function:

```
cv2.circle(img, center, radius, color, thickness)
```

The parameters:

`img`	The image on which you want to draw the circle.
`center`	The center of the circle, specified as a tuple of (x, y) coordinates.
`radius`	The radius of the circle in pixels.
`color`	The color of the circle, specified as a tuple of (B, G, R) values.
`thickness`	The thickness of the circle outline. Use a negative value to fill the circle.

This example works in this way, when the left key of the mouse is pressed the center of the circle is decided, then hold the left key and move the mouse, the radius of the circle is continuously calculated while the mouse is moving. When the mouse left key is released the radius is finalized and the final circle is drawn on the canvas, the center coordinates and the radius are also shown on the canvas. While the mouse is moving with the left key down, a thin circle is drawn alone with the mouse moving in order to indicate how the circle looks like.

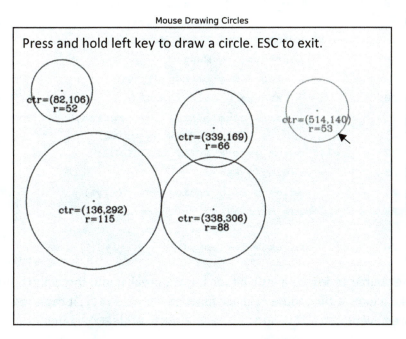

Figure 4-2 Draw Circles with Mouse

Here are the codes:

```
1   import cv2
2   import numpy as np
3   import math
4   import common.Draw as dw
5
6   drawing = False
7   final_color = (255, 255, 255)
8   drawing_color = (125, 125, 125)
9
10  def on_mouse(event, x, y, flags, param):
```

```
11          global drawing, ctr, radius, img, img_bk
12          if event == cv2.EVENT_LBUTTONDOWN:
13              drawing = True
14              ctr = x, y
15              radius = 0
16              draw_circle(img, ctr, radius,
                              drawing_color)
17          elif event == cv2.EVENT_MOUSEMOVE:
18              if drawing == True:
19                  img = img_bk.copy()
20                  radius = calc_radius(ctr, (x,y))
21                  draw_circle(img, ctr, radius,
                                  drawing_color)
22          elif event == cv2.EVENT_LBUTTONUP:
23              drawing = False
24              radius = calc_radius(ctr, (x,y))
25              draw_circle(img, ctr, radius,
                              final_color, 2, True)
26              img_bk = img.copy()
```

The source codes are a little bit longer, we break it into three parts, first take a look at the mouse callback function `on_mouse()`, it captures three events: EVENT_LBUTTONDOWN, EVENT_MOUSEMOVE and EVENT_RBUTTONDOWN.

Line 4	Import a module from `common.Draw`, which includes the wrapper functions for drawing shapes as we explained in section 3.5.
Line 6 - 8	Define the global variables, the flag of drawing, the colors for drawing.
Line 10	Define the mouse callback function.
Line 12 - 16	When the left button is pressed, start drawing by setting the drawing flag to True, and draw the center point of the circle.
Line 17 - 21	When the mouse is moving, calculate the radius based on the center and current points, then draw

	the indicator (a thin) circle with the `drawing_color.`
Line 22 - 26	*When the left button is released, finish the drawing, and draw the final circle with* `final_color.`

The next part of the source codes is to define several functions, `calc_radius()` is using a math function `math.hypot()` to calculate the radius based on the center point and current point; `draw_circle()` is to draw a circle, which includes drawing a point for the center, and drawing texts to display the center coordinates and radius. `print_instruction()` is to display the instruction texts on the top of the canvas.

```
28  def calc_radius(center, current_point):
29      cx, cy = current_point
30      tx, ty = center
31      return int(math.hypot(cx - tx, cy - ty))
32
33  def draw_circle(img, center, r, color,
                    line_scale=1, is_final=False ):
34      txtCenter = "ctr=(%d,%d)" % center
35      txtRadius = "r=%d" % radius
36      if is_final == True:
37          print("Completing circle with %s and %s" %
                  (txtCenter, txtRadius))
38      dw.draw_circle(img, center, 1, color,
                      line_scale)    # draw center
39      dw.draw_circle(img, center, r, color,
                      line_scale)    # draw circle
40      dw.draw_text(img, txtCenter, (center[0]-60,
                     center[1]+20), 0.5, color)
41      dw.draw_text(img, txtRadius, (center[0]-15,
                     center[1]+35), 0.5, color)
42
43  def print_instruction(img):
44      txtInstruction = "Press and hold left key to
                          draw a circle. ESC to exit."
45      dw.draw_text(img,txtInstruction, (10, 20), 0.5,
```

```
                          (255, 255, 255))
46          print(txtInstruction)
```

The final part of the source code is the *main* function, which is similar to previous example codes and straightforward, we will not explain it in detail here.

```
48  def main():
49          global img, img_bk
50          windowName = 'Mouse Drawing Circles'
51          img = np.zeros((500, 640, 3), np.uint8)
52          print_instruction(img)
53          img_bk = img.copy()
54          cv2.namedWindow(windowName)
55          cv2.setMouseCallback(windowName, on_mouse)
56          while (True):
57              cv2.imshow(windowName, img)
58              if cv2.waitKey(20) == 27:
59                  break
60          cv2.destroyAllWindows()
61
62  if __name__ == '__main__':
63          main()
```

Execute the codes in *DrawCircleWithMouse.py*, you will be able to draw circles on the canvas with mouse operations, the results are something like Figure 4-2.

4.3   Draw Polygon with Mouse

```
Source:     DrawPolygonWithMouse.py
Library:    common/Draw.py
```

Similar to above example of drawing circles, this example will draw polygons with the mouse. OpenCV provides cv2.polylines() function to draw polylines or polygons.

```
cv2.polylines(img, points, is_closed,
               color, thickness)
```

`points` specify the vertexes (the corner points of a polygon) of the polygons/polylines, `is_closed=True` will draw a closed polygon, if `False`, draw the polylines. Other parameters are the same as the `cv2.circle()` in the previous section.

This example works in this way, every time the mouse left key is clicked, a point is added to the polygon, when the mouse is moving a thin line is drawn between the last point and the mouse current point to indicate where the line will be drawn. When the right key is clicked the final polygon will be drawn with all points.

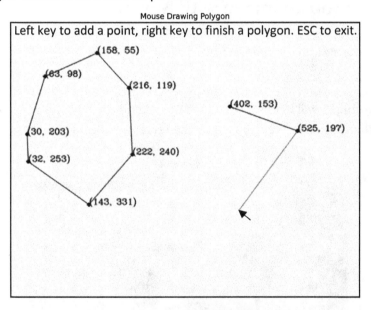

Figure 4-3 Draw Polygon with Mouse

The full source codes are in the *DrawPolygonWithMouse.py* in the Github repository. The source codes are very similar to the previous example of drawing circles, we will not explain it line by line here. The only difference is that an array is used to store the vertexes for the polygon when the `EVENT_ LBUTTONDOWN` (left button down) events happen, the polygon is drawn based on the array of the vertexes.

When the mouse is moving, a thin line is drawn with `drawing_color` between the last point in the array and the current mouse point, this thin line is changing along with the mouse moving to indicate the line.

When the mouse right click happens, the `EVENT_RBUTTONDOWN` event is captured, then the drawing is completed, and the final polygon will be drawn with `final_color`.

Execute the code in *DrawPolygonWithMouse.py* and you are able to draw polygons with your mouse, the results are something like Figure 4-3.

4.4   Crop an Image with Mouse

```
Source:      CropImageWithMouse.py
Library:     common/Draw.py
```

This example will load an image and use the mouse to draw a rectangle, and then crop the image based on the rectangle, like in Figure 4-4:

Figure 4-4 Crop Image with Mouse

When the mouse left button is clicked on the image, the first point is captured, normally it is the top-left of the rectangle however it depends on which direction the mouse is moving, we will resolve it later.

Then hold the left button and move the mouse, similar to previous sections a rectangle is drawn while the mouse is moving to indicate how the rectangle looks like, at the same time the coordinates of the first point and the mouse's current location are shown, as Figure 4-4.

When the left button is released, the second point is captured, and the final rectangle is drawn, at the same time a separate window is shown with cropped image.

The full source code is in the *CropImageWithMouse.py* file in the Github repository, it's similar to the previous examples of drawing circles and polygons.

Now we only focus on the cropping image part of the source code. As mentioned earlier, when the left mouse button is down the first point is captured and recorded, and when it is released the second point is recorded.

To crop an image, an array operation will simply do the job.

```
cropped_image = image[y_start:y_end, x_start:x_end]
```

The image data is in `image` array, its first dimension is y coordinate and the second is x. `y_start:y_end` will select only rows between `y_start` and `y_end`, similarly `x_start:x_end` will select only columns between the two.

Depending on which direction the mouse is moving the first point might not always be the top-left, and the second point might not always be the bottom-right. We resolve this in the `crop_image()` function by comparing the x and y values of the first and second points, the smaller x and y will be the top-left point, the bigger ones will be the bottom right. The code snippets are show as below:

```
1    def crop_image(img, pt_first, pt_second):
2        # top-left point
         x_tl, y_tl = pt_first
3        # bottom-right point
```

```
     x_br, y_br = pt_second
4    # swap x value if opposite
     if x_br < x_tl:
5        x_br, x_tl = x_tl, x_br
6    # swap y value if opposite
     if y_br < y_tl:
7        y_br, y_tl = y_tl, y_br
8    cropped_image = img[y_tl:y_br, x_tl:x_br]
9    cv2.imshow("Cropped Image", cropped_image)
```

Explanations:

Line 1	*Define the* `crop_image()` *function.*
Line 2 - 3	*Retrieve the* x *and* y *values from the first and second points.*
Line 4 - 5	*Compare both* x *values, and swap the values if the second value is smaller.*
Line 6 - 7	*Compare both* y *values, and swap the values if the second is smaller.*
Line 8	*Create a cropped image using Python array operations, the cropped image is a subset of the original image based on the top-left and bottom-right values.*
Line 9	*Show the cropped image.*

Execute the code in *CropImageWithMouse.py* file, you can crop the image with the mouse operations, looks something like Figure 4-4.

4.5   Input Values with Trackbars

Source: UserInputWithTrackbar.py

A Trackbar, or a Slider, is a graphical user interface component that allows the user to adjust a parameter within a range by sliding a knob with the mouse along a horizontal bar, as shown in Figure 4-5. It is commonly used in computer vision applications for real-time parameter tuning, for example, the users can adjust brightness from the range of 0 to 100 by dragging the knob along the bar.

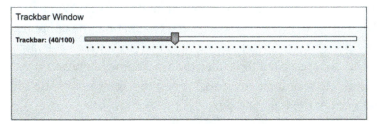

Figure 4-5 A Sample Trackbar

In OpenCV, `cv2.createTrackbar()` function is used to create a trackbar. The function takes several arguments, including the name of the trackbar, the name of the window in which it will appear, the initial value of the trackbar, the maximum value, and a callback function that will be called when the trackbar is moved. When a user moves the knob the callback function will be invoked, and the actions defined in the callback function will be performed.

Here are the code snippets to create a sample trackbar,

```
1   import cv2
2   import numpy as np
3   def on_trackbar(val):
4       print("Trackbar value:", val)
5
6   cv2.namedWindow("Trackbar Window")
7   cv2.createTrackbar("Trackbar", "Trackbar Window",
8                      0, 100, on_trackbar)
9   canvas = np.zeros((100, 800, 3), np.uint8)
10  canvas[:] = 235,235,235
11
12  while True:
13      cv2.imshow("Trackbar Window", canvas)
14      if cv2.waitKey(1) & 0xFF == 27:
15          break
16  cv2.destroyAllWindows()
```

The range of the trackbar is from 0 to a maximum value of 100, a callback function `on_trackbar()` is called whenever the knob is moved by the mouse, and it simply prints the current value of the trackbar to the console.

The trackbar is displayed in a window named "Trackbar Window", which is created using the `cv2.namedWindow()` function, the content of the window is a light gray canvas as we did previously. Inside the main loop, `cv2.imshow()` is called to display the trackbar window and `cv2.waitKey()` to wait for a key press. When the user presses the ESC key, it breaks out of the loop and destroys the window using `cv2.destroyAllWindows()`.

When the user interacts with the trackbar by moving the knob, the `on_trackbar()` function is called with the current value of the trackbar as its parameter. This value can then be used to adjust a parameter in real-time, such as the brightness for an image processing algorithm.

The below example will display a webcam, as in previous section 3.3, together with four trackbars for adjusting the brightness, contrast, saturation and hue of the webcam.

Open the *UserInputWithTrackbar.py* file in the Github repository, the four callback functions are defined below:

```
1    import cv2
2
3    def change_brightness(value):
4        global cap
5        print("Brightness: " + str(value))
6        cap.set(cv2.CAP_PROP_BRIGHTNESS, value)
7
8    def change_contrast(value):
9        print("Contrast: " + str(value))
10       cap.set(cv2.CAP_PROP_CONTRAST, value)
11
12   def change_saturation(value):
13       print("Saturation: " + str(value))
14       cap.set(cv2.CAP_PROP_SATURATION, value)
```

```
15
16   def change_hue(value):
17       print("Hue: " + str(value))
18       cap.set(cv2.CAP_PROP_HUE, value)
```

Explanations:

Line 3	Define a trackbar callback function for brightness. The value from user input via Trackbar will be passed to this function as a parameter.
Line 4	Declare `cap` as a global variable.
Line 5	Print out the value from the trackbar.
Line 6	Set the camera property with the value.
Line 8 - 18	Define the other three trackbar callback functions in the same way, for contrast, saturation and hue.

Then, define the main function to setup the trackbars and display the webcam,

```
20   def main():
21       global cap
22       # read from webcam
         cap = cv2.VideoCapture(0, cv2.CAP_DSHOW)
23       # set width
         cap.set(cv2.CAP_PROP_FRAME_WIDTH, 800)
24       # set height
         cap.set(cv2.CAP_PROP_FRAME_HEIGHT, 480)
25       # set initial brightness
         cap.set(cv2.CAP_PROP_BRIGHTNESS, 100)
26       # set initial contrast
         cap.set(cv2.CAP_PROP_CONTRAST, 50)
27       # set initial saturation
         cap.set(cv2.CAP_PROP_SATURATION, 90)
28       # set initial hue
         cap.set(cv2.CAP_PROP_HUE, 15)
29
30       cv2.namedWindow('Webcam')
31       cv2.createTrackbar('Brightness', 'Webcam', 100,
```

```
                                    300, change_brightness)
32          cv2.createTrackbar('Contrast', 'Webcam', 50, 300,
                                    change_contrast)
33          cv2.createTrackbar('Saturation', 'Webcam', 90,
                                    100, change_saturation)
34          cv2.createTrackbar('Hue', 'Webcam', 15, 360,
                                    change_hue)
35
36          success, img = cap.read()
37          while success:
38              cv2.imshow("Webcam", img)
39
40              # Press ESC key to break the loop
41              if cv2.waitKey(10) & 0xFF == 27:
42                  break
43              success, img = cap.read()
44
45          cap.release()
46          cv2.destroyWindow("Webcam")
47
48  if __name__ == '__main__':
49      main()
```

Explanations:

Line 21	Declare `cap` as a global variable, which is used for above Line 4 as a global variable.
Line 22	Open the Webcam channel and read it into a capture object `cap`.
Line 23 - 28	Set the initial properties for the Webcam capture object.
Line 30 - 34	Create a named window and create four trackbars in the window. Here set the above defined callback function to the trackbars via the last parameter. The range of each trackbar is set here.
Line 36 – 46	Same as displaying a webcam in section 3.3.
Line 48 - 49	The main entrance of the execution.

Execute the code, there are four trackbars shown together with the webcam window, for adjusting brightness, contrast, saturation and hue. The below Figure 4-6 only shows the trackbars' area, the webcam screen also shows in the window. You will see the camera screen changes accordingly when each slider is moved by the mouse.

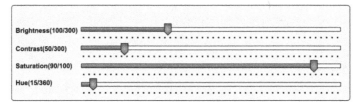

Figure 4-6 Trackbars

5. Image Processing

To recap the previous discussions, a digital image is represented as an array of pixel values. Each pixel in the array represents a tiny element of the image, and its value determines the color or intensity of that element. The pixel values are represented as integers in the range of 0 to 255 for grayscale images, where 0 represents black and 255 represents white. For color images, pixel values are represented as a combination of blue, green, and red (BGR) channels, where each channel is in grayscale with a value between 0 and 255.

Digital images are represented by multi-dimensional arrays in OpenCV, a grayscale image is represented by a 2D array, and a color one is by a 3D array.

Image processing is a technique to apply some mathematical algorithms and use various functions and techniques to manipulate digital images in order to get the desired outcomes with enhanced effects, such as improving their quality or extracting useful information from them.

OpenCV provides a number of methods for image processing, this chapter will introduce some commonly and widely used methods for image processing.

This chapter begins with the color space conversion in section 5.1 which is the basics of image processing, we will introduce the conversion between grayscale, BGR and HSV color spaces.

Section 5.2 will explain how to resize, crop and rotate the images. This chapter will also introduce the object-oriented features of Python, we will create classes to include the functions and write codes to instantiate the classes and invoke those functions.

Section 5.3 will explain how to adjust the Brightness and Contrast, and section 5.4 to adjust Hue, Saturation and Value of the images. By adjusting these values, the color and brightness of the images can be changed accordingly, this is a very important part of image processing.

Section 5.5 will introduce image blending which is to mix two images based on an algorithm. And Section 5.6 will introduce the bitwise operation and blending or mixing two images based on the bitwise operation, which can achieve a different effect.

Section 5.7 will describe image warping, a method to transform a skewed and distorted image into a straightened one.

Section 5.8 will introduce image blurring, it's a technique to make the image smooth by removing the noises from the image. There are many different ways to do it, this section will focus on two types of image blurring methods, Gaussian Blur and Median Blur.

Lastly, section 5.9 will introduce the histogram which gives us important information about the color distributions of the images.

Enjoy the Image Processing with OpenCV and Python.

5.1 Conversion of Color Spaces

> Source: ColorSpace.py

Section 3.4 has explained that the color image can be represented using either BGR or HSV color spaces, and a color image can also be converted to a grayscale image. OpenCV provides many methods for the conversion of color spaces, here we introduce two of them: BGR to and from Grayscale, and BGR to and from HSV.

5.1.1 Convert BGR to Gray

There are two ways to obtain a grayscale image from the color one, 1) use `cv2.cvtColor()` function with `cv2.COLOR_BGR2GRAY` as its second parameter, and 2) load the image with grayscale mode by using `cv2.imread()` function with `cv2.IMREAD_GRAYSCALE` as the second parameter.

The first method loads the color image and then converts it to grayscale, then we have both the color and grayscale images available in the memory.

However, if the color image is not needed, the second method loads the image in grayscale only, the color one is not available in this case and could save some memory. Below code snippets show the two methods:

```
1   def convert_bgr2gray(image):
2       gray = cv2.cvtColor(image, cv2.COLOR_BGR2GRAY)
3       return gray
4
5   def load_image_gray(file_name):
6       gray = cv2.imread(file_name,
                          cv2.IMREAD_GRAYSCALE)
7       return gray
```

Line 1 to 3 is the first method, the color image in `image` is passed as a parameter, `cv2.cvtColor()` function will convert it to grayscale one.

Line 5 to 7 is the second method, it loads the image in grayscale mode directly from the file.

Color Image   *Grayscale Image*

Figure 5-1 Convert BGR to Grayscale

As shown in Figure 5-1 above, the color image (left) is converted to a grayscale one (right).

As discussed earlier, in OpenCV the default color space for an image is BGR, so a color image can be split into three channels of blue, green and red, each channel is in grayscale, as shown in Figure 5-2.

Color Image

Blue, Green and Red channels

Figure 5-2 Color Image is Made of Blue, Green and Red Channels

The `cv2.split()` function can be used to split a color image into the three channels:

```
1  def split_image(image):
```

```
2        ch1, ch2, ch3 = cv2.split(image)
3        return ch1, ch2, ch3
```

And each channel is in grayscale.

5.1.2 Convert Grayscale to BGR

A grayscale image can also be converted to BGR color space, in this case the source is a grayscale image which only has one channel and does not have any color information, therefore the result BGR image looks the same as the original grayscale one. But the difference is the BGR image has three channels although looks the same as the grayscale one, while the original gray image only has one channel.

To convert a grayscale image to BGR, use cv2.cvtColor() function with cv2.COLOR_GRAY2BGR as the second parameter,

```
1    def convert_gray2bgr(image):
2        bgr = cv2.cvtColor(image,cv2.COLOR_GRAY2BGR)
3        return bgr
```

Figure 5-3 below shows the idea:

Grayscale (one channel)   BGR (three channels)

Figure 5-3 Convert Grayscale to BGR

The left image is the original grayscale image, which has only one channel. The right image, however, is in BGR color space although looks same as the grayscale one, it can be split into three channels.

Since the right image looks same as the left one, why we should convert it? There are several reasons to do it, sometimes in the image processing, some operations need to be performed on two or more images, it's important that all the images are in the same color space. For example, if we want to blend, or mix, two images together, but one is color image and another is grayscale, the grayscale one must be converted into BGR before blending them.

Sometimes when you want to colorize a grayscale image, it must be converted to BGR first, then paint colors on different channels, because you are not able to paint colors on a single-channel grayscale image.

5.1.3   Convert BGR to HSV

As explained in section 3.4, an image can be represented not only in BGR but also in HSV color spaces, OpenCV can easily convert the image between BGR and HSV. Like converting it to grayscale, the same function `cv2.cvtColor()` is used but the second parameter is different, `cv2.COLOR_BGR2HSV` in this case.

The HSV image can also be split into three channels, hue, saturation and value. Then each channel can be adjusted to achieve some different effects, later we will explain how to adjust each channel to change the image.

Below code snippets are to convert an image to HSV color space:

```
1   def convert_bgr2hsv(image):
2       hsv = cv2.cvtColor(image, cv2.COLOR_BGR2HSV)
3       return hsv
```

As shown in Figure 5-4, the color image is converted to HSV color space, and then it can be further split into three channels in hue, saturation and value by using `cv2.split()` function.

Color Image

Hue, Saturation and Value channels

Figure 5-4 Convert BGR to HSV

5.1.4 Convert HSV to BGR

When OpenCV displays an image, the function `cv2.imshow()` is used and by default in BGR color space. If an image is converted to HSV and followed by some image processing operations, it can not be directly sent to `cv2.imshow()` for displaying, instead it must be converted back to BGR, then sent to `cv2.imshow()` for displaying, otherwise the image will not be displayed correctly.

In last section an image is converted to HSV, and here we will convert it back to BGR with the same function `cv2.cvtColor()` but different parameter `cv2.COLOR_HSV2BGR`.

```
1  def convert_hsv2bgr(image):
2      bgr = cv2.cvtColor(image, cv2.COLOR_HSV2BGR)
3      return bgr
```

The example in section 5.4 later will show how to convert a BGR image to HSV, and make some adjustments to hue, saturation and value to achieve some effects, and then convert it back to BGR for displaying.

5.2 Resize, Crop and Rotate an Image

> Source: ResizeCropRotate.py
> Library: common/ImageProcessing.py

Python is an excellent language to support object-oriented programming, this chapter will start to use object-oriented techniques to write the codes. We will create classes to include properties and functions, then instantiate the classes and invoke their functions.

Now create a class called ImageProcessing, and define three functions inside, resize(), rotate() and crop(). When a class is created it always has a built-in __init__() function, which is always executed when the class is instantiated. It's used to assign initial values to the properties or other operations that are necessary when the object is created. Here we set the window_name and image_name properties inside __init__() function.

The full source code is in the *ImageProcessing.py* in the common folder of the Github repository.

```python
1    import cv2
2
3    class ImageProcessing(object):
4        def __init__(self, window_name, image_name):
5            self.window_name = window_name
6            self.image_name = image_name
7            self.image = cv2.imread(self.image_name)
8
9        def show(self, title=None, image=None):
10           if image is None:
11               image = self.image
12           if title is None:
13               title = self.window_name
14           cv2.imshow(title, image)
```

Explanations:

Line 3	*Define the* ImageProcessing *class*

Line 4	The built-in `__init__()` function, it's always executed when the class is instantiated. The parameters should be passed when instantiating the class.
Line 5 - 7	Set the class properties, `window_name` and `image_name`, then load the image using `cv2.imread()`.
Line 9 - 14	Define `show()` function, which will show the image using `cv2.imshow()`. When the parameters specify the image or window name then show that image with window name, otherwise use the image and window name specified at `__init()__` function when the class is initialized.

To continue, add three functions, `resize()`, `crop()` and `rotate()`, to the class:

```python
16      def resize(self, percent, image=None):
17          if image is None:
18              image = self.image
19          width = int(image.shape[1]*percent/100)
20          height = int(image.shape[0]*percent/100)
21          resized_image = cv2.resize(image,
                                       (width, height) )
22          return resized_image
23
24      def crop(self,pt_first,pt_second,image=None):
25          if image is None:
26                  image = self.image
27          # top-left point
            x_tl, y_tl = pt_first
28          # bottom-right point
            x_br, y_br = pt_second
29          # swap x value if opposite
            if x_br < x_tl:
30              x_br, x_tl = x_tl, x_br
31          # swap y value if opposite
            if y_br < y_tl:
32              y_br, y_tl = y_tl, y_br
```

```
33              cropped_image=image[y_tl:y_br,x_tl:x_br]
34              return cropped_image
35
36          def rotate(self,angle,image=None,scale=1.0):
37              if image is None:
38                  image = self.image
39              (h, w) = image.shape[:2]
40              center = (w / 2, h / 2)
41              rot_mat = cv2.getRotationMatrix2D(center,
                                    angle, scale)
42              rotated_image = cv2.warpAffine(image,
                                    rot_mat, (w, h))
43              return rotated_image
```

Explanations:

Line 16	Define `resize()` function, specify percentage as parameter, and optionally the image as parameter.
Line 17 - 18	If `image` is not specified in the parameters, then use the class property's image.
Line 19 - 22	Calculate the resized width and height based on the percentage. Then call `cv2.resize()` function to resize the image.
Line 24 - 34	Define `crop()` function, similar to what we did in Section 4.4.
Line 36 – 44	Define `rotate()` function, pass `angle` as a parameter and optionally `image` and `scale`. Use `cv2.getRotationMatrix2D()` and `cv2.warpAffine()` functions to perform the rotation.

Reference the OpenCV documents for `getRotationMatrix2D()` and `warpAffine()` functions at the below link:

https://docs.opencv.org/4.7.0/da/d54/group__imgproc__transform.html

The class definition for `ImageProcessing` is done for now, more functions will be added later.

Now the class can perform the resize, crop and rotate operations.

In the source codes of *ResizeCropRotate.py* in the Github repository, the class is imported in Line 2, this is a typical way to include another Python file for reference.

```
1    import cv2
2    import common.ImageProcessing as ip
3
4    if __name__ == "__main__":
5        # Create an ImageProcessing object
6        ip = ip.ImageProcessing("Resize,Crop and Rotate",
                                   "../res/flower005.jpg")
7
8        # Show original image
9        ip.show()
10
11       # Resize the original image and show it
12       resized_image = ip.resize(50)
13       ip.show("Resized -- 50%", resized_image)
14
15       # Rotate the resized image and show it
16       rotated_image = ip.rotate(45, resized_image)
17       ip.show("Rotated -- 45 degree", rotated_image)
18
19       # Crop the original image and show it
20       cropped_image = ip.crop((300, 10), (600, 310))
21       ip.show("Cropped", cropped_image)
22
23       cv2.waitKey(0)
24       cv2.destroyAllWindows()
```

Explanations:

Line 2	Import the class file we defined earlier, because it is in common *folder,* common.file_name *is used to locate the file.*

Line 4	The main entrance, when the code is executed, it starts from here.
Line 6	Instantiate `ImageProcessing` class with parameters, the window's name and the path of an image, which are set as properties of this class.
Line 9	Show the default image and default window name, which are specified at the class instantiation.
Line 12 – 13	Invoke the `resize()` function to resize the image, and show it.
Line 16 – 17	Invoke the `rotate()` function and show the result with 45-degree rotated.
Line 20 – 21	Invoke the `crop()` function and pass two points to crop the image, and show it.

Below are the results, Figure 5-5 shows the original image:

Resize, Crop and Rotate

Figure 5-5 Original Image

Figure 5-6 shows the 50% resized image:

Resized -- 50%

Figure 5-6 Resized Image

Figure 5-7 shows the cropped image:

Cropped

Figure 5-7 Cropped Image

And finally, Figure 5-8 shows the 45-degree rotated image:

Rotated -- 45 degree

Figure 5-8 45 Degree Rotated Image

Feel free to play with the source codes, for example change an image file, change the degree of rotation, change the percentage of the resizing, and observe how the image is processed.

5.3 Adjust Contrast and Brightness of an Image

```
Source:      ContrastBrightness.py
Library:     common/ImageProcessing.py
```

Section 4.5 has an example to adjust the brightness and contrast for a webcam, however unfortunately OpenCV doesn't provide functions to adjust the brightness and contrast for an image. But OpenCV official document recommends an alternative way to do it, see the link at:

https://docs.opencv.org/4.7.0/d3/dc1/tutorial_basic_linear_transform.html

This book is not intended to deep dive into the algorithms or theories, instead, we focus on the implementation of the techniques using OpenCV with Python. However, in order to make things clear, sometimes we will summarize, or quote from other sources, the related algorithms or theories.

To summarize the techniques of contrast and brightness adjustment, the below formula from OpenCV official document depicts the calculation of the contrast and brightness,

$$g(i,j) = \alpha f(i,j) + \beta$$

from OpenCV official document at
https://docs.opencv.org/4.7.0/d3/dc1/tutorial_basic_linear_transform.html

$f(i,j)$ is the original image and $g(i,j)$ is the result. α changes the contrast, greater than 1 for higher contrast, less than 1 for lower contrast. It should be greater than 0. β changes the brightness, values vary from -127 to +127. (i,j) indicates the coordinates of the image pixels.

The OpenCV official document provides an example to explain how to use the Python array and matrix operations to implement the above formula.

Alternatively, OpenCV provides `cv2.addWeighted()` function which is designed for blending two images with weight added on each, we will use this function to implement the above formula to adjust the contrast and brightness.

```
cv2.addWeighted(image, contrast, zeros, 0, brightness)
```

The function `cv2.addWeighted()` implements the below formular:

$$g(i,j) = \alpha_1 f_1(i,j) + \alpha_2 f_2(i,j) + \beta$$

$g(i, j)$ is the result, $f1(i, j)$ is the image and passed to `cv2.addWeighted()` as the first parameter, α_1 is the second parameter which is contrast; because only one image is interested in this example, so $f2(i, j)$ is an all-zero image, and α_2 is also a zero, therefore the third and fourth parameters of the function are an all-zero array and a zero value. β is the last parameter, which is brightness, this value will be added to the result.

Now add a new `contrast_brightness()` function to the class `ImageProcessing`, which we have defined in section 5.2.

```
45   def contrast_brightness(self, contrast,
                                brightness, image=None):
46       # contrast:
         # between 0 and 1: less contrast;
47       #           > 1: more contrast;
48       #           1: unchanged
49       # brightness: -127 to 127;
50       #           0 unchanged
51       if image is None:
52           image = self.image
53       zeros = np.zeros(image.shape, image.dtype)
54       result = cv2.addWeighted(image, contrast,
                                    zeros, 0, brightness)
55       return result
```

Explanations:

Line 45	Define `contrast_brightness()` function, specify contrast and brightness as parameters, and optionally an image.
Line 53	Create an all-zero array, because `cv2.addWeighted()` requires two images, we don't use the second one, so pass the all-zero array to it.
Line 54	Call `cv2.addWeighted()` function to apply the weights to the image.

Below is the code to adjust the brightness and contrast using the function just created above. Like Section 4.5, two trackbars are added for users to adjust the brightness and contrast.

```python
1   import cv2
2   import common.ImageProcessing as ip
3
4   def change_brightness(value):
5       global brightness
6       brightness = value - 128
7
8   def change_contrast(value):
9       global contrast
10      contrast = float(value)/100
11
12  if __name__ == "__main__":
13      brightness = 0
14      contrast = 1.0
15      title = "Adjust Brightness and Contrast"
16      ip = ip.ImageProcessing(title,
                                "../res/flower003.jpg")
17      cv2.createTrackbar('Brightness', title, 128,
                           255, change_brightness)
18      cv2.createTrackbar('Contrast', title, 100,
                           300, change_contrast)
19
20      while True:
21          adjusted_image = ip.contrast_brightness(
```

```
                              contrast, brightness)
22            ip.show(image=adjusted_image)
23            if cv2.waitKey(10) & 0xFF == 27:
24                break
25        cv2.destroyAllWindows()
```

Explanations:

Line 2	*Import the* ImageProcessing *class.*
Line 4 - 6	*Define the callback function for the trackbar to adjust the brightness.*
Line 8 - 10	*Define the callback function for the trackbar to adjust the contrast.*
Line 12	*Main entrance.*
Line 16	*Instantiate the* ImageProcessing *object.*
Line 17 - 18	*Create two trackbars for brightness and contrast.*
Line 21 – 22	*Call* contrast_brightness()*, the function we just defined, to adjust brightness and contrast.*

Execute the code, the result shows the image together with two trackbars, as Figure 5-9, one is for adjusting brightness and another for contrast:

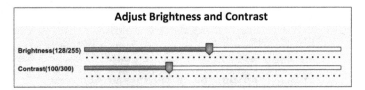

Figure 5-9 Trackbars to Adjust Brightness and Contrast

Use the mouse to drag the two trackbars to change the brightness and contrast values, the image will be changed accordingly in real-time.

The range of contrast in trackbar is from 0 to 300, and the default is 100. In the callback function change_contrast(), the value is divided by 100, therefore the contrast range is from 0.0 to 3.0, default is 1.0.

Feel free to play with the codes by changing the image files and adjusting the two trackbars and observe how the image is changing accordingly.

5.4 Adjust Hue, Saturation and Value

> Source: HueSaturation.py
> Library: common/ImageProcessing.py

Section 3.4.3 has explained a color image can be split not only to BGR channels but also HSV channels, the former represents blue, green and red channels, the latter represents hue, saturation and value. The hue represents the color of the image, different hue values have different colors; saturation represents the purity of the color, a higher saturation means a more colorful image; while value represents the brightness of the image, a higher value means a brighter image.

In this section we will explain how to adjust hue, saturation and value of an image, three trackbars will be created for the three variables, we will see how the image is changing when users adjust these variables in real-time.

The first thing is to convert the image into HSV using `cv2.cvtColor()` with `cv2.COLOR_BGR2HSV` parameter, then split it into hue, saturation and value channels using `cv2.split()`.

Then add weights to hue, saturation and value channels respectively, and merge them back to HSV. Finally convert the HSV to BGR for displaying.

Same as the previous section, `cv2.addWeighted()` is used to adjust each channel with a weight. The below line of code is to add a weight `h_weight` to the `hue` channel,

```
1   hue = cv2.addWeighted(hue, 1.0, zeros, 0, h_weight)
```

And add the weights to other channels in the same way.

Here are the codes, the function `hue_saturation_value()` is added into our `ImageProcessing` class:

```
1    def hue_saturation_value(self, hue, saturation,
                                value, image=None):
2       if image is None:
3          image = self.image
4       hsvImage = cv2.cvtColor(image, cv2.COLOR_BGR2HSV)
5       h, s, v = cv2.split(hsvImage)
6       zeros = np.zeros(h.shape, h.dtype)
7       h = cv2.addWeighted(h, 1.0, zeros, 0, hue)
8       s = cv2.addWeighted(s, 1.0, zeros, 0, saturation)
9       v = cv2.addWeighted(v, 1.0, zeros, 0, value)
10      result = cv2.merge([h, s, v])
11      result = cv2.cvtColor(result, cv2.COLOR_HSV2BGR)
12      return result
```

Explanations:

Line 1	*Define the function in `ImageProcessing` class, the parameters are* hue, saturation *and* value.
Line 4	*Convert the image into HSV image.*
Line 5	*Split the HSV image into separate* h, s, v *channels.*
Line 7 - 9	*Add the weights to the three channels. The* hue, saturation *and* value *are the weights to* h, s, *and* v *channels respectively.*
Line 10	*Merge the* h, s, v *channels into the HSV image.*
Line 11	*Convert the HSV image back to BGR image.*

This function is called from the *HueSaturation.py* file, in this example we add a feature to save the image into a file on the local disk drive, in addition to pressing ESC key to exit, when press "s" key the file will be saved to a specified file using `cv2.imwrite()` function.

```
1    import cv2
2    import common.ImageProcessing as ip
```

```
3
4   def change_hue(value):
5       global hue
6       hue = (value * 2) - 255
7
8   def change_saturation(value):
9       global sat
10      sat = (value * 2) - 255
11
12  def change_value(value):
13      global val
14      val = (value * 2) - 255
15
16  if __name__ == "__main__":
17      hue, sat, val = 0, 0, 0
18      title = "Adjust Hue, Saturation and Value"
19      ip = ip.ImageProcessing(title,
                               "../res/flower003.jpg")
20      cv2.createTrackbar('Hue', title, 127, 255,
                          change_hue)
21      cv2.createTrackbar('Saturation', title,
                          127, 255, change_saturation)
22      cv2.createTrackbar('Value', title, 127,
                          255, change_value)
23      ip.show("Original")
24      print("Press s key to save image,
               ESC to exit.")
25
26      while True:
27          adjusted_image =
                ip.hue_saturation_value(hue, sat, val)
28          ip.show(image=adjusted_image)
29          ch = cv2.waitKey(10)
30          if (ch & 0xFF) == 27:
31              Break
32          elif ch == ord('s'):
```

```
33                    # press 's' key to save image
34                    filepath = "C:/temp/flower003.png"
35                    cv2.imwrite(filepath, adjusted_image)
36                    print("File saved to " + filepath)
37          cv2.destroyAllWindows()
```

Explanations:

Line 4 - 15	Define three callback functions for trackbars for hue, saturation and value. The value is changing from -255 to 255 for each. You can modify the range base on your needs.
Line 19	Instantiate the `ImageProcess` class with a title and an image.
Line 20 - 22	Create three trackbars for hue, saturation and value respectively.
Line 23	Show the original image.
Line 27	Call the function we just defined in `ImageProcess` class with parameters of the adjusted hue, saturation and value.
Line 28	Show the result image.
Line 32 - 36	Save the result image when pressing "s" key.

Execute the code, the result shows the original image and the adjusted image together with three trackbars, as Figure 5-10, for adjusting hue, saturation and value respectively.

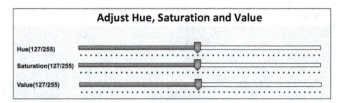

Figure 5-10 Trackbars to Adjust Hue, Saturation and Value

The original image and adjusted image are omitted here, feel free to change different images in the codes and observe how they are changing when adjusting the hue, saturation and value by moving the knobs of the trackbars.

5.5   Blend Image

```
Source:      BlendImage.py
Library:     common/ImageProcessing.py
```

Blending images refers to the process of combining two images to create a single image that has the characteristics of both original images. The result is a combination of the corresponding pixel values of the two original images with weights.

The blending process involves specifying a weight for each pixel in one of the original images, computing (1 – weight) for each pixel in another image, and then merging them together to produce the output image.

Blending images is a common operation in computer vision and image processing, and is used for a variety of applications, such as creating panoramas, compositing images, and generating special effects in videos and images.

Say, there are two images, Original Image 1 and Original Image2, as shown in Figure 5-11 and Figure 5-12.

Original Image 1

Figure 5-11 Blend Image: Original Image 1

Original Image 2

Figure 5-12 Blend Image: Original Image 2

The OpenCV documents describe the algorithm to blend them together,

$$g(i,j) = \alpha f_o(i,j) + (1 - \alpha) f_1(i,j)$$

from OpenCV official document at
https://docs.opencv.org/4.7.0/d5/dc4/tutorial_adding_images.html

$f_o(i, j)$ and $f_1(i, j)$ are the two original images, and $g(i, j)$ is the output image. α is the weight (value from 0 to 1) on the first image, $(1 - \alpha)$ is the weight on the second image.

By adjusting the value of α, we can achieve different blending effects. Same as the previous sections, cv2.addWeighted() function is used to blend the two images.

The blend() function is to be added to the ImageProcessing class:

```
1    def blend(self, blend, alpha, image=None):
2        if image is None:
3            image = self.image
4        blend = cv2.resize(blend,
                    (image.shape[1], image.shape[0]))
5        result = cv2.addWeighted(image, alpha,
                        blend, (1.0 - alpha), 0)
6        return result
```

Explanations:

Line 1	Define `blend()` function, the parameters are the image to blend, and alpha which is between 0 and 1.
Line 4	The two images must be in the same size, make them the same using `cv2.resize()`.
Line 5	Use `cv2.addWeighted()` function to implement the blending algorithm.

Here are the main codes:

```python
1   def change_alpha(value):
2       global alpha
3       alpha = float(value)/100
4   def blendTwoImages(imageFile1, imageFile2):
5       global alpha
6       alpha = 0.5
7       title = "Blend Two Images"
8       iproc = ip.ImageProcessing(title, imageFile1)
9       toBlend = cv2.imread(imageFile2)
10      cv2.createTrackbar("Alpha",title,50,100,change_alpha)
11      iproc.show("Original Image 1", )
12      iproc.show("Original Image 2", toBlend)
13      print("Press s key to save image, ESC to exit.")
14      while True:
15          blended_image = iproc.blend(toBlend, alpha)
16          iproc.show(image=blended_image)
17          ch = cv2.waitKey(10)
18          if (ch & 0xFF) == 27:
19              break
20          elif ch == ord('s'):
21              # press 's' key to save image
22              filepath = "C:/temp/blend_image.png"
23              cv2.imwrite(filepath, blended_image)
24              print("File saved to " + filepath)
25      cv2.destroyAllWindows()
26
27  if __name__ == "__main__":
28      image1 = "../res/sky001.jpg"
29      image2 = "../res/bird002.jpg"
30      blendTwoImages(image1, image2)
```

A trackbar is created for adjusting `alpha` from 0 to 100, with a default value of 50. The callback function `change_alpha()` divides the value by 100, then it's from 0 to 1.0.

The result looks something like Figure 5-13:

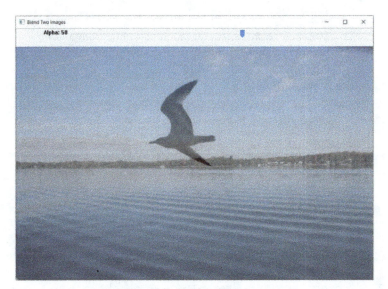

Figure 5-13 Blend Images

The default `alpha` of 50 makes the two original images blend evenly. By adjusting the `alpha` value, the output image will be changing. If `alpha=100`, the result becomes pure Original Image 1; if `alpha=0`, the result is pure Original Image 2. If the `alpha` is in between, the result is mixed, but the weight of each image is different based on the `alpha` value.

5.6   Bitwise Operation

```
Source:      BlendImageBitwise.py
Library:     common/ImageProcessing.py
```

The last section introduced image blending by implementing the algorithm introduced by the OpenCV document. As you can see from the result in Figure 5-13, the image looks a little bit faded out, and both original images become transparent to some extent. It depends on what effects you want to achieve, sometimes this kind of faded-out effect is not ideal, you might want the images to be opaquely added together without fading out.

This section will introduce another way to blend two images, a blending mask will be used in the image blending. The blending mask is a grayscale image that specifies the contribution of each pixel in the input images to the output image. It is also referred to as an alpha mask or alpha matte.

The blending mask is used as a weighting function to compute the weighted average of the pixel values from the input images. The values of the blending mask typically range from 0 to 255, where 0 represents complete opacity and 255 represents complete transparency. The blending mask is usually a grayscale image, but it can also be a color image in some cases. However, in this section we use a binary mask, the values are either 0 or 255, with no values in between.

In this section we will create a mask from the image of Figure 5-12, the bird image, and apply it to both images as a bitwise operation to achieve a different blending effect.

OpenCV provides bitwise operations – AND, OR, NOT and XOR. It is very useful when we want to extract something partially from an image and put it in another image. These bitwise operations can be used here to achieve the effects we want.

`cv2.bitwise_and(img1,img2)`	Perform bitwise AND for img1 and img2
`cv2.bitwise_or(img1,img2)`	Perform bitwise OR for img1 and img2
`cv2.bitwise_not(img1)`	Perform bitwise NOT for img1
`cv2.bitwise_xor(img1,img2)`	Perform bitwise XOR for img1 and img2

The algorithm is as following:

$$g(i,j) = mask \,\&\, f_o(i,j) + (1-mask) \,\&\, f_1(i,j)$$

$f_o(i,j)$ and $f_1(i,j)$ are the original images to blend, and $g(i,j)$ is the result image; $\&$ is the bitwise AND operation.

The bitwise blending process is shown in Figure 5-14, a *mask* is created based on Original Image 2 which is Figure 5-12. And *(1 - mask)* is created based on the *mask*.

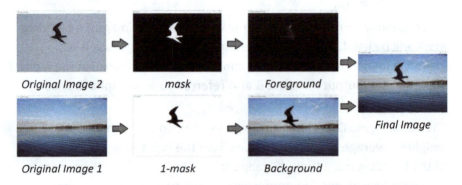

Original Image 2   mask   Foreground

Final Image

Original Image 1   1-mask   Background

Figure 5-14 Blending Images with Bitwise

The *mask* is applied to Original Image 2 by bitwise AND, and produces the foreground of the output image, only the bird appears transparently in the foreground image, and other pixels are opaque and appear as black in the foreground, as shown in Figure 5-15.

Then *(1 -mask)* is applied to the Original Image 1 by bitwise AND, and produces the background image. The bird appears black here, and all other pixels appear transparently.

Finally, the foreground and background are joined together by bitwise OR to produce the result, as shown in Figure 5-14.

There are different ways to create a mask based on an image. An effective way to create a mask is introduced in Section 6.8.1 later, the image is converted to HSV color space, and find out the lower and upper range of HSV value to pick up the interested part of the image, in our case the bird. Then use `cv2.inRange()` function to get the mask. And lastly convert the mask image from grayscale to BGR color space.

Below are the code snippets to create our mask. Note, the creation of masks depends on the images, different images have different methods to create masks, section 6.8 will explain it in detail. Below code snippets are using the technique introduced in Section 6.8.1,

```
1   def remove_background_by_color (
                self,hsv_lower,hsv_upper,image=None) :
2      if image is None:
3        image = self.image
4      imgHSV = cv2.cvtColor(image, cv2.COLOR_BGR2HSV)
5      mask = cv2.inRange(imgHSV, hsv_lower, hsv_upper)
6      mask = 255 - mask
7      mask = cv2.cvtColor(mask, cv2.COLOR_GRAY2BGR)
8      bg_removed = cv2.bitwise_and(image, mask)
9      return bg_removed, mask
```

Figure 5-15 shows the foreground image by applying the *mask* on the bird image with bitwise AND operation.

Figure 5-15 Foreground Image After *mask* Applied

As shown in the above result, all the background from the original image is removed, only the bird is left, which is the interesting part of this image.

This implements the first part of the above formula:

$$g(i,j) = mask \& f_o(i,j) + (1 - mask) \& f_1(i,j)$$

Next is to create *(1 − mask)*, technically this is 255 − *mask*, because the mask is created in a grayscale channel, which has values ranging from 0 to 255. However, in this case we deal it with the binary channel, the values are either 0 or 255, meaning either 100% opacity or 100% transparency, no other values in between. Although in other cases the values in between could indicate the percentage of transparency.

Figure 5-16 shows the result of *(1 − mask)*,

Figure 5-16 *(1 - mask)* Created based on *mask*

Then apply *(1 − mask)* to the second image as bitwise AND operation to produce the background image, the result is shown in Figure 5-17.

Figure 5-17 Background Image After *(1-mask)* Applied

The pixels of the bird are removed, and all others remain on the result image. This implements the second part of the formula:

$$g(i,j) = mask \ \& \ f_o(i,j) + (1 - mask) \ \& \ f_1(i,j)$$

Finally, the two images are merged by bitwise OR operation, or just simply add them up, the result is shown as Figure 5-18:

Figure 5-18 Blended Image with Bitwise Operations

This implements the whole formula:

$$g(i,j) = mask \ \& \ f_o(i,j) + (1 - mask) \ \& \ f_1(i,j)$$

By comparing it with the one in the last section, the difference is obvious, this one does not have any faded-out effect.

In this case the foreground and background are merged with 100% transparency. In real-world projects, depending on what effects you want to achieve, different methods can be selected.

Below is the code snippet in the `ImageProcessing` class,

```
1  def blend_with_mask(self, blend, mask, image=None):
2      if image is None:
3          image = self.image
4      blend = cv2.resize(blend, image.shape[1::-1])
5      mask = cv2.resize(mask, image.shape[1::-1])
```

```
6     result = cv2.bitwise_and(blend, mask) +
                 cv2.bitwise_and(image,(255-mask))
7     return result
```

Explanations:

Line 1	*Define* `blend_with_mask()` *function, the blend image and mask image are passed as parameters.*
Line 4 - 5	*The mask and blend images must be in the same size as the original image, use* `cv2.resize()` *to make them the same dimension, in case they are not.*
Line 6	*Use bitwise AND on blend image and mask image to produce the foreground image.*
	Use bitwise AND again on the original image with (255-mask) to produce the background image.
	Then add both images using plus operation to make the resulting image. `cv2.bitwise_or()` *can also be used, they are the same in this case.*

The full source codes for this example are in *BlendImageBitwise.py* file.

```
1    import cv2
2    import common.ImageProcessing as ip
3
4    def blendTwoImagesWithMask(imageFile1, imageFile2):
5        title = "Blend Two Images"
6        iproc = ip.ImageProcessing(title, imageFile1)
7        iproc.show(title="Original Image1",
                     image=iproc.image)
8        toBlend = cv2.imread(imageFile2)
9        iproc.show(title="Original Image2", image=toBlend)
10       _, mask = iproc.remove_background_by_color(
                       hsv_lower = (90, 0, 100),
11                      hsv_upper = (179,255,255),
12                      Image = toBlend    )
13       iproc.show(title="Mask from Original Image2",
                     image=mask )
14       iproc.show(title=" (1-Mask)", image= (255-mask))
15       blend = iproc.blend_with_mask(toBlend, mask)
```

```
16          iproc.show(title=title, image=blend)
17          cv2.waitKey(0)
18          cv2.destroyAllWindows()
19
20   if __name__ == "__main__":
21          image1 = "../res/sky001.jpg"
22          image2 = "../res/bird002.jpg"
23          blendTwoImagesWithMask(image1, image2)
```

Line 10 – 12 is to call `remove_background_by_color()` function in `ImageProcessing` class to get the mask of the bird image, the details will be explained in Section 6.8.1. The value of parameters of `hsv_lower` and `hsv_upper` are specific only to this image, different images should have different values to get a mask.

5.7   Warp Image

```
Source:      WarpImage.py
Library:     common/ImageProcessing.py,
             common/Draw.py
```

Warp image refers to the process of geometrically transforming an image into different shapes. It involves applying a perspective or affine transformation to the image, which can change its size, orientation, and shape.

This section introduces *perspective warping*, also known as *perspective transformation*, which is a type of image warping that transforms an image from one perspective to another. It is a geometric transformation that changes the viewpoint of an image, as if the observer's viewpoint has moved or rotated in space.

It is often used to correct the distortion caused by the camera's perspective when capturing an image. This distortion causes objects in the image to appear different in size and shape depending on their position in the image. For example, objects closer to the camera appear larger and more distorted than those farther away.

The perspective warping process includes defining four points in the original image and mapping them to four corresponding points in the output image. These points are known as the *source points* and *destination points*, respectively. Once the corresponding points are identified, a transformation matrix is calculated, which maps each pixel in the original image to its new location in the output image. As shown in Figure 5-19, there is an original image in the left, and the output image in the right. The four source points from the original image are A, B, C and D, the perspective warping process will transform them to the output image in the right, so that A is mapped to A', B to B', C to C' and D to D'.

The real-world use case is, for example, using a camera to take a picture of a document, there are some distortions that make the document looks like the left-side image where A, B, C and D are the four corners of the document. A perspective warping will be able to transform the document into the right-side image, which is corrected and aligned properly.

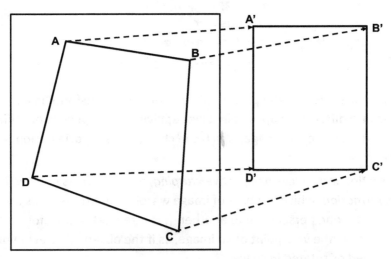

Figure 5-19 Perspective Warping

OpenCV documents have descriptions of the algorithms for image geometric transformations, we do not focus on that in this book, please reference them, if interested, at:

https://docs.opencv.org/4.7.0/da/d54/group__imgproc__transform.html

Perspective warping is commonly used in computer vision and image processing applications, such as image correction, where in many cases images can be distorted due to the angle of the camera, by applying perspective warping the image can be corrected and aligned properly. Another example is image stitching where multiple images are combined to create a larger panorama, warping can be used to align the images properly so that they fit seamlessly.

In this section, as an example in Figure 5-20 below, the left picture is taken by a tablet camera from the homepage of OpenCV.org, the picture looks distorted, the perspective warping will be used to correct it and make it aligned properly, the result will be shown in the right side of Figure 5-20.

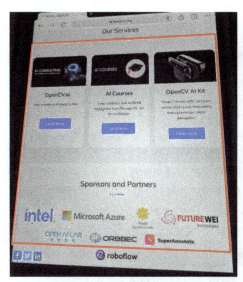

Figure 5-20 An Example of Image Perspective Warping

The picture is taken from the homepage of OpenCV.org

OpenCV provides two functions to perform perspective warping, `cv2.getPerspectiveTransform()` is to calculate the transformation matrix, it takes the four source points and four target points as input. Then `cv2.warpPerspective()` is to perform the perspective warping, it takes the original image, the transformation matrix and the output size.

We will take the four source points from the original image, which indicate the area to transform, and then use them to do the perspective warping.

In the `ImageProcessing` class, add the function `perspective_warp()`:

```
1    def perspective_warp(self, points, width, height
                               image=None):
2      if image is None:
3        image = self.image
4      pts_source = np.float32([points[0], points[1],
                              points[3], points[2]])
5      pts_target = np.float32([[0, 0],[width, 0],
                             [0,height],[width,height]])
6      matrix = cv2.getPerspectiveTransform(
                            pts_source, pts_target)
7      result = cv2.warpPerspective(
                            image,matrix,(width,height))
8      return result
```

Explanations:

Line 1	Define the function for perspective warping, the parameters: `points`: coordinates of the four points from the source image `width`/`height`: the width and height of the warping image. Image: the source image, if `None` then use the default image of the `ImageProcessing` class.
Line 4	Define the coordinates of four points for the source.
Line 5	Define the coordinates of four points for the target.
Line 6	Use `cv2.getPerspectiveTransform()` function to generate the transformation matrix, pass the coordinates of source points and target points as parameters.
Line 7	Use `cv2.warpPerspective()` to perform the perspective transformation.

Now let's look at the codes for image warping, open *WarpImage.py* file from the Github repository. Remember in section 4.3 we used the mouse to draw polygons, every time when left click happens, a point is added to an array; on right click, the drawing is finished, and the polygon is shown, the points in the array are its vertices. Now we reuse the codes to collect the four source points by slightly modifying them, a point is added to the array on left-click, when the number of points is counted to 4, it is finished and a red polygon is drawn to indicate the selected area, at the same time call above `perspective_warp()` function to obtain the warped image, and show the result.

Here are the source codes,

```python
1   import cv2
2   import numpy as np
3   import common.Draw as dw
4   import common.ImageProcessing as ip
5   drawing = False
6   final_color = (0, 0, 255)
7   drawing_color = (0, 0, 125)
8   width, height = 320, 480
9   points = []
10  def on_mouse(event, x, y, flags, param):
11      global points, drawing, img, img_bk, iproc, warped_image
12      if event == cv2.EVENT_LBUTTONDOWN:
13          drawing = True
14          add_point(points, (x, y))
15          if len(points) == 4:
16              draw_polygon(img, points, (x, y), True)
17              drawing = False
18              img_bk = iproc.copy()
19              warped_image = iproc.perspective_warp(points,
                                            width, height)
20              points.clear()
21              iproc.show("Perspective Warping", image=warped_image)
22      elif event == cv2.EVENT_MOUSEMOVE:
23          if drawing == True:
24              img = img_bk.copy()
25              draw_polygon(img, points, (x, y))
26
27  def add_point(points, curt_pt):
28      print("Adding point #%d with position(%d,%d)"
29              % (len(points), curt_pt[0], curt_pt[1]))
```

```
30        points.append(curt_pt)
31
32   def draw_polygon(img, points, curt_pt, is_final=False):
33     if (len(points) > 0):
34       if is_final == False:
35         dw.draw_polylines(img, np.array([points]),
                             False, final_color)
36         dw.draw_line(img, points[-1], curt_pt,
                         drawing_color)
37       else:
38         dw.draw_polylines(img, np.array([points]),
                             True, final_color)
39       for point in points:
40           dw.draw_circle(img, point, 2, final_color, 2)
41           dw.draw_text(img, str(point), point,
                          color=final_color,
                          font_scale=0.5)
42
43   def print_instruction(img):
44     txtInstruction = "Left click to specify four
                         points to warp image.
                         ESC to exit, 's' to save"
45     dw.draw_text(img,txtInstruction, (10, 20), 0.5,
                                        (255, 255, 255))
46     print(txtInstruction)
47
48   if __name__ == "__main__":
49     global img, img_bk, iproc, warped_image
50     title = "Original Image"
51     iproc = ip.ImageProcessing(title,
                                   "../res/skewed_image001.jpg")
52     img = iproc.image
53     print_instruction(img)
54     img_bk = iproc.copy()
55     cv2.setMouseCallback(title, on_mouse)
56     iproc.show()
57     while True:
58       iproc.show(image=img)
59       ch = cv2.waitKey(10)
60       if (ch & 0xFF) == 27:
61         break
62       elif ch == ord('s'):
63         # press 's' key to save image
64         filepath = "C:/temp/warp_image.png"
```

106

```
65              cv2.imwrite(filepath, warped_image)
66              print("File saved to " + filepath)
67      cv2.destroyAllWindows()
```

The source codes are not explained line by line here, because it's basically the same as the one for drawing polygons in section 4.3. Execute the codes in *WarpImage.py*, left click on the image to specify the four points in the same way as we did in drawing polygons, the coordinates are shown in the image. After all four points are collected, it will draw the polygon, and then call `perspective_warp()` function to transform the specified area and show the resulting image.

5.8   Blur Image

```
Source:     BlurImage.py
Library:    common/ImageProcessing.py
```

Blurring an image is a common image processing technique used to reduce noises, smooth out edges, and simplify the image. This section will introduce two types of image blurring techniques, Gaussian Blur and Median Blur.

5.8.1   What is Gaussian Blur

Gaussian Blur is a widely used effect for image processing and is available in many image-editing software. Basically it reduces noises and hides details of the image, and makes the image smoothing.

Figure 5-21 shows what it looks like, the left one is the original image, and the right one is a Gaussian blurred image. By changing the Kernel size, the level of blurring will be changed.

Figure 5-21 Gaussian Blur

Let's take a close look at how the Gaussian blur works, notice the small area highlighted by a white square pointed by a white arrow in Figure 5-21 above. Now zoom in this area and show the details in pixel level, as shown in Figure 5-22, this square is 9 by 9 pixels. Apply a Gaussian blur on this 9×9 area, we get the right-side image in Figure 5-22, the edge of the flower becomes blurred. The size of this area is called *kernel size*, in this example the area is a square of 9×9 pixels, then its kernel size is 9. It doesn't have to be a square, it could be a rectangle, say 5×9 pixels. However, the kernel size must be odd numbers.

This small area is called *filter*, the Gaussian filter will be applied throughout the entire image starting from the top-left corner, moving from left towards right and from top towards down until the bottom-right corner, in another word the filter swept over the whole image, this is the image blurring process.

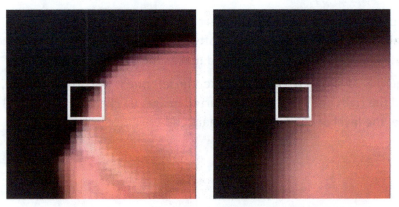

Figure 5-22 Gaussian Blur in Detailed Pixels' Level

Now, let's look at how the Gaussian function works, in other words how the filter is calculated and applied to the area.

Gaussian filter does not simply calculate the average value of the area, in this case the 9×9 area. Instead, it calculates a weighted average of the value for this area, the pixels near the center get more weights, and the pixels far away from the center get less weights. And the calculation is done on a channel-by-channel basis, which means it calculates the blue, green and red channels respectively.

Let's dig a little deeper and see how the Gaussian function works, this is the formula in one dimension:

$$p(x) = \frac{1}{\sigma\sqrt{2\pi}} e^{-\frac{x^2}{2\sigma^2}}$$

However, a pixel is determined by x and y coordinates in an image, so the two-dimensional Gaussian formula should be used for image processing, it's shown as Figure 5-23.

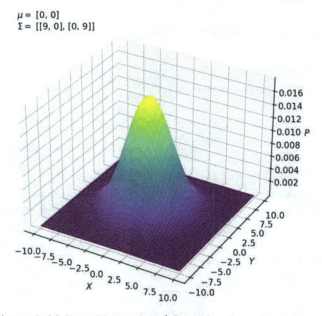

Figure 5-23 Two-Dimensional Gaussian Function

This is generated by the source codes at common/gaussian.py

The two-dimensional Gaussian formula is:

$$p(x, y) = \frac{1}{\sigma\sqrt{2\pi}} e^{-\frac{x^2+y^2}{2\sigma^2}}$$

Now imagine the Gaussian filter mentioned above, in our case an area of 9 x 9 pixels, is overlaying on the vertex of the above plot, the height is the weight for calculation. The pixels near the center are more important and then get more weights, the pixels near the edge are less important and then get less weights.

This is a basic idea of how Gaussian blur works in general, although the algorithm is not as simple as described above. Fortunately, OpenCV provides a function for this purpose, cv2.GaussianBlur(), and all the complexities are hidden behind the scenes. All we need to do is to call this function and specify the kernel size in width and height, which doesn't have to be the same, but must be odd numbers.

5.8.2   Gaussian Blur

Now we add the Gaussian blur function to the ImageProcessing class,

```
1  def blur(self, ksize=(1,1), image=None):
2      if image is None:
3          image = self.image
4      if ksize[0] % 2 == 0:
5          ksize = (ksize[0] + 1, ksize[1])
6      if ksize[1] % 2 == 0:
7          ksize = (ksize[0], ksize[1] + 1)
8      result = cv2.GaussianBlur(image,ksize,
                              cv2.BORDER_DEFAULT)
9      return result
```

Explanations:

Line 1	Define the blur() function, pass ksize as parameter.
Line 4 − 7	ksize must be odd numbers, check ksize if not odd then change it to odd.
Line 8	Invoke cv2.GaussianBlur() function.

BlurImage.py file has the source codes to perform the Gaussian blur, a trackbar is added to change the kernel size, by changing the kernel size we can observe how the blurring effects are different. In this example a square kernel is used, meaning the width and height are equal. Feel free to modify the codes to use a rectangle kernel and observe the blurring effects.

```
1   import cv2
2   import common.ImageProcessing as ip
3
4   def change_ksize(value):
5       global ksize
6       if value % 2 == 0:
7           ksize = (value+1, value+1)
8       else:
9           ksize = (value, value)
10
11  if __name__ == "__main__":
12      global ksize
13      ksize = (5,5)
14      iproc = ip.ImageProcessing("Original",
                                "../res/flower003.jpg")
15      iproc.show()
16
17      cv2.namedWindow("Gaussian Blur")
18      cv2.createTrackbar("K-Size", "Blur", 5, 21,
                        change_ksize)
19
20      while True:
21          blur = iproc.blur(ksize)
22          iproc.show("Blur", blur)
23
24          ch = cv2.waitKey(10)
25          # Press 'ESC' to exit
            if (ch & 0xFF) == 27:
26              break
27          # Press 's' to save
            elif ch == ord('s'):
28              filepath = "C:/temp/blend_image.png"
```

```
29                  cv2.imwrite(filepath, blur)
30                  print("File saved to " + filepath)
31          cv2.destroyAllWindows()
```

Explanations:

Line 4 – 9	*Trackbar callback function, get kernel size from trackbar, and change it to odd number if it's not.*
Line 14 – 15	*Instantiate the `ImageProcessing` class with an image and show it as original image.*
Line 17 – 18	*Create a trackbar in another window called "Gaussian Blur".*
Line 21	*Call `blur()` function defined above in `ImageProcessing` class, pass the kernel size as a parameter.*
Line 22	*Show the blurred image in the "Gaussian Blur" window.*

Figure 5-24 is the result, as the K-Size trackbar is changing, the degree of blurring is also changing in real-time.

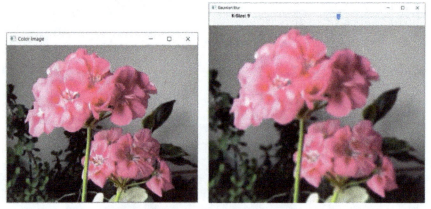

Figure 5-24 Gaussian Blur Results

5.8.3   Median Blur

Same as Gaussian Blur, the Median Blur is also widely used in image processing, it is often used for noise reduction purposes.

112

Similar to the Gaussian Blur filter, instead of applying the Gaussian formula, the Median Blur calculates the median of all the pixels inside the kernel filter and the central pixel is replaced with this median value. OpenCV also provides a function for this purpose, `cv2.medianBlur()`.

Here is the code in `ImageProcessing` class to apply the median blur function,

```
1  def median_blur(self, ksize=1, image=None):
2    if image is None:
3      image = self.image
4    result = cv2.medianBlur(image, ksize)
5    return result
```

In *BlurImage.py* file the codes for Median Blur are quite similar to the Gaussian Blur, a trackbar can change the kernel size, and the effects can be observed in real-time. Below shows the original image vs. the median-blurred image.

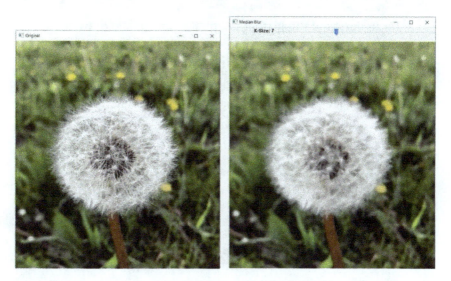

Figure 5-25 Median Blur Results

5.9   Histogram

Source: Histogram.py
Library: common/ImageProcessing.py

5.9.1   About Histogram

A histogram is a graphical representation of the distribution of pixel values in an image. In image processing, a histogram can be used to analyze the brightness, contrast, and overall intensity of an image. It is plotted in a x-y chart, the x-axis of a histogram represents the pixel values ranging from 0 to 255, while the y-axis represents the number of pixels in the image that have a given value. A histogram can show whether an image is predominantly dark or light, and whether it has high or low contrast. It can also be used to identify any outliers or unusual pixel values.

To better understand the histogram, plot an image and draw some squares and rectangles and fill them with the color value of 0, 50, 100, 150, 175, 200 and 255, as shown in the left-side of Figure 5-26. The coordinates of each square/rectangle are also displayed in the image, so we can easily calculate how many pixels for each color.

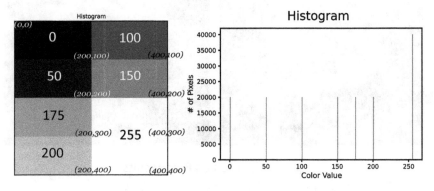

Figure 5-26 Histogram

In the histogram plot in the right-side, x-axis is the color value from 0 to 255, and y-axis is the number of pixels. The y value is 20,000 at $x=0$, meaning there are 20,000 pixels that have a color value of 0, from the left-side image we can see the black rectangle (color: 0) is from (0, 0) to (200, 100), the total number of black pixels is 200 x 100 = 20,000. The histogram plot also shows the color value 0 has 20,000 pixels. The white square (color: 255) has 40,000 pixels. In the same way, calculate the number of pixels for other colors, there are 20,000 pixels for color values of 50, 100, 150, 175 and 200.

This is how the histogram works, the number of pixels and the color values are shown in the histogram.

Below is the code to create the above image and histogram plot.

```
1   def show_histogram():
2       img = np.zeros((400, 400), np.uint8)
3       cv2.rectangle(img, (200,0), (400, 100), (100), -1)
4       cv2.rectangle(img, (0, 100), (200, 200), (50), -1)
5       cv2.rectangle(img, (200, 100), (400, 200), (150), -1)
6       cv2.rectangle(img, (0,200), (200, 300), (175), -1)
7       cv2.rectangle(img, (0, 300), (200, 400), (200), -1)
8       cv2.rectangle(img, (200,200), (400, 400), (255), -1)
9       fig = plt.figure(figsize=(6, 4))
10      fig.suptitle('Histogram', fontsize=20)
11      plt.xlabel('Color Value', fontsize=12)
12      plt.ylabel('# of Pixels', fontsize=12)
13      plt.hist(img.ravel(), 256, [0, 256])
14      plt.show()
```

Explanations:

Line 2	*Create a numpy array as a blank canvas with all zeros.*
Line 3 - 8	*Draw squares and rectangles and fill them with specific color values.*
Line 9 – 12	*Define a plot using matplotlib library, set title and X, Y-axis labels.*
Line 13	*Create a histogram using matplotlib function.*
Line 14	*Show the histogram plot*

Histograms can be used for various purposes in image processing, below is a list of some of the use cases,

Image equalization, by modifying the distribution of pixel values in the histogram, it is possible to improve the contrast and overall appearance of an image.

Thresholding, by analyzing the histogram, it is possible to determine the optimal threshold value for separating the foreground and background of an image.

Color balance, by analyzing the histograms of individual color channels, it is possible to adjust the color balance of an image.

In conclusion, histograms are an important tool in image processing for analyzing and manipulating the distribution of pixel values in an image.

5.9.2   Histogram for Grayscale Images

There are two ways to compute and display histograms. First, OpenCV provides `cv2.calcHist()` function to compute a histogram for an image, second, use `matplotlib` to plot the histogram diagram, `matplotlib` is a Python library for creating static, animated, and interactive visualizations.

Figure 5-27 shows the histogram of a real image.

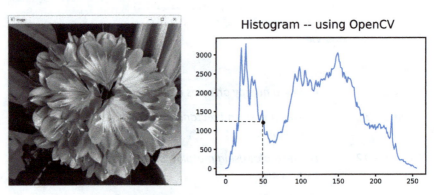

Figure 5-27 Histogram for a Grayscale Image

Look at a specific point, i.e. the ● point in the histogram at the right-side of Figure 5-27, it means there are about 1,200 pixels with color value of 50 in the left-side grayscale image.

This is how to read the histogram which gives an overall idea of how the color value is distributed.

Here are the codes to produce the histogram in Figure 5-27:

```
1    # Get histogram using OpenCV
2    def show_histogram_gray(image):
3        hist = cv2.calcHist([image], [0], None, [256], [0, 256])
4        fig = plt.figure(figsize=(6, 4))
5        fig.suptitle('Histogram - using OpenCV', fontsize=18)
6        plt.plot(hist)
7        plt.show()
```

The second way to display a histogram is to use `matplotlib`, which provides `plt.hist()` function to generate a histogram plot, it does the exact same thing just looks a little bit differently, as Figure 5-28:

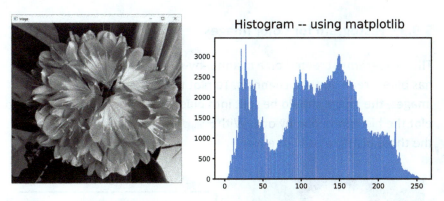

Figure 5-28 Histogram for a Grayscale Image

Here are the codes to produce the histogram in Figure 5-28,

```
9     # Alternative way for histogram using matplotlib
10    def show_histogram_gray_alt(image):
11        fig = plt.figure(figsize=(6, 4))
12        fig.suptitle('Histogram - using matplotlib',fontsize=18)
13        plt.hist(image.ravel(), 256, [0, 256])
14        plt.show()
```

Explanations:

Line 1 - 7	Use OpenCV cv2.calchist to generate a histogram.

Line 3	Call $cv2.calcHist()$ function, pass the image as the parameter.
Line 4 - 6	Create a plot using $matplotlib$, specify the plot size, set the title, and plot the histogram created in line 3.
Line 7	Show the plot
Line 10 - 14	Alternatively, use $matplotlib$ function to generate a histogram.
Line 11 -12	Create a plot using $matplotlib$, specify the plot size, set the title.
Line 13	Call $plt.hist()$ function to create a histogram of the image.

5.9.3 Histogram for Color Images

The histogram is created on a channel-by-channel basis, a color image has blue, green and red channels. To plot the histogram for color images, the image should be split into blue, green and red channels, and plot the histogram one by one. With $matplotlib$ library we can put the three histograms in one plot.

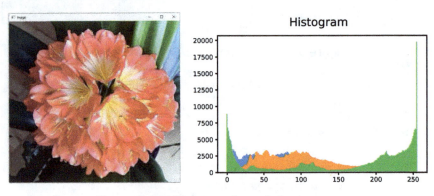

Figure 5-29 Histogram for a Color Image

Below is the code to generate above histogram for color image:

```
1    def show_histogram_color(image):
```

```
2      blue, green, red = cv2.split(image)
3      # cv2.imshow("blue", blue)
4      # cv2.imshow("green", green)
5      # cv2.imshow("red", red)
6      fig = plt.figure(figsize=(6, 4))
7      fig.suptitle('Histogram', fontsize=18)
8      plt.hist(blue.ravel(), 256, [0, 256])
9      plt.hist(green.ravel(), 256, [0, 256])
10     plt.hist(red.ravel(), 256, [0, 256])
11     plt.show()
```

Explanations:

Line 2	Split the color image into blue, green and red channels
Line 3 - 5	Optionally show the blue, green and red channels.
Line 6 - 7	Create a plot, set the title.
Line 8 - 10	Add the histograms for blue, green and red to the plot
Line 11	Show the histogram plot.

In summary, the shape of the histogram can provide information about the overall color distributions, as well as valuable insights into the overall brightness and contrast of an image. If the histogram is skewed towards the higher intensity levels, the image will be brighter, while a skew towards lower intensity levels indicates a darker image. A bell-shaped histogram indicates a well-balanced contrast.

Histogram equalization is a common technique used to enhance the contrast of an image by redistributing the pixel intensities across a wider range. This technique can be used to improve the visual quality of images for various applications, such as medical imaging, satellite imaging, and digital photography.

6. Object Detection

O bject detection is a technique used in image processing to identify and locate objects within an image or video. The goal of object detection is to accurately identify the presence, location, and extent of objects within an image or video frame. It's an important application for computer vision, it applies algorithms to identify the objects in the images, such as shapes of triangles, circles, rectangles, as well as human, faces and eyes, or texts.

OpenCV provides lots of methods for detecting different types of objects. Here is a high-level overview of the steps involved in object detection:

1. The first step is to load the image or video file that you want to analyze using OpenCV.
2. Before running the object detection algorithm, it's usually necessary to preprocess the images by resizing, adjusting the contrast, adjusting HSV or converting to grayscale, etc. Some commonly used techniques like canny, dilation and erosion might also be used for preprocessing.
3. Depending on the specific object detection task, we may choose to use one of the built-in object detection algorithms provided by OpenCV or implement some third-party algorithms.

4. Finally, visualize the results of the object detection algorithm by drawing bounding boxes around the detected objects and displaying the annotated image or video.

This chapter begins with the basics of detection by introducing the Canny Edge Detection in section 6.1, as well as Dilation and Erosion in section 6.2, these techniques are necessary for image detection.

Section 6.3 will introduce shape detection, OpenCV provides methods to identify the shapes like triangles, circles or squares, and calculate their boundaries, areas and perimeters.

Section 6.4 will detect the colors of images by detecting the hue, saturation and value in HSV color space.

Section 6.5 will introduce Optical Character Recognition (OCR), which is to recognize texts in the images. A third-party tool, Tesseract, will be used together with OpenCV to achieve text recognition.

Section 6.6 and section 6.7 will introduce machine learning based approaches, *Haar Cascade classifiers* for face and eye detection and *Histograms of Oriented Gradients (HOG)* for human detection. They are very fast algorithms and can be used in real-time detection in videos. We will focus only on the implementation of these methods, instead of the theory or mathematics details of the algorithms.

Section 6.8 introduces several ways to detect the foreground from images and remove the background. It's a common practice in image processing to detect and remove background from an image, which is called Semantic Segmentation.

At last, in section 6.9, since we are able to detect the foreground separated from the background, we will introduce how to blur the background to make the foreground stand out.

Enjoy the Object Detection with OpenCV and Python.

6.1 Canny Edge Detection

Source: Canny.py

Canny Edge Detection is a widely used algorithm in image processing and computer vision to detect the edges in images. It was proposed by John F. Canny in 1986, the algorithm and theory are beyond the scope of this book, if interested please reference the paper of *Canny, J., A Computational Approach To Edge Detection, IEEE Transactions on Pattern Analysis and Machine Intelligence, 8(6):679–698, 1986, at: https://scirp.org/reference/referencespapers.aspx?referenceid=1834431*

The goal of edge detection is to identify the boundaries of objects within an image. The Canny Edge Detection algorithm achieves this by detecting sharp changes in intensity or color within an image.

There are multiple steps involving the detection of the edges using Canny Edge Detection, OpenCV documents describe the algorithm and steps, see the below link for details: *https://docs.opencv.org/4.7.0/d7/de1/tutorial_js_canny.html*

OpenCV provides `cv2.Canny()` function for this purpose, in order to implement it, the image should be converted to grayscale before using the function. This function needs to specify two thresholds – lower and upper thresholds. They are used to determine which edges in the image are real edges, which are false edges. The pixel gradient is compared with the upper and lower thresholds, if higher than the upper one then the pixel is determined as an edge; if below the lower one then it is a false edge and is discarded; if between the upper and lower and if it is connected with a real edge then accepted as an edge, otherwise discarded.

In this example we use two trackbars to change upper and lower thresholds, and see the edges are changing accordingly.

Notice in line 4 of the source codes, the trackbar callback function is doing nothing with a statement of `pass`, in previous examples the callback function is used to retrieve the values though. Now, alternatively, we use `cv2.getTrackbarPos()` function within the while loop, in line 19 and 20, to retrieve the trackbar value.

```
1    import cv2
2
3    def nothing(x):
4        pass
5
6    def canny_edge_detection():
7        lower, upper = 100, 200
8        image = cv2.imread("../res/flower001.jpg")
9        gray = cv2.cvtColor(image, cv2.COLOR_BGR2GRAY)
10
11       cv2.namedWindow("Canny")
12       cv2.createTrackbar("Lower","Canny",lower,500,nothing)
13       cv2.createTrackbar("Upper","Canny",upper,500,nothing)
14
15       cv2.imshow("Original", image)
16       cv2.imshow("Gray", gray)
17
18       while True:
19           lower = cv2.getTrackbarPos("Lower", "Canny")
20           upper = cv2.getTrackbarPos("Upper", "Canny")
21           canny = cv2.Canny(gray, lower, upper)
22           cv2.imshow("Canny", canny)
23
24           ch = cv2.waitKey(10)
25           # Press 'ESC' to exit
             if (ch & 0xFF) == 27:
26               break
27           # Press 's' to save
             elif ch == ord('s'):
28               filepath = "C:/temp/canny.png"
29               cv2.imwrite(filepath, canny)
30               print("File saved to " + filepath)
31       cv2.destroyAllWindows()
32
33   if __name__ == "__main__":
34       canny_edge_detection()
```

Explanations:

Line 3 - 4	Define a trackbar callback function that is doing nothing.
Line 6	Define `canny_edge_detection()` function.
Line 7	Set initial lower and upper threshold values.

Line 8 - 9	Load an image and convert it to grayscale.
Line 11 - 13	Define a named window and create two trackbars.
Line 15 - 16	Show the original image and grayscale image.
Line 19 - 20	Use `cv2.getTrackbarPos()` to retrieve the lower and upper threshold values from trackbars.
Line 21	Use `cv2.Canny()` function to do the Canny Edge Detection.
Line 22	Show the canny image.
Line 24 – 30	Press ESC to exit and 's' to save the file.
Line 31	Close all windows and exit.
Line 33	The main entrance, call `canny_edge_detection()`.

The results are shown in Figure 6-1. If move both trackbars towards left, more detailed edges will be shown; if move both towards right, less edges will be shown. This is how the thresholds can determine the details of the edges.

Figure 6-1 Canny Edge Detection

The Canny edge detection algorithm is widely used because it is very effective at detecting edges while minimizing noise and other unwanted features. It is also relatively fast and can be applied to a wide range of images and applications. This technique will be applied for object detection in the later sections.

6.2   Dilation and Erosion

Source: DilationErosion.py

Dilation and erosion are two fundamental operations in image processing that are used to manipulate the shape and size of objects in an image. They are the most basic operations of Morphological Image Processing, which is a collection of operations related to the shape or morphology in an image.

Dilation is a morphological operation that is used to enlarge the boundaries of an object in an image. It works by adding pixels to the boundaries of the object based on the defined structuring element. The structuring element is a small matrix or shape that is used to determine which pixels are added to the boundaries of the object. The dilation operation is useful for filling in small gaps, connecting broken parts of an object, and thickening the boundaries of an object.

Erosion is also a morphological operation that is used to shrink the boundaries of an object in an image. It works by removing pixels from the boundaries of the object based on the defined structuring element. The erosion operation is useful for removing small objects, smoothing the boundaries of an object, and separating objects that are close together.

Simply put, dilation will expand the shape or boundaries to make it thicker. Erosion is in opposite of dilation, it erodes away the shape or boundaries and makes it thinner.

Both dilation and erosion are typically used as pre-processing steps in image analysis tasks, such as segmentation and feature extraction. They are often used in combination to achieve specific effects, such as removing small objects while preserving the overall shape of larger objects.

A *structuring element*, also known as *kernel*, is a 2-dimensional matrix that dilation and erosion will use to slide through the entire image to detect pixels. In both operations, the structuring element is swept over the image, and the output image is determined by the interaction between the structuring element and the image pixels. In the case of dilation, a pixel in a binary image (either 1 or 0) will be converted to 1 if any pixels under the kernel are 1, and will be 0 if all pixels under the kernel are 0. In case of erosion, a pixel will be converted to 1 only if all the pixels under the kernel are 1, otherwise 0.

These operations are often used in combination with other image processing techniques to perform tasks such as edge detection, noise removal, and object recognition. For example, erosion can be used for noise removal, the small not connected pixels will be removed after image erosion. But sometimes the real boundaries are also eroded, normally first apply dilation then erosion, and adjust the kernel size, therefore the noises can be removed effectively.

Canny Edge Detection is introduced in the last section, with Canny we can obtain the edge of the boundary of the image. Now apply dilation to make the boundaries thicker. The left-side image in Figure 6-2 below is the one we got from the last section – Canny Edge Detection, the right-side image is the dilation of it. The kernel size is 3 x 3.

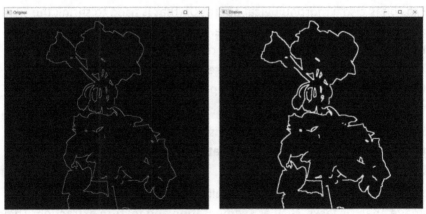

Figure 6-2 Dilation from Canny Edge Detection

Then use this dilated image as the input and apply the erosion on it, the results are shown in Figure 6-3, the kernel size is also 3 x 3, the left-side image is the dilated image from above, the right-side is the result of the erosion.

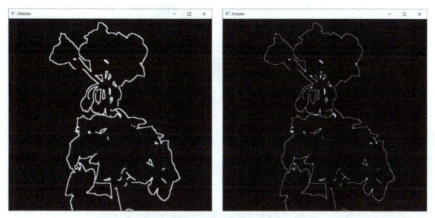

Figure 6-3 Erosion from Dilated Image

Below are the codes to generate above results:

```
1   import cv2
2   import numpy as np
3
4   def dilation(image, ksize=(1,1)):
5       kernel = np.ones(ksize, np.uint8)
6       dilation = cv2.dilate(image, kernel, iterations=1)
7       cv2.imshow("Original", image)
8       cv2.imshow("Dilation", dilation)
9       while True:
10          ch = cv2.waitKey(10)
11          if (ch & 0xFF) == 27:    # Press 'ESC' to exit
12              break
13          elif ch == ord('s'):     # Press 's' to save
14              filepath = "C:/temp/dilation.png"
15              cv2.imwrite(filepath, canny)
16              print("File saved to " + filepath)
17      cv2.destroyAllWindows()
18      return dilation
19
20  def erosion(image, ksize=(1,1)):
21      kernel = np.ones(ksize, np.uint8)
22      erosion = cv2.erode(image, kernel, iterations=1)
23      cv2.imshow("Original", image)
```

127

```
24        cv2.imshow("Erosion", erosion)
25        while True:
26            ch = cv2.waitKey(10)
27            if (ch & 0xFF) == 27:    # Press 'ESC' to exit
28                break
29            elif ch == ord('s'):     # Press 's' to save
30                filepath = "C:/temp/erosion.png"
31                cv2.imwrite(filepath, canny)
32                print("File saved to " + filepath)
33        cv2.destroyAllWindows()
34        return erosion
35
36    if __name__ == "__main__":
37        image = cv2.imread("../res/flower001.jpg")
38        gray = cv2.cvtColor(image, cv2.COLOR_BGR2GRAY)
39        lower, upper = 290, 475
40        canny = cv2.Canny(image, lower, upper)
41        dilation = dilation(canny, (3,3))
42        erosion(dilation, (3,3))
```

Explanations:

Line 4 - 18	Define `dilation()` function.
Line 5	Create a kernel matrix based on the kernel size from the parameter.
Line 6	Call `cv2.dilate()` to perform dilation on the image.
Line 7 - 8	Show original and dilated images.
Line 9 - 17	Press ESC to exit, and "s" to save.
Line 18	Return the dilation result.
Line 20 - 34	Define `erosion()` function.
Line 21	Create a kernel matrix based on the kernel size from the parameter.
Line 22	Call `cv2.erode()` function to perform erosion on the image.
Line 23 – 24	Show original and eroded images.
Line 25 - 33	Press ESC to exit, and "s" to save.
Line 34	Return the erosion result.

Line 36	The main entrance.
Line 37 – 38	Load an image and convert it to a grayscale image.
Line 39 - 40	Apply canny on the grayscale image, see the last section.
Line 41	Apply dilation on the canny image.
Line 42	Apply erosion on the dilated image.

Execute the code and play with the kernel sizes, you will be able to understand how the kernel size affects the results of dilation and erosion.

6.3   Shape Detection

```
Source:      ShapeDetection.py
Library:     common/Detector.py
```

Shape detection is the process of identifying specific geometric shapes in digital images, such as circles, squares, triangles, rectangles, and so on. It is an important task in image processing, computer vision, and pattern recognition.

Suppose there is an image like Figure 6-4 below, there are several different shapes of triangle, circle, rectangle, and square. OpenCV provides functions to detect these shapes, and calculate the area and the perimeter of each shape. Shape detection typically involves several steps, including:

1. Preprocessing: the image is preprocessed to improve its quality, enhance contrast, and remove noise. This step helps to ensure that the detection algorithm can accurately detect shapes in the image.

2. Edge detection: the edges of objects in the image are detected using techniques such as the Canny edge detector. This helps to identify the boundaries of shapes in the image.

3. Contour extraction: the contours of the shapes in the image are extracted from the edge map. Contours are the boundaries of

connected pixels that have similar properties, such as color or intensity.

4. Shape classification: The extracted contours are classified into different shape categories based on their properties. For example, circles have a constant curvature, while squares and rectangles have four straight edges and four right angles.

5. Verification: The detected shapes are verified to ensure that they are valid and accurate. This step may involve filtering out false positives or adjusting the parameters of the shape detection algorithm to improve accuracy.

Figure 6-4 shows an image with several shapes, this will be used as an example for shape detection in this section:

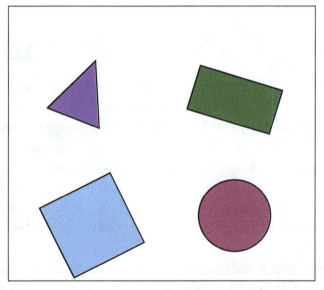

Figure 6-4 Shape Detection

6.3.1   Pre-processing for Shape Detection

There are several steps in pre-processing, the goal of which is to obtain smooth edges with minimized noise.

1. Convert the color image to a grayscale image.

2. Detect edges using Canny edge detection.
3. Adjust edges using Dilation and/or Erosion.

The step 1 and 2 are explained in section 6.1, use `cv2.cvtColor()` with `cv2.COLOR_BGR2GRAY` parameter to convert the color image to grayscale. And then do the Canny edge detection, the lower and upper thresholds need to be adjusted to get the best results. Here we don't repeat the steps in section 6.1 with two trackbars to adjust both thresholds, instead we use fixed values for the thresholds. Then we get the below image with the edges detected.

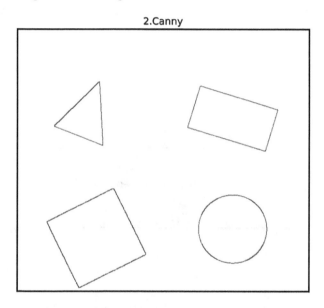

Figure 6-5 Shape Detection, Pre-processing, Canny

Now we have obtained an image with edges detected, in some cases the edges are not good enough for next steps of shape detection because sometimes the edges are not clear enough, or some noises around the edges make it difficult to detect accurately.

If this is the case, it comes to the step 3, adjust the edges to make it smooth. The techniques of dilation and/or erosion will be used in this step to adjust the edges, as explained in section 6.2. The kernel size for dilation and erosion should be adjusted to achieve the best results, and this is an iterative process.

The results of dilation and erosion are shown as Figure 6-6 and Figure 6-7 below.

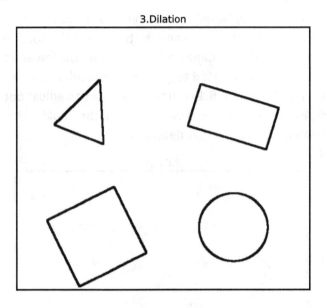

Figure 6-6 Shape Detection, Pre-processing, Dilation

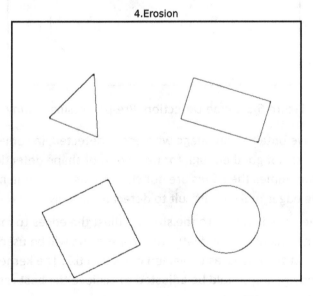

Figure 6-7 Shape Detection, Pre-processing, Erosion

After the dilation and erosion, which is an iterative process, the edges should become smoother than the original edges detected by Canny.

6.3.2   Find Contours

Contours refer to the outlines of objects in an image. They are essentially the boundaries that separate the foreground of an image from the background.

Here is the definition by OpenCV official document:

Contours can be explained simply as a curve joining all the continuous points (along the boundary), having same color or intensity. The contours are a useful tool for shape analysis and object detection and recognition.

From
https://docs.opencv.org/4.7.0/d4/d73/tutorial_py_contours_begin.html

Simply put, the edges of the rectangle in Figure 6-4 is a contour, the edge of a circle is also a contour. OpenCV provides cv2.findContours() function to detect the contours from an image. It returns an array of contours that are detected from an image, each contour is stored as a vector of points. cv2.drawContours() function is used to draw the contours.

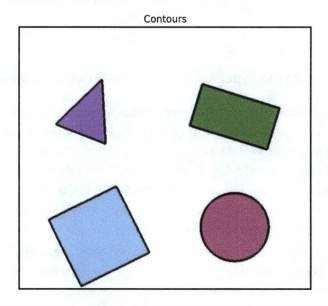

Figure 6-8 Shape Detection, Contours

Now we will find contours from the pre-processed image in the above section, and then draw the contours on top of the original image, as Figure 6-8. The black lines around the shapes are the contours detected.

The details of `cv2.findContours()` function can be found in OpenCV documents, it is used as below,

```
1   contours, hierarchy = cv2.findContours(image,
2                                   cv2.RETR_EXTERNAL,
3                                   cv2.CHAIN_APPROX_NONE)
```

This function takes an input image, finds the contours from it, and returns a list of contours. The contours returned are represented as a list of points, where each point is a coordinate of the contour.

`cv2.RETR_EXTERNAL` specifies the contour retrieval algorithm, specifically it retrieves only the extreme outer contours.

`cv2.CHAIN_APPROX_NONE` specifies the contour approximation algorithm, specifically it stores absolutely all the contour points.

This function returns the `contours` and `hierarchy`, the former is the array that contains all the contours detected from the image, the latter contains the image topology information, which is optional for this example.

6.3.3   Detect the Type, Area and Perimeter of the Shapes

Once the contours are obtained, we can use various OpenCV functions to manipulate and extract information from them. Some of the common functions include `cv2.drawContours()` for drawing the contours on an image, `cv2.contourArea()` for calculating the area of the contour, `cv2.arcLength()` for calculating the perimeter of the contour, and `cv2.boundingRect()` for finding the minimum bounding rectangle of the contour.

Now the contours have been retrieved from the image, and a list of contours is returned from `cv2.findContours()` function. Each item in the contour list is a shape detected from the image. A contour contains the points of the shape, then the type of the shapes can be determined based on the number of points. For example, three-point contour means a triangle, four-point contour means either a rectangle or a square, a circle has eight points in a contour.

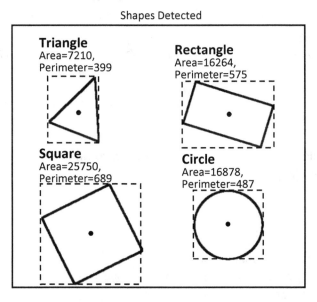

Figure 6-9 Shapes Detected

Figure 6-9 is the result of retrieving the information from the contour list, the black lines are the contours of the shapes, the black dot in the center of each shape is the center of the contour. The rectangular box in dashed line that encloses each contour is the bounding rectangle.

The type of each shape (e.g. triangle, circle, etc.), its area and perimeter are also obtained and shown in Figure 6-9.

The following OpenCV functions are used in this example:

findContours()	*Find the contours from the image, the black thick lines in the above images are contours.*
boundingRect(contour)	*Find the rectangle that includes the contour, the dotted lines are bounding rectangles.*
contourArea(contour)	*Calculate the area of the contour.*

`arcLength(contour, True)`	*Calculate the perimeter of the contour, the second parameter specifies if it is a closed contour (True) or a curve (False).*
`moments(contour)`	*Calculate the center of the contour.*
`approxPolyDP(contour, epsilon, True)`	*Apply Douglas-Peucker algorithm to approximate a contour with a smaller number of vertices. It can repair the "bad shape" of the original contour by reducing some noises. Check OpenCV documents for details.*

A class called `ShapeDetector` is created in common folder in *Detector.py* file,

```
1   class ShapeDetector:
2     def __init__(self):
3       self.epsilon = 0.02
4       self.shapes = {
5         "Triangle": 3,
6         "Square": 4,
7         "Pentagon": 5,
8         "Hexagon": 6,
9         "Circle": 8
10        }
11
12    def get_shape(self, vertices, ratio=1.0):
13      shape = "Other"
14      for (i, (lbl, vrt)) in
                    enumerate(self.shapes.items()):
15        if vertices == vrt:
16          if vrt == 4:
17            if ratio > 0.95 and ratio < 1.05:
18              shape = "Square"
19            else:
20              shape = "Rectangle"
21          else:
22              shape = lbl
23      return shape
24
```

```
25    def detect(self, contour):
26        area = cv2.contourArea(contour)
27        perimeter = cv2.arcLength(contour, True)
28        approximation = cv2.approxPolyDP(contour,
                              self.epsilon * perimeter, True)
29        x, y, w, h = cv2.boundingRect(approximation)
30        vertices = len(approximation)
31        shape = self.get_shape(vertices,
                              (float(w) / float(h)))
32        return shape, area, perimeter, vertices
33
34    def get_bounding_rect(self, contour):
35        perimeter = cv2.arcLength(contour, True)
36        approximation = cv2.approxPolyDP(contour,
                              self.epsilon * perimeter, True)
37        x, y, w, h = cv2.boundingRect(approximation)
38        return x, y, w, h
39
40    def get_center(self, contour):
41        M = cv2.moments(contour)
42        cx = int(M['m10'] / M['m00'])
43        cy = int(M['m01'] / M['m00'])
44        return cx, cy
```

Explanations:

Line 4 - 10	Create a dictionary for shape and its number of vertices. E.g. a triangle has 3 vertices, a square has 4, etc.
Line 12 - 23	Define a function to retrieve a shape from vertices. A special case of square and rectangle is processed here, when the vertices=4, it will check the ratio of width/height to decide square or rectangle.
Line 25	Define the function to detect shape from a contour. The area and perimeter are calculated here, the vertices and shape are also decided here.
Line 26 - 27	Calculate the area and perimeter of the contour.
Line 28	Get an approximation of contour with less number of vertices, some noises in the original contour might cause

	some false vertices, this function will reduce the unnecessary vertices. See OpenCV documents for details.
Line 29	*Find the bounding rectangle of the approximated contour.*
Line 30 - 31	*Get the number of vertices, and determine the shape based on it. E.g. vertices=3 for triangle, vertices=5 for pentagon, etc.*
Line 34 - 38	*Get bounding rectangle, same as Line 27 - 29.*
Line 40 - 44	*Get center point of the contour.*

The source code for this example is in *ShapeDetection.py*, it is straightforward and not explained line by line here.

Execute the codes, the above figures are displayed, and the results are also displayed below:

```
Circle : Vertices=8, Area=16878, Perimeter=487
Square : Vertices=4, Area=25750, Perimeter=689
Rectangle : Vertices=4, Area=16264, Perimeter=575
Triangle : Vertices=3, Area=7210, Perimeter=399
```

6.3.4   Other Contour Features

OpenCV also provides additional functionalities for advanced contour processing, such as approximating contours with polygonal curves, finding the convex hull of a contour, and detecting the orientation of a contour.

Below table lists some other features that are not used in the above example, OpenCV documents have the explanation and code samples, *https://docs.opencv.org/4.7.0/dd/d49/tutorial_py_contour_features.html*

Checking Convexity	*Check if a curve is convex or not, return True or False.*
Minimum Enclosing Circle	*Find the minimum circle that includes the contour.*
Fitting an Ellipse	*Find an ellipse that includes the contour.*

| Convex Hull | Similar to Approximation, see Wikipedia or other sources for details. |

6.4   Color Detection

Color detection is the process of identifying and extracting specific colors from the images. This technique is often used in image processing and computer vision applications to extract information from images or videos.

There are several approaches for color detection, and the choice of method depends on the specific task and the nature of the images being processed. One common approach of color detection is to use color segmentation, which involves dividing the image into regions based on color. This can be done using techniques such as thresholding and clustering. Thresholding is to select a threshold value for a particular color channel and assigning all pixels with values above that threshold to the corresponding color region. Clustering is to group similar colors together based on some distance metric, this will be introduced in the chapter of machine learning in section 7.1.

Another approach to color detection is to use a histogram, which is a graphical representation of the distribution of colors in an image, see section 5.9. It can be used to identify specific colors or color ranges by comparing the histogram of the image to a reference histogram.

Color detection can also be combined with other image processing techniques such as edge detection, object detection, or extracting information from images or videos. For example, in object detection, color can be used as a feature to identify objects through a video sequence.

This section will introduce the color segmentation with thresholds in HSV color space. A minimum threshold and a maximum threshold are defined for a particular color, any pixels between the two thresholds are identified as the color region.

6.4.1 Find Color from an Image

> Source: FindColor.py, common/color_wheel.py

As explained in section 3.4.3 earlier, a color image can be represented in HSV space where a pixel has hue, saturation and value. Hue is for color, saturation for the purity of the color, and value for the brightness. Each color has a range of these values, let's look at how to find out the range of each color.

To recap the concept, see the color wheel in Figure 6-10, the circle is divided by 360 degrees, each degree represents a different color. The color is distributed based on the hue from 0 to 359.

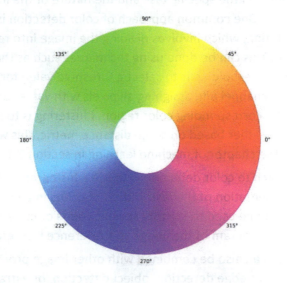

Figure 6-10 Color Wheel

Generated by source codes at common/color_wheel.py

The colors can be identified by changing the hue, saturation and value. First, the original image must be converted to HSV space using cv2.cvtColor() function,

```
1   imgHSV = cv2.cvtColor(img, cv2.COLOR_BGR2HSV)
```

140

Then create six trackbars for adjusting minimum and maximum thresholds of hue, saturation and value. These thresholds are retrieved from the trackbars as they are changing, see Figure 6-11 below:

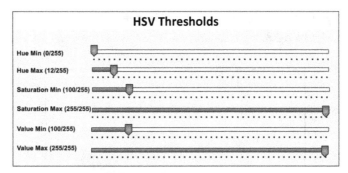

Figure 6-11 HSV Thresholds

These thresholds are used to create a mask that can obtain a portion of the image that only have pixels in the range of [mix, max], all the pixels that are not in the range are filtered out. The cv2.inRange() function is used to create the mask.

Figure 6-12 Find Color, Mask

Here are the codes:

```
2  lower = np.array([h_min, s_min, v_min])
3  upper = np.array([h_max, s_max, v_max])
```

141

```
4   mask = cv2.inRange(imgHSV, lower, upper)
```

The mask is created and is shown in Figure 6-12, it includes only the pixels within the thresholds of hue, saturation and value.

Then applying this mask to the original image of Figure 6-10, we get the results as Figure 6-13.

Color Detected

Figure 6-13 Color Detected

Please note, the mask is obtained from the HSV image, and then it's converted back to BGR and applied to the original image to display. As we mentioned earlier the HSV image is not used for displaying but for image processing.

When changing the trackbars for the thresholds, the mask and the color detected are changing accordingly. The source codes are in *FindColor. py*, by changing the thresholds in trackbars we get different values of the color as shown in the below table. These values will be used in the next section for detecting colors.

Color	Min/Max	Hue	Saturation	Value
Red	Min	0	90	100
	Max	10	255	255

Yellow	Min	11	90	100
	Max	35	255	255
Green	Min	36	90	100
	Max	70	255	255
Cyan	Min	71	90	100
	Max	100	255	255
Blue	Min	101	90	100
	Max	130	255	255
Magenta	Min	131	90	100
	Max	160	255	255
Red	Min	161	90	100
	Max	179	255	255

Let's take a look at the next example, we want to detect the red color from the image in Figure 6-14 below.

It's noticed from the above table that the red has two ranges of hue: [0, 10] and [161, 179], that is because the red color wraps around 359 and 0 in the color wheel of Figure 6-10. Both ranges should be considered when detecting red.

Figure 6-14 Detect Red Color

143

First load the image into `img`, and convert it to HSV in `imgHSV`. Then create two masks, `mask1` and `mask2`, the hue ranges are `[0, 10]` and `[161, 179]` respectively. Then merge the two masks by bitwise OR operation:

```
1   img = cv2.imread("../res/flower002.jpg")
2   imgHSV = cv2.cvtColor(img, cv2.COLOR_BGR2HSV)
3   mask1 = cv2.inRange(imgHSV, (161,  90, 100),
4                              (179, 255, 255) )
5   mask2 = cv2.inRange(imgHSV, (  0,  90, 100),
6                              ( 10, 255, 255) )
7   mask = cv2.bitwise_or(mask1, mask2)
```

The mask looks like Figure 6-15, it's the combination of `mask1` and `mask2`, it should cover all red pixels in the image

Mask

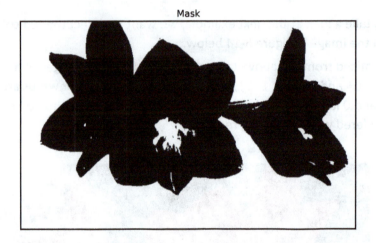

Figure 6-15 Mask for Red Color

Finally, apply `mask` to `img` by bitwise AND operation.

```
8    result = cv2.bitwise_and(img, img, mask=mask)
9    cv2.imshow("Mask", mask)
10   cv2.imshow("Result", result)
```

The result looks like Figure 6-16,

Result

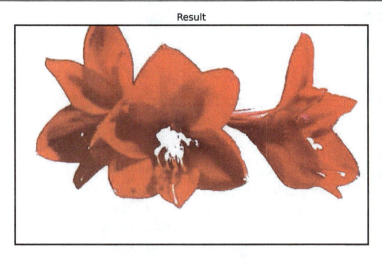

Figure 6-16 Red Color Detected

In summary, because the red color wraps around 359 and 0 in the hue color wheel, in order to detect red, we have to create two masks and merge them together. It should be easier for detecting other colors, only one mask is needed.

6.4.2   Find Color Labels

```
Source:      ColorDetection.py
Library:     common/Detector.py
```

In the last section we have obtained the range of hue, saturation and value for different colors, based on these values we can find out the color labels.

Define a class called ColorDetector and define a dictionary with the color label and the lower and upper HSV values for that color. Then look up the dictionary with an HSV value, if the values are within the range of a color, its color label can be obtained.

For example, say a HSV value is (50,120,234), by looking up the dictionary it's found that this value is within the range of green, then the color label is green.

145

Learn OpenCV with Python by Examples

Here are the codes:

```
1   class ColorDetector:
2     def __init__(self):
3       self.colors = {
4         "Red_1":   ([[0,90,100],   [10,255,255]]),
5         "Yellow":  ([[11,90,100],  [35,255,255]]),
6         "Green":   ([[36,90,100],  [70,255,255]]),
7         "Cyan":    ([[71,90,100],  [100,255,255]]),
8         "Blue":    ([[101,90,100],[120,255,255]]),
9         "Violet":  ([[121,90,100],[130,255,255]]),
10        "Magenta":([[131,90,100],[159,255,255]]),
11        "Pink":    ([[161,90,100],[166,255,255]]),
12        "Red_2":   ([[167,90,100],[190,255,255]]),
13      }
14
15    def get_color_label(self, hsv, mask):
16      color_label = "Unknown"
17      masked_hsv = cv2.bitwise_and(hsv, hsv, mask=mask)
18      mean = cv2.mean(masked_hsv, mask=mask)[:3]
19      for (i, (label, (lower, upper))) in
                      enumerate(self.colors.items()):
20        if np.all(np.greater_equal(mean, lower)) and
21            np.all(np.less_equal(mean, upper)):
22          color_label = label
23      return color_label, mean
```

Explanations:

Line 4 - 12	Create a dictionary with the color labels and the lower/upper HSV values.
Line 15	Define a function to look up the color label dictionary, the HSV image and a mask is passed in as a parameter.
Line 17	Apply the mask to the HSV image.
Line 18	Get the mean value of the masked area. E.g. if a masked area is the red portion of the image, the mean value of this area will be in red range.

146

Line 19 - 22	Look up the dictionary to check the mean value within which color range.
Line 23	Return the color label and the mean value.

Now look at this example, the image is the same as what we did in shape detection, as Figure 6-17. There are different shapes with different colors in this image, previously we detected the shapes, but now we want to find the color labels for each shape.

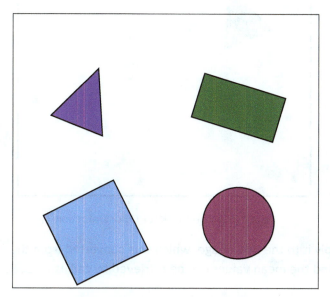

Figure 6-17 Color Label Detection

Similar to the shape detection in section 6.3, first find out all the contours of the shapes in this image, then create a mask for each contour, `cv2.drawContours()` function is used to create the mask, the parameter `cv2.FILLED` is to draw the closed contour with inside filled, as below code snippet:

```
1  contours, hierarchy = cv2.findContours(image,
2                              cv2.RETR_EXTERNAL,
                              cv2.CHAIN_APPROX_NONE)
3      for contour in contours:
4          mask = np.zeros(image.shape[:2], np.uint8)
5          cv2.drawContours(mask, [contour], -1, (255),
```

```
cv2.FILLED)
```

A mask is created and looks like Figure 6-18, the triangle at the upper left of the image:

Mask

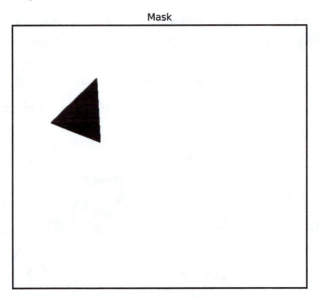

Figure 6-18 The Mask for Color Detection

Then apply it to the HSV image, which was converted from the original image. And the mean values can be retrieved by calling `cv2.mean()` function.

```
6      masked_hsv = cv2.bitwise_and(hsv,hsv,mask=mask)
7      mean = cv2.mean(masked_hsv, mask=mask)[:3]
```

The mean HSV values will be used to look up the color label dictionary that was defined in the `ColorDetector` class earlier. The below code snippets are to look up the dictionary for the color label, it checks whether the mean value is between the lower and upper value for a color.

```
8      for (i, (label, (lower, upper))) in
                   enumerate(self.colors.items()):
9          if np.all(np.greater_equal(mean, lower)) and
10             np.all(np.less_equal(mean, upper)):
```

```
11                    color_label = label
```

The color label for the upper-left triangle is detected as:

```
Violet [129. 128. 170.]
```

The above steps will be repeated for every shape in the image, the results are shown as Figure 6-19 below, the color label as well as the HSV values are displayed along with each shape.

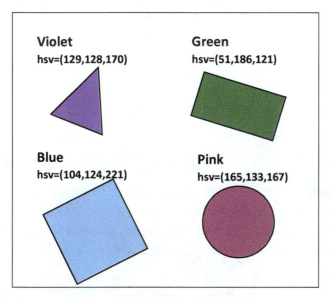

Figure 6-19 Color Labels Detected

The results are also printed out as:

```
Pink [165. 133. 167.]
Blue [104. 124. 221.]
Green [ 51. 186. 121.]
Violet [129. 128. 170.]
```

In this example we defined the color label in a broader range, e.g. both yellow and orange are identified as Yellow; the green, dark green and light green are all identified as Green. If you want, you can define it on a more granular level in the dictionary in ColorDetector class.

For example, instead of only one entry for the yellow,

```
1    "Yellow":    ([[11, 90, 100],   [35, 255, 255]]),
```

You might think to break it down into more entries for the yellows, like gold, orange, honey and canary, as below code snippets. The lower and upper values need to be figured out one by one though.

```
1    "Gold":    ([[11, 90, 100], [xxx, xxx, xxx]]),
2    "Orange": ([[xxx, xxx, xxx], [xxx, xxx, xxx]]),
3    "Yellow": ([[xxx, xxx, xxx], [xxx, xxx, xxx]]),
4    "Honey":  ([[xxx, xxx, xxx], [xxx, xxx, xxx]]),
5    "Canary": ([[xxx, xxx, xxx], [35, 255, 255]]),
```

6.5   Text Recognition with Tesseract

```
Source:        TextRecognition.py
```

Text recognition, or Optical Character Recognition (OCR) is a process to detect texts from an image which could be a scanned document or handwritten texts, and convert them into machine readable texts that can be used for various purposes, such as editing, searching, and storing.

This process involves several steps, including image preprocessing, text detection, character segmentation, and character recognition. In the first step, the image is preprocessed to improve the quality of the scanned or handwritten texts. This may involve removing noises, enhancing contrast, and sharpening the image.

Next, text detection algorithms are used to locate the areas of the image that contain text. This is done by analyzing the image for patterns that resemble text, such as lines and curves, and then extracting those regions for further processing.

Once the text has been detected, the image is segmented into individual characters or words. This involves separating the text into its constituent parts, which are then recognized using character recognition algorithms.

OCR technology has a wide range of applications, including document digitization, text translation, and automated data entry. It is commonly used in industries such as finance, healthcare, and government, where the ability to quickly and accurately process large amounts of text data can be critical to decision-making and operations.

Tesseract is an open-source text recognition library developed by Google, it is considered as one of the most accurate open-source OCR engines. It's designed to recognize text in a variety of languages and formats, including scanned documents, PDFs, and images. It can be used from the command line or as a library in other programming languages, such as Python.

Python has a wrapper library called `pytesseract`, which can be used to access the Tesseract features for recognizing texts from images. The details can be found in the URL at: *https://github.com/tesseract-ocr/tesseract*

6.5.1   Install and configure Tesseract

In order to use Tesseract, it must be installed first. Go to the Tesseract website at *https://tesseract-ocr.github.io/tessdoc/Installation.html*, there are different installation packages for different operating systems, grab one for yours and do the installation following the instructions.

In Windows, download the latest package for Windows and execute it until completion, it's a straightforward process.

Next, find the location of Tesseract executables, this information is needed later in the Python code. The default location is here:

```
C:\Program Files\Tesseract-OCR\tesseract.exe
```

Now run the command from the Windows CMD window,

```
"C:\Program Files\Tesseract-OCR\tesseract.exe" -
version
```

The results look something like below:

```
tesseract v5.0.0-alpha.20201127
  leptonica-1.78.0
```

```
   libgif 5.1.4 : libjpeg 8d (libjpeg-turbo 1.5.3) :
libpng 1.6.34 : libtiff 4.0.9 : zlib 1.2.11 :
libwebp 0.6.1 : libopenjp2 2.3.0
...
```

The above result indicates Tesseract is ready on the system, although it could be different versions. The above version is the latest at the time of this writing.

On Ubuntu, simply execute the following command, it's super easy because Tesseract is already part of the apt-get repository.

```
$ sudo apt install tesseract-ocr
```

To verify the installation on Ubuntu, execute the below command, similar results will be shown to indicate the version of the installed Tesseract:

```
$ tesseract -v
```

After it's installed on the operating systems, the Python library `pytesseract` must also be installed on the environment. Reference section 2.3.2 to install the package

When successfully installed, it should appear in the Python Interpreter package list in Figure 2-6.

6.5.2   Text Recognition

It's important to note that the accuracy of text recognition can vary depending on the quality of the input image and the complexity of the text being recognized. Preprocessing techniques such as image enhancement and noise reduction can be used to improve OCR accuracy. Additionally, training Tesseract on specific fonts and languages can also improve its recognition capabilities.

In this example, there is an image like Figure 6-20, the image looks inclined. Performing OCR on an inclined or rotated image can be challenging as the texts are not aligned with the horizontal axis, which can affect the accuracy of the OCR.

In section 5.7 we have introduced the technique of perspective warping, it can be used here to de-skew the image in order to align the texts with the horizontal axis.

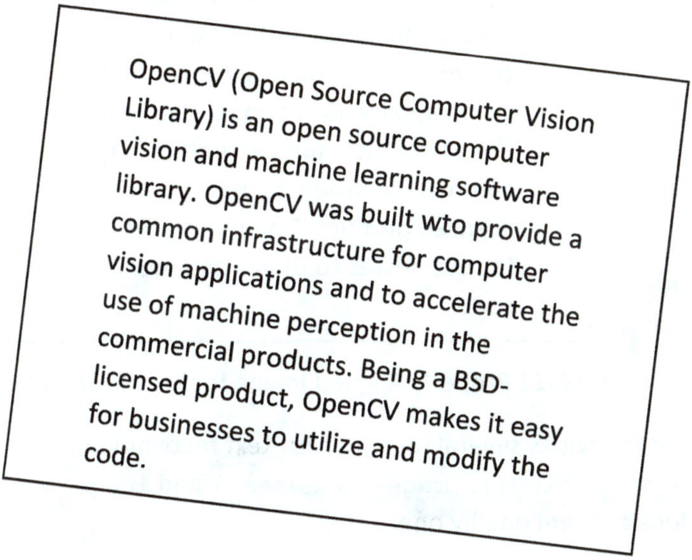

Figure 6-20 Original Image for Text Recognition

Below codes apply the perspective warping introduced in section 5.7:

```
1  def perspective_warp(points, width, height, image):
2      pts_source = np.float32([points[0], points[1],
                                points[3], points[2]])
3      pts_target = np.float32([[0, 0],[width, 0],[0,
                                height],[width, height]])
4      matrix = cv2.getPerspectiveTransform(pts_source,
                                pts_target)
5      result = cv2.warpPerspective(image, matrix,
                                (width, height))
6      return result
```

Then we get a better aligned image as Figure 6-21. This will be used for text recognition. This pre-processing technique can also be used for distorted images taken by cameras, for details please reference the previous section 5.7 for image warping.

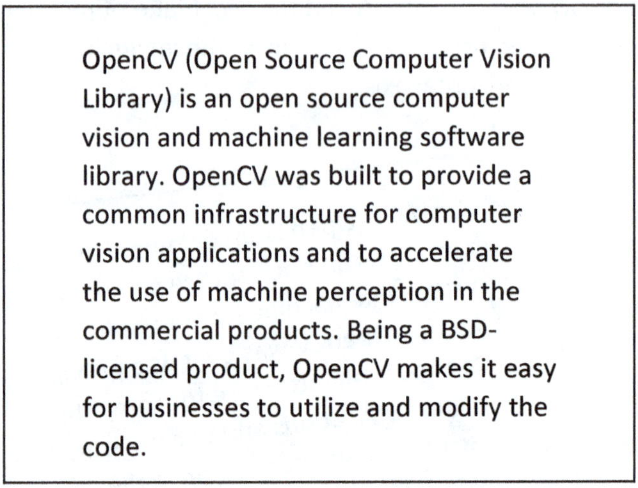

OpenCV (Open Source Computer Vision Library) is an open source computer vision and machine learning software library. OpenCV was built to provide a common infrastructure for computer vision applications and to accelerate the use of machine perception in the commercial products. Being a BSD-licensed product, OpenCV makes it easy for businesses to utilize and modify the code.

Figure 6-21 Properly Aligned Image for Text Recognition

Tesseract provides several functions for text recognition, `image_to_string()`, `image_to_boxes()` and `image_to_data()`. Let's look at them one by one.

In order to use Tesseract in Python codes, it's necessary to import `pytesseract` library and specify the location of Tesseract executable, like following,

```
1  import pytesseract
2  pytesseract.pytesseract.tesseract_cmd =
3       "C:/Program Files/Tesseract-OCR/tesseract.exe"
```

6.5.2.1   Recognize Texts from Image to String

The function `image_to_string()` takes an image as a parameter and returns a string of all recognized texts.

```
1  def recognize_to_string(image):
2      text = pytesseract.image_to_string(image)
3      return text
```

The results are displayed as below:

```
OpenCV (Open Source Computer Vision
Library) is an open source computer
```

vision and machine learning software
library. OpenCV was built to provide a
common infrastructure for computer
vision applications and to accelerate the
use of machine perception in the
commercial products. Being a BSD-
licensed product, OpenCV makes it easy
for businesses to utilize and modify the
code.

6.5.2.2 Recognize Texts by Word

The `image_to_data()` function takes the image as an input parameter, recognizes the text word by word and returns a dictionary that includes the information of each word in the image.

```python
1  def recognize_by_word(image):
2      words = pytesseract.image_to_data(image)
3      for i, word in enumerate(words.splitlines()):
4          if i != 0:
5              word = word.split()
6              print(word)
7              if len(word) == 12:
8                  t,x,y,w,h = word[11], int(word[6]),
                                int(word[7]),
9                                int(word[8]), int(word[9])
10                 cv2.rectangle(image, (x,y), (w+x,h+y),
                                (0,0,255),1)
11                 cv2.putText(image, t, (x,y),
                                cv2.FONT_HERSHEY_COMPLEX,
12                                0.6, (0,0,255), 1)
```

The dictionary returned by `image_to_data()` function looks something like below table,

Level	Page#	Line#	Word#	Left	Top	Width	Height	Text
5	1	1	1	133	87	123	46	OpenCV
5	1	1	2	278	87	124	46	(Open

5	1	1	3	419	87	122	46	Source
5	1	1	4	556	87	158	46	Computer
5	1	1	5	723	87	119	46	Vision
4	1	2	0	134	176	635	37	
5	1	2	1	134	176	131	37	Library)
5	1	2	2	280	176	25	29	is
5	1	2	3	319	184	40	21	an
5	1	2	4	374	184	85	29	open
5	1	2	5	473	184	117	21	source
5	1	2	6	604	178	165	35	computer
...	...	...	...	...	...	...	...	...

Each item in the dictionary contains information about the recognized text, including the text itself, its position on the image, and other details. The position includes its left, top, width and height, which are coordinates of the bounding rectangles of the words.

Draw the results as Figure 6-22:

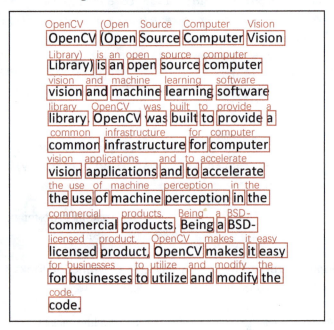

Figure 6-22 Recognize Texts by Word

The bounding rectangle of each word is used to draw a box around the word, and the recognized text is also drawn on the resulting image in Figure 6-22.

With this function, we can recognize the texts in the image and extract the individual words as a list of strings. Note that Tesseract may not recognize every word correctly, especially if the image has poor quality or the text is distorted in some way.

6.5.2.3 Recognize Texts by Characters

Similarly, the function `image_to_boxes()` takes the image as an input parameter, recognizes the texts character by character and returns a dictionary that includes the information of each character.

```
1  def recognize_by_char(image):
2      height, weight = image.shape[:2]
3      chars = pytesseract.image_to_boxes(image)
4      for char in chars.splitlines():
5          print(char)
6          char = char.split(" ")
7          c,x,y,w,h = char[0],int(char[1]),int(char[2]),
8                              int(char[3]), int(char[4])
9          cv2.rectangle(image, (x,height-y), (w,height-h),
                               (0,0,255),1)
10         cv2.putText(image, c, (x,height-y-20),
                               cv2.FONT_HERSHEY_COMPLEX,
11                             0.5, (0,0,255), 1)
```

The `image_to_boxes()` function returns a dictionary with information about each character recognized in the image, including its position on the image, which looks something like below table.

O	133	899	161	929	0
p	165	892	183	921	0
e	186	899	205	921	0
n	209	900	226	921	0
C	213	887	252	933	0

V	231	899	256	929	0
(	278	891	307	929	0
O	310	899	338	929	0
p	320	887	359	933	0
e	342	892	360	921	0
n	363	899	402	921	0
S	419	899	441	928	0
o	445	899	464	921	0
u	447	887	486	933	0
r	468	899	495	920	0
c	495	899	520	921	0
e	522	899	541	921	0
...	...	...	...	...	...

Each item in the dictionary has four coordinates to indicate the bounding rectangle around each character, below is the formula to get the character and the bounding rectangle from each item of the dictionary:

```
Character = Column 0
x = Column 1
y = Image height - Column 2
width = Column 3
height = Image height - Column 4
```

We can extract the recognized characters and their bounding rectangles from this dictionary and draw them on the image.

The result is similar to Figure 6-22 above, but the boxes are around each character instead of each word.

With this code, we can recognize the texts in an image and extract each individual character along with its position on the image. Note that Tesseract may not recognize every character correctly, especially if the image has poor quality or the text is distorted in some way.

Below are the full source codes,

```
1    import cv2
2    import numpy as np
3    import pytesseract
```

158

```
4
5    def perspective_warp(points, width, height, image):
6        pts_source = np.float32([points[0], points[1],
                                          points[3], points[2]])
7        pts_target = np.float32([[0, 0], [width, 0],
                                          [0, height],
                                          [width, height]])
8        matrix = cv2.getPerspectiveTransform(pts_source,
                                                  pts_target)
9        result = cv2.warpPerspective(image, matrix,
                                          (width, height))
10       return result
11
12   def recognize_to_string(image):
13       text = pytesseract.image_to_string(image)
14       return text
15
16   def recognize_by_char(image):
17       height, weight = image.shape[:2]
18       chars = pytesseract.image_to_boxes(image)
19       for char in chars.splitlines():
20           print(char)
21           char = char.split(" ")
22           c,x,y,w,h = char[0], int(char[1]), int(char[2]),
                                  int(char[3]), int(char[4])
23           cv2.rectangle(image, (x,height-y), (w,height-h),
                            (0,0,255),1)
24           cv2.putText(image, c, (x,height-y-20),
                          cv2.FONT_HERSHEY_COMPLEX,
                          0.5, (0,0,255), 1)
25
26   def recognize_by_word(image):
27       words = pytesseract.image_to_data(image)
28       for i, word in enumerate(words.splitlines()):
29           if i != 0:
30               word = word.split()
31               print(word)
32               if len(word) == 12:
33                   t,x,y,w,h = word[11], int(word[6]),
                                      int(word[7]),
                                      int(word[8]),
                                      int(word[9])
34                   cv2.rectangle(image, (x,y), (w+x,h+y),
                                    (0,0,255),1)
```

```
35                              cv2.putText(image, t, (x,y),
                                    cv2.FONT_HERSHEY_COMPLEX,
                                    0.6, (0,0,255), 1)
36
37   def text_recognition():
38       img = cv2.imread("../res/text_for_ocr.jpg")
39       width, height = 880, 760
40       points = [(69, 1), (1089, 83), (1020, 947), (0, 866)]
41       warped = perspective_warp(points, width, height, img)
42       cv2.imshow("Original", img)
43       cv2.imshow("Warped", warped)
44
45       text = recognize_to_string(warped)
46       print(text)
47
48       result1 = warped.copy()
49       result2 = warped.copy()
50       recognize_by_char(result1)
51       recognize_by_word(result2)
52
53       cv2.imshow("Text Recognition by Char", result1)
54       cv2.imshow("Text Recognition by Word", result2)
55       cv2.waitKey(0)
56       cv2.destroyAllWindows()
57
58   if __name__ == "__main__":
59       pytesseract.pytesseract.tesseract_cmd =
                "C:/Program Files/Tesseract-OCR/tesseract.exe"
60       text_recognition()
```

6.5.2.4   Recognize Texts Directly from Tesseract

Since Tesseract is installed in the operating system, it can be directly invoked from the command line to recognize the text in an image, without Python.

From Windows cmd window, execute the following command, and pass the image file and the output file name as the arguments.

```
"C:\Program Files\Tesseract-OCR\tesseract.exe"
text_for_ocr.jpg output.txt
```

The recognized texts are in the `output.txt` file.

6.6   Human Detection

> Source: HumanDetection.py

OpenCV provides the algorithm called *HOG (Histograms of Oriented Gradients)* which is a very fast human detection method. It is pre-trained to detect human mostly standing up and fully visible, such as pedestrians, it doesn't work well in other cases.

We don't focus on the theory and algorithm of *HOG*, instead we want to show how it is used in Python with OpenCV. There are several papers and articles in the References section to help better understand it.

To perform human detection using OpenCV with HOG, there are several basic steps:

1. Load the image or video frame.
2. Convert the image or video frame to grayscale.
3. Create a HOG descriptor using `cv2.HOGDescriptor()` function.
4. Use the `hog.setSVMDetector()` function to compute the HOG features for the image, it sets the support vector machine (SVM) detector for object detection. It is trained on a large dataset of human images and is optimized for detecting standing or walking human in typical environments.
5. Use the `hog.detectMultiScale()` function to detect objects in the image. This function takes the HOG features as input and returns the bounding rectangles of the detected objects.
6. Draw the bounding rectangle on the original image using the `cv2.rectangle()` function.

6.6.1   Human Detection from Pictures

It's quite simple and straightforward to use *HOG* to detect human in Python and OpenCV, as following code snippets, the first two lines are to initialize *HOG*, line 3 is to detect human from an image.

```
1  hog = cv2.HOGDescriptor()
2  hog.setSVMDetector(cv2.HOGDescriptor_
                   getDefaultPeopleDetector())
```

```
3   boxes, weights = hog.detectMultiScale(image,
                                winStride=(8, 8))
```

The `boxes` that returned from the function `detectMultiScale()` contain an array of bounding rectangles for persons detected from the image, the bounding rectangles can be drawn to highlight the persons in the image.

Below are the codes for this example. The `human_detection()` function detects human using `hog.detectMultiScale()`, and draws rectangles for each item in the returned `boxes`, as well as the number of persons detected. In the `__main__` block, initialize the HOG and load three pictures for human detection.

```
1    import cv2
2    def human_detection(image):
3        boxes, weights = hog.detectMultiScale(image,
                                        winStride=(8, 8))
4        person = 1
5        for x,y,w,h in boxes:
6            cv2.rectangle(image,(x, y),(x+w,y+h),(0,255,0),2)
7            cv2.putText(image, f'person-{person}', (x, y-10),
8                    cv2.FONT_HERSHEY_SIMPLEX,0.5,(0,255,0),1)
9            person += 1
10       return image
11
12   if __name__ == "__main__":
13       # initialize HOG for human/person detector
14       hog = cv2.HOGDescriptor()
15       hog.setSVMDetector(cv2.HOGDescriptor_
                            getDefaultPeopleDetector())
16       img1 = cv2.imread("../res/pexels-charlotte-may-
                        5965704.jpg")
17       cv2.imshow("Human Detection 1", human_detection(img1))
18       img2 = cv2.imread("../res/pexels-catia-matos-
19                       1605936.jpg")
20       cv2.imshow("Human Detection 2", human_detection(img2))
21       img3 = cv2.imread("../res/pexels-daniel-frese-
22                       574177.jpg")
23       cv2.imshow("Human Detection 3", human_detection(img3))
24       cv2.waitKey(0)
```

```
25      cv2.destroyAllWindows()
```

Below Figure 6-23 and Figure 6-24 show the results of human detection.

Figure 6-23 Human Detection 1

Photo by Charlotte May: https://www.pexels.com/photo/unrecognizable-women-walking-along-paved-pathway-5965704/

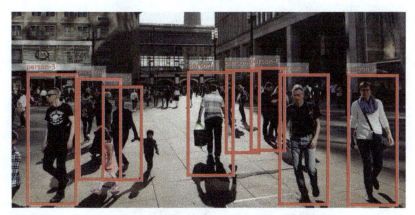

Figure 6-24 Human Detection 2

Photo by Daniel Frese: https://www.pexels.com/photo/man-in-black-crew-neck-t-shirt-walking-near-building-574177

6.6.2   Human Detection from Videos

The HOG algorithm is so fast that can be used for videos, which is similar to that for images. The only difference is to loop over the frames of the video and apply the HOG detector to each frame.

Here's an example code snippet that demonstrates how to detect human from the webcam using HOG:

```
1    import cv2
2    def human_detection_from_video(url):
3        cap = cv2.VideoCapture(0)
4        success, image = cap.read()
6        while success:
7            cv2.imshow("Human Detection from Video",
                    human_detection(image))
8            # Press ESC key to break the loop
9            if cv2.waitKey(5) & 0xFF == 27:
10               break
11           success, image = cap.read()
12       cap.release()
13       cv2.destroyAllWindows()
```

Explanations:

Line 2	*Define* human_detection_from_video().
Line 3	*Load video from the default webcam.*
Line 4	*Load a frame from the video capture object, the frame is stored in* image, *and the result is stored in* success *indicating True or False.*
Line 6 - 11	*Loop frame by frame from the video capture object until ESC key is pressed, and human detection is performed for each frame inside the loop.*
Line 7	*Call* human_detection() *to detect human and show the results.*
Line 9	*Press ECS to exit.*

Execute the codes, the video from the webcam will be played, and the human detection is in action. When a person is captured by the webcam, there will be a box shown around the person in the video, something like Figure 6-23.

The HOG algorithm can detect human in most cases and very fast, however it's not 100% accurate. The accuracy depends on several factors such as the size of the person, the resolution of the image or video, and the HOG parameters used for detection.

In general, HOG-based human detection is considered to be a reliable method, especially for detecting standing or walking persons. However, it may not perform well in detecting persons in unusual postures or when they are partially captured.

To improve the accuracy of HOG-based human detection, it's important to select appropriate parameters for the HOG descriptor, such as the size of the image window, the number of cells in each block, and the size of the stride. These parameters can affect the accuracy of the HOG detector, as well as the speed of the detection.

It's also important to note that HOG-based human detection is often used in combination with other methods, such as cascade classifiers or deep learning models, to improve the overall accuracy of the detection. For example, some researchers use a cascade of HOG detectors to improve the accuracy of human detection in complex scenes.

Overall, the accuracy of HOG-based human detection is affected by several factors, and it's important to select appropriate parameters and use them in combination with other methods to achieve the best possible accuracy.

6.7   Face and Eye Detection

> Source: FaceEyeDetection.py

OpenCV provides another method for object detection using Haar feature-based cascade classifiers, it is an effective object detection method proposed by Paul Viola and Michael Jones in their paper, *"Rapid Object Detection using a Boosted Cascade of Simple Features"* in

2001. It is a machine learning based approach where a cascade function is pre-trained with the input data.

The Haar cascade classifier is trained using thousands of positive and negative images as the input data. The positive images are those that contain the object to be detected, while the negative images are those that do not contain the object. The classifier is trained using a machine learning algorithm called AdaBoost, which selects a small set of important features (called Haar features) from the training set and trains a classifier using these features. The Haar features are calculated by subtracting the sum of pixel intensities in one rectangular region of an image from the sum of pixel intensities in another rectangular region adjacent to it.

The Haar classifier works by sliding a window of a fixed size over an image and computing the Haar features for each position of the window. The classifier then applies the trained model to determine if the object is present in that window. If the object is present, the window is classified as positive, and if not, it is classified as negative. By sliding the window over the entire image, the classifier can detect the object in different locations and scales.

There are a number of articles online to explain how the cascade classifier works, which is out of the scope of this book, please reference those materials if you want to understand the theories and algorithms. There are several articles listed in the References section as well, this book however only focuses on the implementation.

OpenCV comes with some pre-trained classifiers which can be used to detect different objects from images. There are two ways to get those cascade classifiers,

1. They come with OpenCV installation, located at the folder specified by `cv2.data.haarcascades`.
2. Download the latest version from the below link, *https://github.com/opencv/opencv/tree/master/data/haarcascades*

The cascade classifiers only work on grayscale images, make sure the images are converted to grayscale before calling the cascade functions.

In this example we will detect faces and eyes from the images, there are two cascade classifiers for this purpose, one for faces (`haarcascade_frontalface_default.xml`) and another for eyes (`haarcascade_eye.xml`).

We use the ones that come with OpenCV installation, as below line 25 – 29.

```python
1   import cv2
2   def detect_face_and_eye(image):
3     gray = cv2.cvtColor(image, cv2.COLOR_BGR2GRAY)
4     faces = face_cascade.detectMultiScale(gray,
5                       scaleFactor = 1.1,
6                       minNeighbors = 4  )
7     print('Faces found: ', len(faces))
8     for (x, y, w, h) in faces:
9       cv2.rectangle(image, (x, y), (x + w, y + h),
10                    (0, 255, 0), 2)
11      face_gray = gray[y:y + h, x:x + w]
12      face_color = image[y:y + h, x:x + w]
13      eyes = eye_cascade.detectMultiScale(
14                      face_gray,
15                      scaleFactor=1.1,
16                      minNeighbors=3)
17      print('Eyes found: ', len(eyes))
18      for (ex, ey, ew, eh) in eyes:
19        cv2.rectangle(face_color, (ex, ey),
20                    (ex + ew, ey + eh),
21                    (255, 0, 0), 2)
22    return image
23
24  if __name__ == "__main__":
25    face_cascade = cv2.CascadeClassifier(
26            cv2.data.haarcascades +
27            "haarcascade_frontalface_default.xml" )
28    eye_cascade = cv2.CascadeClassifier(
29        cv2.data.haarcascades + "haarcascade_eye.xml")
30    img = cv2.imread("../res/pexels-bess-hamiti-35188.jpg")
31    cv2.imshow("Face and Eye Detection",
32              detect_face_and_eye(img) )
33    cv2.waitKey(0)
34    cv2.destroyWindow("Face and Eye Detection")
```

Explanations:

Line 24	The start point of the execution.
Line 25 - 27	Load face cascade classifier from OpenCV default installation.
Line 28 - 29	Load eye cascade classifier from OpenCV default installation.
Line 30	Load an image.
Line 31 - 32	Call detect_face_and_eye() function and show the result.
Line 2	Define detect_face_and_eye() function.
Line 3	Convert the image to grayscale.
Line 4 - 6	Call detectMultiScale() function of the face cascade classifier to detect faces. It takes three parameters: 1. Input image in grayscale, 2. scaleFactor specifies how much the image size is reduced with each scale, 3. minNeighbours specifies how many neighbors each candidate rectangle should have to retain it The function returns a list that contains the coordinates of the bounding rectangles for the faces detected. These coordinates are used to draw the boxes in the image.
Line 8	Do while loop for each face in the list returned from detectMultiScale() function.
Line 9 - 10	Draw the bounding rectangle for the face.
Line 11 – 12	Create the grayscale and color region of the face, which are used for eye detection.
Line 13 - 16	Use detectMultiScale() function of eye cascade classifier to detect eyes, similar to line 4 - 6.
Line 18 – 21	Draw the bounding rectangle for each eye detected.

The results are shown in Figure 6-25:

Figure 6-25 Face and Eye Detection

Photo by Bess Hamiti: https://www.pexels.com/photo/two-children-standing-near-concrete-fence-35188/

Similar to the Human Detection in the previous section, the cascade classifier method is fast enough for video. `detect_face_and_eye()` function in line 2 above can be put in the while loop of the video processing as we did in section 6.6.2, then the faces and eyes can be detected and highlighted from the video.

Below table is the list of all available cascade classifiers at the time of this writing, not only face and eye, but also body, smile and license plate etc. They can be used to detect different objects from images or videos in the same way.

haarcascade_eye.xml
haarcascade_eye_tree_eyeglasses.xml
haarcascade_frontalcatface.xml
haarcascade_frontalcatface_extended.xml
haarcascade_frontalface_alt.xml
haarcascade_frontalface_alt2.xml
haarcascade_frontalface_alt_tree.xml
haarcascade_frontalface_default.xml
haarcascade_fullbody.xml

haarcascade_lefteye_2splits.xml
haarcascade_licence_plate_rus_16stages.xml
haarcascade_lowerbody.xml
haarcascade_profileface.xml
haarcascade_righteye_2splits.xml
haarcascade_russian_plate_number.xml
haarcascade_smile.xml
haarcascade_upperbody.xml

Haar cascade classifiers are a powerful tool for object detection and have many advantages, including speed, accuracy, robustness, and portability. However, they also have some drawbacks, training a Haar cascade classifier requires a large number of positive and negative examples, and the training process can be computationally expensive, therefore OpenCV comes with a limited number of pre-trained cascade classifiers. The Haar cascade classifiers are sensitive to object pose and occlusion, which could lead to false negatives or missed detections. They may not work well for detecting small objects or images with low contrast, as the Haar features may not be able to capture the relevant information.

6.8   Remove Background

In some circumstances we want to detect the foreground and background of an image and want to separate them. This is called *semantic segmentation* of the image.

Semantic segmentation is a technique used in image processing to assign semantic labels to each pixel in an image, which means grouping together pixels that belong to the same object class. It is a type of image segmentation that focuses on identifying and labeling objects in an image based on their semantic meaning.

In contrast to simple image segmentation, which only divides an image into regions or objects, semantic segmentation can differentiate between objects of the same class (e.g., different cars in an image) and accurately label each pixel according to the class it belongs to. This makes it a powerful tool for various computer vision tasks, such as object detection, scene understanding, and image recognition.

There are several applications of *semantic segmentation* in image processing, including object detection, autonomous driving, medical image analysis, and video analysis. For example, semantic segmentation can be used to detect and track objects in a video stream, or to segment medical images into different anatomical structures for diagnosis and treatment planning.

This section will apply the concept of semantic segmentation to separate the foreground from the background of an image and remove the background. The specific area or pixels of the image will be identified as the foreground, and another area as the background. There are different ways to do so, depending on the image itself maybe one way is more efficient than the others.

Four methods will be introduced in this section to remove background:

- Remove Background by Color
- Remove Background by Contour
- Remove Background by Machine Learning
- Remove Background by Mask

6.8.1 Remove Background by Color

```
Source:      RemoveBackgroundByColor.py
Library:     common/ImageProcessing.py
```

The background of the image can be identified and removed based on the colors, if the color of the foreground of an image is significantly different from that of the background, it's worthwhile to try this method.

Let's take a look at the image shown in Figure 6-26, the color of the flower looks significantly different from the background.

Figure 6-26 Remove Background
by Color

Section 6.4 has introduced the method to detect colors by adjusting the hue, saturation and value. We can use the same technique to create a mask and apply it to the original image to remove the background.

The first step is to convert the image into HSV color space, then find the lower and upper thresholds of the hue, saturation and value. Then the mask is created using `cv2.inRage()` function.

The below function is to create a mask and remove the background by color, it is added to the `ImageProcessing` class that defined in chapter 5.

```
1    def remove_background_by_color(
                        self,
2                       hsv_lower=(10,10,10),
3                       hsv_upper=(179,255,255),
4                       image=None ):
5      if image is None:
6        image = self.image
7      imgHSV = cv2.cvtColor(image, cv2.COLOR_BGR2HSV)
8      mask = cv2.inRange(imgHSV, hsv_lower, hsv_upper)
9      mask = 255 - mask
10     mask = cv2.cvtColor(mask, cv2.COLOR_GRAY2BGR)
11     bg_removed = cv2.bitwise_and(image, mask)
12     return bg_removed, mask
```

Explanations:

Line 1	*Define* remove_background_by_color() *function, the parameters are the lower and upper thresholds of HSV values.*

Line 5 - 6	The `ImageProcessing` class already has a default image at initialization, if there is no image passed from the parameter then use the default image.
Line 7	Convert the image into HSV color space.
Line 8	Obtain the mask using `cv2.inRange()` function based on the upper and lower thresholds of HSV values.
Line 9	In this example the mask selected is the background only, now perform 255 – mask to get the mask of foreground.
Line 10	The mask created by `cv2.inRange()` function is grayscale, now convert it to BGR color space to make it in the same space as the original image.
Line 11	Apply the mask to the original image with bitwise AND operation to remove the background from original image.
Line 12	Return the background removed image as well as the mask.

Similar to the previous sections, in the main codes we create a `Parameters` window that has six slider bars to adjust the hue, saturation and values, as shown in Figure 6-27.

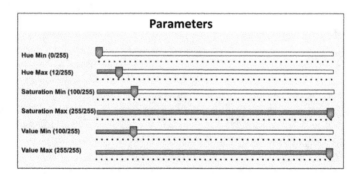

Figure 6-27 Parameters Window

At the same time the `Mask` and `Background Removed` windows are shown side by side, as Figure 6-28. Adjusting the minimum and maximum thresholds of hue, saturation and values from the `Parameters` window, the `Mask` window and `Background Removed` window are changing in real-time.

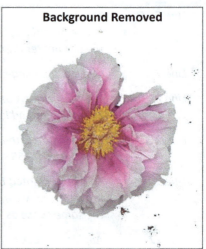

Figure 6-28 The Mask and Background Removed

The mask in the left side of Figure 6-28 does not look perfect, it comes with some noises, as a result the final image also includes the noises. You might want to use some techniques like dilation and erosion as discussed in section 6.2 to reduce the noises. Or alternatively, you can simply save the mask to a file, then use a third-party image processing software to manually remove those noises, we will introduce this manual approach in section 6.8.4.

Below are the full source codes:

```python
1    import cv2
2    import common.ImageProcessing as ip
3
4    def empty(a):
5      pass
6
7    if __name__ == "__main__":
8      iproc = ip.ImageProcessing("Original",
                                    "../res/flower012.jpg")
9      iproc.show(image=iproc.resize(65,iproc.image))
10     h_min, h_max = 25, 81
11     s_min, s_max = 0, 255
12     v_min, v_max = 0, 162
13     cv2.namedWindow("Parameters")
```

```
14      cv2.resizeWindow("TrackBars", 640, 240)
15      cv2.createTrackbar("Hue Min","Parameters",h_min,179,empty)
16      cv2.createTrackbar("Hue Max","Parameters",h_max,179,empty)
17      cv2.createTrackbar("Sat Min","Parameters",s_min,255,empty)
18      cv2.createTrackbar("Sat Max","Parameters",s_max,255,empty)
19      cv2.createTrackbar("Val Min","Parameters",v_min,255,empty)
20      cv2.createTrackbar("Val Max","Parameters",v_max,255,empty)
21      while True:
22         h_min = cv2.getTrackbarPos("Hue Min", "Parameters")
23         h_max = cv2.getTrackbarPos("Hue Max", "Parameters")
24         s_min = cv2.getTrackbarPos("Sat Min", "Parameters")
25         s_max = cv2.getTrackbarPos("Sat Max", "Parameters")
26         v_min = cv2.getTrackbarPos("Val Min", "Parameters")
27         v_max = cv2.getTrackbarPos("Val Max", "Parameters")
28         bg_removed, mask = iproc.remove_background_by_color(
29                         hsv_lower=(h_min, s_min, v_min),
30                         hsv_upper=(h_max, s_max, v_max) )
31         iproc.show(title="Mask", image=iproc.resize(65,mask))
32         iproc.show(title="Background Removed",
                    image=iproc.resize(65,bg_removed))
33         ch = cv2.waitKey(10)
34         if (ch & 0xFF) == 27:   # Press 'ESC' to exit
35            break
36      cv2.destroyAllWindows()
```

6.8.2   Remove Background by Contour

```
Source:      RemoveBackgroundByContour.py
Library:     common/ImageProcessing.py
```

Contour was introduced in previous sections when detecting shapes from images. To recap, a contour is a curve that represents the boundary of an object in an image, it's a sequence of connected pixels that form a continuous line around the object.

The background of the images can also be identified and removed based on the contours, if an image has a significant contour, it's worthwhile to try this method.

Take a look at Figure 6-29, we want to remove the background:

Original

Figure 6-29 Remove Background by Contour

As introduced in section 6.1, the Canny edge detection will be used to find out the edges of the object in the image (in our case, the bird), and use dilation and erosion to modify the edges. Then we find contours as introduced in section 6.3, and draw the contours as the mask.

Remember in the last section, the final mask has some noises, and we did not handle them. Now in this example we will use dilation, erosion and Gaussian blur to minimize the noises in the mask.

Add the following function to the `ImageProcessing` class,

```
1    def remove_background_by_contour(self,
2                                      gs_blur=3,
3                                      canny_lower=10,
4                                      canny_upper=200,
5                                      dilate_iter=1,
6                                      erode_iter=1,
7                                      image = None):
8        if image is None:
9            image = self.image
10       gray = cv2.cvtColor(image, cv2.COLOR_BGR2GRAY)
11       edges = cv2.Canny(gray, canny_lower, canny_upper)
12       edges = cv2.dilate(edges, None)
13       edges = cv2.erode(edges, None)
14       mask = np.zeros_like(edges)
```

```
15    contours, _ = cv2.findContours(edges, cv2.RETR_LIST,
16                            cv2.CHAIN_APPROX_NONE)
17    for contour in contours:
18      cv2.fillConvexPoly(mask, contour, (255))
19      mask = cv2.dilate(mask, None, iterations=dilate_iter)
20      mask = cv2.erode(mask, None, iterations=erode_iter)
21      if gs_blur % 2 == 0:
22        gs_blur = gs_blur + 1
23      elif gs_blur <= 0:
24        gs_blur = 1
25      mask = cv2.GaussianBlur(mask, (gs_blur, gs_blur), 0)
26      mask = cv2.cvtColor(mask, cv2.COLOR_GRAY2BGR)
27      bg_removed = cv2.bitwise_and(image, mask)
28      return bg_removed, mask
```

Explanations:

Line 1 - 7	*Define* `remove_background_by_contour()` *function, the parameters are lower and upper thresholds of Canny, kernel size for Gaussian blur and iteration numbers for dilation and erosion.*
Line 8 - 9	*The* `ImageProcessing` *class already has a default image at initialization, if there is no image passed from the parameter then use that default image.*
Line 10	*Convert the image into a grayscale one.*
Line 11	*Obtain the edges from the grayscale image by applying Canny with upper and lower thresholds.* *Optionally, add* `cv2.imshow()` *after this line to see its result.*
Line 12 - 13	*Apply dilation and erosion to modify the edges.* *Optionally, add* `cv2.imshow()` *after each line to see the results.*
Line 14	*Create an empty mask based on the edges.*
Line 15 - 16	*Find contours from the edges, see section 6.3.2 for details.*
Line 18	*Draw the contours on the mask.* *Optionally, add* `cv2.imshow()` *after this line to see its result.*

Line 19 - 20	Apply dilation and erosion to remove noises from the mask. It's different from Line 12 and 13.
Line 21 - 25	Apply Gaussian blur to modify the mask. The kernel size must be odd numbers, if it's not odd then change it to odd. See section 5.8 for details.
Line 26	The mask is in grayscale, convert it to BGR space which is same as the original image.
Line 27	Apply the mask to the original image with bitwise AND operation to remove the background from the original image.
Line 28	Return the background-removed image as well as the mask.

Similar to previous sections, in the main code we create a `Parameters` window that has slider bars to adjust the following parameters, as Figure 6-30:

- Kernel size for Gaussian blur
- Lower thresholds of Canny
- Upper thresholds of Canny
- Iteration numbers for dilation
- Iteration numbers for erosion

The `Mask` window and `Background Removed` window are shown side by side to indicate the real-time results, as Figure 6-31 and Figure 6-32. The initial kernel size for Gaussian is specified as 3, the initial lower and upper thresholds of Canny are 103 and 153 respectively. The initial iterations for dilation and erosion are 1 and 1 respectively.

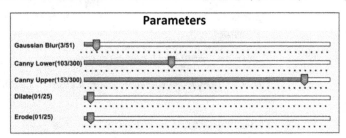

Figure 6-30 Parameters for Remove Background by Contour

When adjusting the parameters, the images are changing at real-time.

178

Figure 6-31 Mask for the Foreground

Figure 6-32 Background Removed

Below are the full source codes:

```
1   import cv2
2   import common.ImageProcessing as ip
3
4   def empty(a):
5     pass
6
7   if __name__ == "__main__":
8     iproc = ip.ImageProcessing("Original",
                                  "../res/bird001.jpg")
9     iproc.show(image=iproc.resize(65,iproc.image))
10    gs_blur = 3
```

```
11    lower, upper = 103, 153
12    dilate, erode = 1, 1
13    cv2.namedWindow("Parameters")
14    cv2.createTrackbar("GS_Blur","Parameters",gs_blur,51,empty)
15    cv2.createTrackbar("Lower", "Parameters", lower, 300,empty)
16    cv2.createTrackbar("Upper", "Parameters", upper, 300,empty)
17    cv2.createTrackbar("Dilate", "Parameters", dilate,25,empty)
18    cv2.createTrackbar("Erode", "Parameters", erode, 25, empty)
19
20    while True:
21      gs_blur = cv2.getTrackbarPos("GS_Blur", "Parameters")
22      lower = cv2.getTrackbarPos("Lower", "Parameters")
23      upper = cv2.getTrackbarPos("Upper", "Parameters")
24      dilate = cv2.getTrackbarPos("Dilate", "Parameters")
25      erode = cv2.getTrackbarPos("Erode", "Parameters")
26      bg_removed,mask=iproc.remove_background_by_contour(
                        gs_blur, lower, upper,
                        dilate, erode)
27      cv2.imshow("Mask", iproc.resize(65,mask))
28      cv2.imshow("Background Removed",
                        iproc.resize(65,bg_removed))
29      ch = cv2.waitKey(10)
30      # Press 'ESC' to exit
        if (ch & 0xFF) == 27:
31        break
32    cv2.destroyAllWindows()
```

This example shows the effects of adjusting Gaussian blur kernel size, dilation and erosion, and then finding the contour of the foreground, and removing the background by bitwise AND operation.

Execute the code and play with the parameters to observe how the results are changing. You might also want to change different images to see how it works.

6.8.3   Remove Background by Machine Learning

> Source: RemoveBackgroundByML.py

PixelLib is a Python library that provides an easy-to-use interface for various computer vision tasks, including image segmentation, object detection, and image and video processing. It utilizes deep learning models to perform these tasks and simplifies the process of building custom object detection and segmentation models. It comes with pre-trained models to support background editing of images and videos using a few lines of codes. The website of PixelLib is located at: *https://github.com/ayoolaolafenwa/PixelLib*

With a few lines of codes, we can simply implement the following operations:

- Remove background – remove the background.
- Gray background – make the background grayscale while keeping the color of foreground object.
- Blur background – make the background blurred while keeping the foreground object clear.
- Change background – change a different image as background while keeping the foreground object.

The PixelLib can also work on videos, please reference its official website for details and tutorials. This section focuses only on the above four operations on the images.

Before starting, the following two libraries need to be added to the Python environments, if they are already installed on your environment, make sure they are upgraded to the latest version.

- tensorflow
- pixellib

Follow the instructions in section 2.3.2 to install or upgrade the libraries. *tensorflow* is used for machine learning, and it will be used in next chapter for machine learning as well.

Below are the codes to initialize PixelLib,

```
1  import pixellib
2  from   pixellib.tune_bg import alter_bg
3  change_bg = alter_bg()
4  change_bg.load_pascalvoc_model(
5                  "../res/deeplabv3_xception_tf_
                   dim_ordering_tf_kernels.h5")
```

This example will use *deeplabv3+* model trained on *PASCAL VOC (PASCAL Visual Object Classes)* dataset. The dataset contains 20 object categories including person, bicycle, boat, bus, car, motorbike, train, bottle, chair, dining table, potted plant, sofa, TV/monitor, bird, cat, cow, dog, horse and sheep. This dataset has been widely used as a benchmark for object detection, background segmentation and classification tasks, see material #10 in the References section.

deeplabv3+ is a semantic segmentation algorithm that uses a convolutional neural network (CNN) to identify and classify different objects and regions within an image. Semantic segmentation involves assigning a label to every pixel in an image, based on the object or region it belongs to.

deeplabv3+ achieves state-of-the-art performance on several benchmark datasets, including PASCAL VOC and others. It has been used in a wide range of computer vision applications, including object recognition, scene understanding, and autonomous driving. For image background removal, *deeplabv3+* can be used to accurately identify the foreground objects in an image and segment them from the background. This makes it a useful tool for tasks such as video conferencing, virtual backgrounds, and photo editing.

The model *deeplabv3_xception_tf_dim_ordering_tf_kernels.h5* is available for download from PixelLib website, at below link (at the time of this writing):

https://github.com/ayoolaolafenwa/PixelLib/releases/download/1.1/deeplabv3_xception_tf_dim_ordering_tf_kernels.h5

It's a big file about 150MB, so it is not included in our Github repository. Download the file and put it in the /res directory of your local environment, line 4 and 5 of the above codes are to load the model.

Please note, the *tensorflow, pixellib* and *deeplabv3+* are also big libraries, it could take some time to load them when executing the codes, maybe several minutes depending on your machine's capabilities. It might also require some hardware specifications, there could be some warning messages if these requirements are not met.

This example will use the image of a bird, as shown in Figure 6-33:

Figure 6-33 Remove Background by Machine Learning

Remove the background with following codes:

```
6   bg_removed = change_bg.color_bg(image_file,
                              colors = (0,0,0))
7   cv2.imshow("Remove Background", bg_removed)
```

Figure 6-34 Background Removed

In line 6, `change_bg.color_bg()` function replaces the background with a solid color, here we specified `colors=(0,0,0)`, then the background is replaced with a solid black color in Figure 6-34.

Similarly, make the background grayscale by `change_bg.gray_bg()` method:

```
8   bg_gray = change_bg.gray_bg(image_file)
9   cv2.imshow("Gray Background", bg_gray)
```

As shown in Figure 6-35 the background is converted to grayscale based on the original background, which is not just simply a solid gray color.

Figure 6-35 Make the Background Gray

We can also blur the background with `change_bg.blur_bg()`, and replace the background with `change_bg.change_bg_img()` method:

```
10   bg_blur = change_bg.blur_bg(image_file, low = True)
11   cv2.imshow("Blur Background", bg_blur)
12   background_file = "../res/background_002.jpg"
13   print("Change Background ...")
14   bg_change = change_bg.change_bg_img(
                    f_image_path = image_file,
15                  b_image_path = background_file)
16   cv2.imshow("Change Background", bg_change)
```

Figure 6-36 is the result of blurring the background:

184

Figure 6-36 Blur the Background

Figure 6-37 is the result of replacing the background with another image:

Figure 6-37 Change Background Image

When using remote video conferencing tools like Microsoft Teams or Google Meet, you might be curious how they remove and change the backgrounds with the "Background Effects" feature, PixelLib is one of the most effective ways to do it.

6.8.4   Remove Background by Mask

> Source: RemoveBackgroundByMask.py

If you cannot achieve the desired background removal effect by all of the above methods, you can always use third-party image-editing software to generate a mask and apply that mask to the original image to remove the background. The third-party software can be Adobe PhotoShop or *GIMP*, or any other image-editing tool.

GIMP (GNU Image Manipulation Program) is a free and open-source image editing software that can be used for a wide range of tasks such as photo retouching, image composition, and image authoring. It has many features that are similar to those found in commercial software like Adobe Photoshop, but is available for free and runs on multiple platforms, including Windows, macOS, and Linux.

This is a manual approach, some efforts are needed to remove the background in the third-party software to achieve the desired results.

In this example the original image looks like Figure 6-38 below:

Figure 6-38 Remove Background by Mask

It's not significant to separate the foreground by color, nor by contour, therefore the methods introduced in previous sections might not work well, and even the machine learning approach might not work.

Load this image into GIMP software, or Adobe PhotoShop or any other image editors, manually create the mask, as shown below. Some efforts are needed since it's a manual work, Figure 6-39 is the mask.

Figure 6-39 Mask Created Manually

Figure 6-40 Background Removed

Apply the mask to the original image by bitwise AND operation to remove the background, see Figure 6-40.

This is the function defined in `ImageProcessing` class,

```
1   def remove_background_by_mask(self, mask,
                                        image = None):
2       if image is None:
3           image = self.image
4       bg_removed = cv2.bitwise_and(image, mask)
5       return bg_removed, mask
```

And below are the codes to generate the above result in Figure 6-40, it loads the original image and the mask, then calls the above function to apply the bitwise AND operation to remove the background.

```
1   import cv2
2   import common.ImageProcessing as ip
3   def remove_background(image, mask):
4       iproc = ip.ImageProcessing("Original", image)
5       iproc.show(image=iproc.image)
6       mask = cv2.imread(mask)
7       iproc.show(title="Mask", image=mask)
8       bg_removed, _ =
                iproc.remove_background_by_mask(mask)
9       iproc.show(title="Background Removed",
                image=bg_removed)
10          cv2.waitKey(0)
11      cv2.destroyAllWindows()
12
13  if __name__ == "__main__":
14      remove_background(
                image = "../res/flower010.jpg",
15              mask = "../res/flower010_mask.jpg")
```

With manual work and effort, the mask created will be accurate, this is always an effective way to achieve the desired results.

6.9 Blur Background

> Source: BlurBackground.py
> Library: common/ImageProcessing.py

Sometimes we want to achieve an effect that makes the foreground stand out. In the previous sections we can separate the foreground from the image, now we will blur the background in order to make the foreground stand out.

As an example, when using remote video conferencing tools like Microsoft Teams or Google Meet, the "Background Effects" can blur the background and make the person distinguished during the video call.

Here are several examples to blur the background, Figure 6-41 uses Gaussian blur on the background with kernel size of (41, 41), and sigma of (52, 52):

Original Image   Gaussian Blurred Image

Figure 6-41 Blur Background with Gaussian

In addition to Gaussian blur, other blur methods can also be used, and kernel size can be adjusted to achieve the desired results. The color of background can also be adjusted, for example use grayscale, or change the bright, contrast, saturation etc.

Similar to previous examples, we create four trackbars in the `Parameters` window. These trackbars are used to control the background processing.

The first trackbar is the kernel size of Gaussian or Median blur. The second is the sigma for Gaussian blur, it doesn't apply to Median blur. The third one is a switch of the two blurring methods, 0 is for Gaussian and 1 for Median. The last one is a switch of color or grayscale. As shown in Figure 6-42:

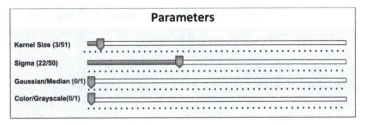

Figure 6-42 Trackbars to Control the Blurring

Optionally, if you want to adjust the brightness, contrast, hue, saturation and value, you can add more trackbars here, and add codes accordingly to process them.

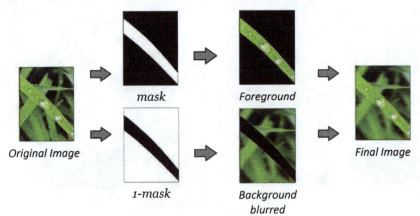

Figure 6-43 The Process to Blur the Background

The above Figure 6-43 is the process to blur the background. The original image is used to create the *mask*, and at the same time create

(1-mask). The mask is applied to the original image with bitwise AND operation to get the foreground; while *(1-mask)* is applied to the original image to get the background, then apply the blur as well as color adjustments on the background. Finally merge the foreground and background with bitwise OR operation to get the final image.

Below are the code snippets to generate foreground and background,

```
1   image = cv2.imread(image)
2   mask  = cv2.imread(mask)
3   foreground = cv2.bitwise_and(image, mask)
```

Line 1 and 2 are to load the original image and mask, the mask can be created based on one of the several methods introduced in section 6.8, here we use the third-party image-editing software to create the mask and save it to a file. Line 2 is to load the mask file. Then use `cv2.bitwise_and()` to apply the *mask* to the original image to get the foreground.

```
4   background = cv2.bitwise_and(image, (255 - mask))
```

Then apply *(1 − mask)* to the original image to get the background. *(1 − mask)* is the inverse of the mask, the mask is binary data, either 0 or 255, so in the code `(255-mask)` represents *(1 − mask)*, as line 4 above.

Then apply either Gaussian or Median blur on the background, in line 5 or line 6 below. Gaussian and Median blur has been introduced in section 5.8.

```
5   background = cv2.GaussianBlur(background,
                          (ksize, ksize),
                          sigma, sigma,
                          cv2.BORDER_DEFAULT )
6   # background = cv2.medianBlur(background, ksize)
```

Please note, it should be either line 5 or line 6, not both.

Sometimes, in order to make the foreground distinguished, you might want to make the background grayscale, or adjust the color.

```
7   background=cv2.cvtColor(background,cv2.COLOR_BGR2GRAY)
```

```
8   background=cv2.cvtColor(background,cv2.COLOR_GRAY2BGR)
```

Line 7 converts the background to grayscale, since grayscale only has one channel, it should be in the same color space as the foreground, i.e. BGR space, so line 8 is to convert it back to BGR.

Optionally, you might want to adjust the brightness, contrast, hue, and saturation of the background in order to achieve some desired effects, follow sections 5.3 and 5.4 to make adjustments to those values.

After the background is completed, use cv2.bitwise_or() function to merge the foreground and background to obtain the result.

```
9   result = cv2.bitwise_or(foreground, background)
```

The full source codes are as below:

```
1    import cv2
2    def chg_ksize(value):
3        global ksize
4        if value % 2 == 0:
5            ksize = value+1
6        else:
7            ksize = value
8
9    def chg_method(value):
10       global blur_method
11       blur_method = value
12
13   def chg_color_gray(value):
14       global is_gray
15       is_gray = value
16
17   def chg_sigma(value):
18       global sigma
19       sigma = value
20
21   def blur_background(image, mask):
22       global ksize, blur_method, is_gray, sigma
23       ksize = 9
24       blur_method = 0
25       is_gray = 0
26       sigma = 22
27       image = cv2.imread(image)
```

```
28      mask = cv2.imread(mask)
29      foreground = cv2.bitwise_and(image, mask)
30      cv2.imshow("Original", image)
31      # cv2.imshow("Mask", (255-mask))
32      # cv2.imshow("Background Removed", foreground)
33      title = "Background Blurred"
34      cv2.namedWindow("Parameters")
35      cv2.createTrackbar("K-Size", "Parameters",
                        ksize, 51, chg_ksize)
36      cv2.createTrackbar("Sigma", "Parameters",
                        sigma, 50, chg_sigma)
37      cv2.createTrackbar("Gaus/Medn", "Parameters",
                        blur_method, 1, chg_method)
38      cv2.createTrackbar("Color/Gray", "Parameters",
                        is_gray, 1, chg_color_gray)
39          while True:
40          background = cv2.bitwise_and(image,(255-mask))
41          if blur_method == 0:
42              background = cv2.GaussianBlur(background,
                            (ksize, ksize),
43                          sigma, sigma,
                            cv2.BORDER_DEFAULT )
44          else:
45              background = cv2.medianBlur(
                            background, ksize)
46          if is_gray == 1:
47              background = cv2.cvtColor(
                            background,
                            cv2.COLOR_BGR2GRAY)
48              background = cv2.cvtColor(
                            background,
                            cv2.COLOR_GRAY2BGR)
49          result = cv2.bitwise_or(foreground,
                        background)
50          cv2.imshow(title, result)
51          ch = cv2.waitKey(10)
52          # Press 'ESC' to exit
            if (ch & 0xFF) == 27:
53              break
54          # Press 's' to save
            elif ch == ord('s'):
55              filepath = "C:/temp/blur_background.png"
56              cv2.imwrite(filepath, result)
```

193

```
57                    print("File saved to " + filepath)
58          cv2.destroyAllWindows()
59
60    if __name__ == "__main__":
61        blur_background(image="../res/flower011.jpg",
62                        mask="../res/flower011_mask.jpg")
```

There are several more examples, Figure 6-44 uses median blur with kernel size of 23 on the grayscale background,

Figure 6-44 Median Blur with Gray Background

Figure 6-45 uses Gaussian blur with a kernel size of 43 and sigma of 12, and then color adjusted by reducing hue, saturation and value.

Figure 6-45 Gaussian Blur with Color Adjustment

Below are several images and their masks in the Github repository, you might want to try them by modifying line 61 and 62 in above code.

- `res/flower011.jpg, res/flower011_mask.jpg`
- `res/flower012.jpg, res/flower012_mask.jpg`
- `res/flower013.jpg, res/flower013_mask.jpg`
- `res/flower014.jpg, res/flower014_mask.jpg`

Section 6.8 has introduced the techniques for image segmentation for background removal, and this section has introduced blurring the background. By combining the techniques of image segmentation and blurring the background, we can achieve the effect of highlighting the foreground object and making it stand out and drawing attention to it. This can be useful in various applications such as product photography, where you want to showcase a particular item.

It can also improve the visual aesthetics, blurring the background can create a pleasing visual effect by reducing distractions and emphasizing the subject of the image. This is commonly used in portrait photography, for example the "Background Effects" feature of remote video conferencing software like Microsoft Teams and Google Meet.

These techniques are also useful for enhancing image analysis, in some fields such as medical imaging or satellite imagery, image segmentation can be used to isolate specific regions of interest for further analysis. For example, in medical imaging, segmenting tumors or other abnormalities can help with diagnosis and treatment planning.

7. Machine Learning

Machine learning has become a fundamental part of computer vision and image processing in recent years. As part of artificial intelligence, it includes many mathematical algorithms and techniques. Machine Learning will automatically "learn" the patterns and features from the massive amount of data and will apply those patterns and features to solve a wide range of problems related to image analysis, processing and detection.

Many state-of-the-art computer vision and image processing techniques are based on machine learning, here are some examples:

- Object detection and recognition: Machine learning algorithms can be trained to recognize and locate specific objects within images or videos, as introduced in section 6.6 and 6.7 to detect human, faces and eyes. This is useful in various applications, such as surveillance, self-driving cars, and medical imaging.
- Image segmentation: Machine learning can be used to segment images into different regions or objects, as introduced in section 6.8.3 to separate the foreground from the backgrounds. This is useful in medical imaging, robotics, and natural language processing.
- Image classification: Machine learning can classify images into different categories based on their features, it's useful in

applications such as content-based image retrieval, face recognition, and automated inspection. This will be introduced in the following sections.

- Image restoration and enhancement: Machine learning can be used to restore or enhance images that are degraded or of low quality. This is useful in applications such as medical imaging, satellite imaging, and forensic analysis. Machine learning algorithms such as generative adversarial networks (GANs) can be used to train models that can restore images.
- Generative models: Machine learning can be used to generate new images that are similar to a given set of images. This is useful in applications such as artistic style transfer, data augmentation, and data synthesis.

Machine learning has revolutionized the field of computer vision and image processing, enabling new applications and improving the accuracy of existing techniques.

What exactly is Machine Learning? As a very high-level overview, Machine Learning (ML) is part of Artificial Intelligence (AI), and Deep Learning (DL) is part of Machine Learning (ML).

Artificial Intelligence refers to the creation of intelligent machines or applications that can perform tasks that typically require human intelligence, such as visual perception, speech recognition, decision-making, and language translation.

Machine learning is a type of AI that involves training algorithms to automatically improve their performance on a specific task, such as image classification or natural language processing. Machine learning algorithms use statistical techniques to identify patterns in data and make predictions or decisions based on those patterns.

Deep learning, on the other hand, is a subset of machine learning that involves the use of artificial neural networks to process and analyze large amounts of data. Deep learning algorithms are inspired by the structure and function of the human brain, and they use layers of interconnected nodes to learn from and make predictions about data.

In this book, the term "Machine Learning" refers to both machine learning (ML) and deep learning (DL), as both are subsets of Artificial Intelligence that involve training algorithms to make predictions or decisions based on data.

There are two key parts of machine learning,

1.   The **data**, is the actual things that it learns from.
2.   The **model**, contains the algorithm and mechanism of how to learn from the data.

The quality of *data* is important for machine learning projects, in real-world projects lots of efforts are needed for preparing the datasets, like clean-up the data, ensuring the accuracy of the data, removing blank records etc. For example, the date field should have all dates in the same format, if most dates are in the format of "2021/06/21", but some are "Jun 21, 2021", this will cause an error when processing the dataset.

In most of cases these activities should also be working together with the subject-matter experts who have the expertise in the domain, like healthcare data needs to be reviewed with health experts to ensure accuracy; housing data to review with real estate experts, and so on.

In this book, however, almost all the datasets are from the Python packages, like `scikit-learn` and `tensorflow`, they are well-prepared and ready to use, with no need for the efforts such as data clean-up etc.

The *model* is another aspect of machine learning, a good model with an effective algorithm will help it to better learn from the data. This chapter will introduce several widely used algorithms in computer vision and image processing, they have different characteristics for different purposes.

There are basically two types of machine learning algorithms, *Supervised Learning* and *Unsupervised Learning*. The former learns from the labeled data, which means the algorithm knows what the data is, for example, the algorithm receives a picture, and is told the picture is a dog, then the algorithm tries to map the picture to the dog. The latter learns from the data without labels, for example the algorithm receives a picture but doesn't know what this picture is, it works on its own to discover the information of the data, and explore the patterns and classifications etc.

OpenCV provides a number of pre-defined machine learning algorithm models. We don't need to know exactly how the algorithms works in terms of mathematics, although it's better to understand it. We will introduce how to use these pre-defined models to solve problems. This chapter will introduce the following models:

- Unsupervised learning
  - o K-Means (Section 7.1)
- Supervised learning
  - o K-Nearest Neighbors (Section 7.2)
  - o Support Vector Machine (Section 7.3)
  - o Artificial Neural Network (Section 7.4)
  - o Convolutional Neural Network (Section 7.5)

The data is very important for machine learning, it is the actual things for the models to learn from. A model can do nothing without the data. There are a number of pre-built datasets for machine learning purposes. This chapter will introduce the following datasets that are widely used for machine learning:

- MNIST (Modified National Institute of Standards and Technology) dataset: contains a large number of handwritten digits from 0 to 9. It is the de facto "Hello World" dataset and is widely used for machine learning purposes. It's available from `keras.datasets` package. We will use this dataset in every section in this chapter, and evaluate the results by comparing the different models.
- CIFAR-10 Dataset: contains 60,000 32x32 color images in 10 classes, with 6,000 images per class. The classes include airplane, automobile, bird, cat and so on. It's also available from `keras.datasets` package.
- IRIS Flower dataset: a small but multivariate dataset with labels. This dataset comes with the `sklearn.datasets` package.
- In addition to the pre-built datasets, we will also learn how to generate sample data using the functions provided by `sklearn.datasets`.

There are several Python packages needed for this chapter, they must be installed before running the example codes, reference section 1.4 for the versions of these packages that are used in this book.

- `sklearn`, or `scikit-learn`: an open source library for machine learning, it supports supervised and unsupervised learning. It also provides various tools and utilities for data preprocessing, model selection and evaluation.
- `keras`: an open source library for machine learning, it's very powerful to support machine learning and deep learning.
- `tensorflow`: an open source library for machine learning, it's usually installed together with `keras`.
- `matplotlib`: an open source library for data visualizations in Python, it has been used in previous chapters.

If these libraries are not installed on your environments, it's strongly suggested installing them following the instructions in section 2.3, then you will be able to execute the source codes for this chapter.

Enjoy the Machine Learning!

7.1 K-Means Clustering

7.1.1 What is K-Means Clustering

```
Source:     K-Means.py
```

K-means clustering is a popular unsupervised machine learning algorithm used to partition a given dataset into k clusters based on their similarities, where k is a predefined number.

It is an unsupervised algorithm because it does not require labeled data to train the model, the model will learn from the data by itself. In other words, it does not rely on any predetermined target variables or output values to guide its learning process.

The goal of the K-means algorithm is to group similar data points together into clusters based on their similarity or distance from each other. It does this by finding a number of *centroids* to represent the center of clusters and iteratively assigning each data point to the nearest cluster centroid, and then updating the centroids based on the new members of the clusters. The *centroids* are arithmetic mean position, or average position, of the clusters of the data. The process is repeated until the centroids no longer move or a maximum number of iterations is reached.

In a real-world use case, for example, a T-shirt maker wants to make products fit for a wide range of people with different heights and weights. The maker is planning to make three sizes: L, M and S for different groups of people. The three sizes are called *centroids* in the terminology of K-means algorithm, each *centroid* represents a group of people, or a cluster of people.

K-Means is an effective algorithm to resolve this type of problem, it will find the three centroids (L, M and S) from the dataset. It is an unsupervised learning method because it will find the results from the data itself by calculation, we don't need to mark each data with a label.

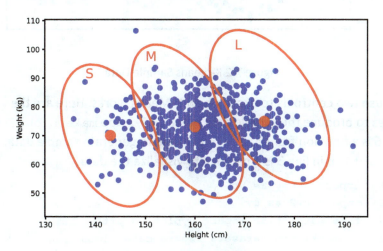

Figure 7-1 T-shirt Example

As shown in Figure 7-1, the horizontal axis represents the height of people, and the vertical axis represents their weight. Each data point represents a person, the data points can be grouped in three clusters: S, M and L.

The arithmetic mean (average) position of each group is the *centroid* and located near the center of each group, shown as red ● in Figure 7-1. Each centroid has its corresponding height and weight, the T-shirt maker will make three sizes of T-shirts based on the three centroids, they will most likely fit all people in different groups.

Let's take a look at how K-Means works in the simplest case, generate random 2D data in 2 clusters and plot the data as Figure 7-2,

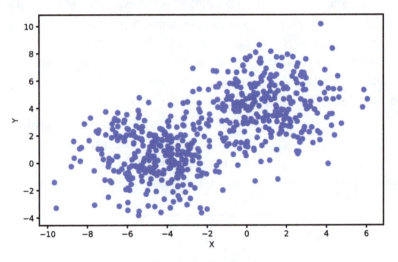

Figure 7-2 K-means Sample Data

We use two centroids to explain how K-Means works. Here are the codes to produce the sample data in Figure 7-2, the `make_blobs()` in line 6 is a function from `sklearn` package to generate sample data. `matplotlib` in line 3 is a package to visualize the data.

```
1   import numpy as np
2   import cv2 as cv
3   from matplotlib import pyplot as plt
4   from sklearn.datasets import make_blobs
5   def sample_cluster():
6       X, y = make_blobs(n_samples=600, centers=2,
                cluster_std=2.8, random_state=1)
7           X = np.float32(X)
```

```
8          plt.figure(figsize=(6, 4))
9          plt.scatter(X[:,0],X[:,1],s=10,cmap='spring')
10         plt.xlabel('X')
11         plt.ylabel('Y')
12         plt.show()
13         return X, y
```

K-Means will perform the following steps,

Step 1: Randomly initialize k centroids, in our case $k=2$, so two centroids: μ_1 and μ_2 are initialized.

Step 2: calculate the distance from each data point to both centroids and label the data. If a data is closer to μ_1, then the data is labeled with 0; if it is closer to μ_2 then labeled with 1. If there are more centroids, then labeled with 2, 3, ..., etc.

Run the codes below for one iteration of K-Means, get the results of Step 2, as in Figure 7-3:

```
15    criteria = (cv.TERM_CRITERIA_MAX_ITER, 1, 1.0)
16    ret,label,center=cv2.kmeans(X, 2, None , criteria, 1,
                                cv2.KMEANS_RANDOM_CENTERS)
```

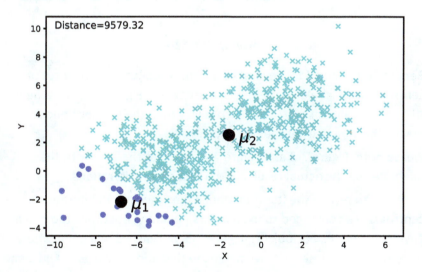

Figure 7-3 K-means, One Iteration

The data points near μ_1 are labeled as 0 and shown as • in Figure 7-3, and the data near μ_2 are labeled as 1 and shown as ×.

The `Distance` displayed in the top-left corner, 9579.32, is the actual value that returned from `cv2.kmeans()` function in line 16 of the above code snippets, it's the sum of squared distance of all data points.

Step 3: Calculate the average of all • data points that becomes the new μ_1, and the average of all × points that becomes the new μ_2.

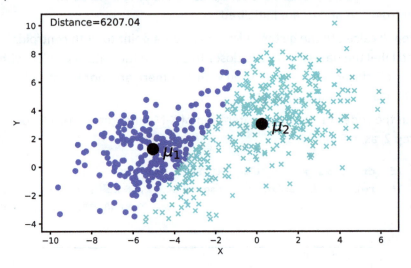

Figure 7-4 K-means, After Several Iterations

Repeat Step 2 and 3 for several iterations, then we get a new set of centroids with labeled data points, as shown in Figure 7-4, and a new `Distance` value of 6207.04, which is less than the previous one. It means this time we get the better centroids.

Please note, Figure 7-3 and Figure 7-4 illustrate the concepts, they might not be the actual results of the first several iterations.

Continue to repeat the iteration until a maximum of 100 iterations, the centroids are converged to fixed points, meaning not move too much anymore. The results look like Figure 7-5, μ_1 reaches to a point where all the data points close to it are marked with 0 and shown as •. And same for μ_2, all data points close to it are marked with 1 and in ×. And `Distance` reaches a minimum value of 3700.15.

204

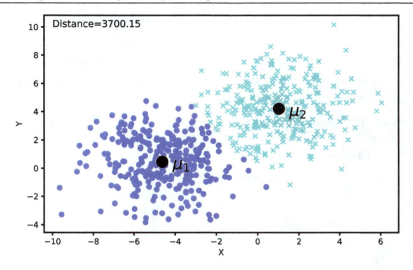

Figure 7-5 K-means, 100 Iterations

The goal of K-Means algorithm is to find out these centroids to represent the data near them. In this case, μ_1 is used to represent all • data points, and μ_2 is to represent all × data points.

Back to the example at the beginning, the T-shirt example. The maker doesn't have to make T-shirts based on the size of each individual, instead use K-means algorithm to calculate three centroids for S, M and L. These three sizes will fit most people of each group. Of cause in real-world, maybe create more centroids for XS, S, M, X, XL and so on.

As explained, the algorithm repeats the steps as iterations, but when the iterations terminate? And how the algorithm knows the final results? This is called *Termination Criteria*, it applies not only to K-means algorithm but also almost all machine learning algorithm models. OpenCV uses two criteria to terminate the iterations,

- Define a maximum number of iterations, the iteration terminates when this maximum number is reached. The results are deemed final.
- Define the convergence metrics, ε (epsilon), this can be understood as a measure of accuracy, the algorithm calculates the results against the metrics, if the results meet the metrics, then

the iteration terminates, meaning the defined accuracy level is reached.

Different algorithm models have different ways to calculate accuracy, OpenCV will take care of them. The examples in the following sections explain how to define the termination criteria.

Here are the details of *kmeans()* function

```
1   distance, bestLabels, centers =
                    cv.kmeans(data,
2                             nclusters,
3                             bestLabels,
4                             criteria,
5                             attempts,
6                             flags,
7                             [centers] )
```

Parameters:

data	*Data for clustering, an array of n-Dimensional data points with a* `float32` *data type.*
nclusters	*Number of clusters.*
bestLabels	*An input/output integer array that stores the labels for every sample, the labels are marked as 0, 1, 2…. If there are labels for the data, then pass them as an input parameter, otherwise pass None.*
criteria	*The algorithm termination criteria, that is, the iteration stops when these criteria are satisfied. It has three parameters:* *1. type of termination criteria,* *cv2.TERM_CRITERIA_EPS - stop the algorithm iteration if the specified accuracy, epsilon, is reached.* *cv2.TERM_CRITERIA_MAX_ITER - stop the algorithm after the specified number of iterations, max_iter.* *2. max_iter - an integer specifying the maximum number of iterations.*

	3. epsilon - required accuracy
attempts	Specify the number of times the algorithm is executed using different initial labeling.
flags	Specify how initial centers are taken: 1. cv2.KMEANS_PP_CENTERS 2. cv2.KMEANS_RANDOM_CENTERS 3. cv2.KMEANS_USE_INITIAL_LABELS

Output:

distance	Sum of squared distance from each point to their corresponding centers.
bestLabels	An array of the labels, same as the above bestLabels for the input parameter.
centers	Array of centroids of the clusters .

Below is an example of how to create the criteria and how to call `cv2.kmeans()` function:

```
1    criteria = ( cv2.TERM_CRITERIA_EPS +
2                 cv2.TERM_CRITERIA_MAX_ITER,
3                 100,
4                 1.0)
5    _,label,center=cv2.kmeans(X,
6                 2,
7                 None ,
8                 criteria,
9                 100,
10                cv2.KMEANS_RANDOM_CENTERS)
```

Line 1 to 4 above specify the termination criteria, it's combined with maximum iteration and accuracy metrics by:
`cv2.TERM_CRITERIA_EPS+cv2.TERM_CRITERIA_MAX_ITER`

The maximum iteration is specified in line 3 as `100`, and the accuracy metrics in line 4 as `1.0`.

Then line 5 to 10 invoke `cv2.kmeans()` to execute K-means algorithm, X in line 5 is the data, `2` in line 6 is the k value which specifies the clusters of the output. Line 7 specifies the labels that come with the input dataset, since K-Means is unsupervised this parameter is not necessary, we give it `None` here. Line 8 specifies the `criteria` that defined earlier. Line 9 specifies the maximum iteration, and line 10 tells the function to randomly initialize the centroids.

7.1.2 Color Quantization

> Source: K-MeansColorQuantization.py,
> common\color_wheel.py

One of the applications of K-Means is Color Quantization, which is the process of reducing the number of distinct colors in an image while preserving its overall appearance. It is a commonly used technique in image processing, computer graphics, and computer vision.

The purpose of color quantization is 1) to reduce the memory and the size to store the image; and 2) to display the images on some devices that have limitations on the number of distinct colors. Sometimes it can also be used to create artistic effects in images, such as posterization or stylization.

By reducing the number of colors in an image, color quantization can help reduce the size of image files, increase image compression, and improve the efficiency of image processing operations. It is commonly used in image compression algorithms, digital art, and computer graphics.

The basic idea behind color quantization is to replace the original colors in the image with a smaller set of colors. This is usually done by clustering similar colors together and replacing them with their average color value.

How many distinct colors can an image have? In theory, an image has three channels of blue, green and red, each can have 256 values, therefore totally 256 * 256 * 256 = 16,777,216 possible distinct colors, although in most cases there are not so many colors in an image. The following code snippets will count the distinct colors in an image,

```
1   def get_distinct_colours(image):
```

```
2     unique, counts = np.unique(
                image.reshape(-1, img.shape[-1]),
                axis=0, return_counts=True)
3     return counts.size
```

Figure 7-6 illustrates how the color quantization works, the original image in the left-side is a color palette, the right-side is the image after color quantization with clusters = 8.

The similar colors in the left-side color wheel are grouped together as a cluster and represented by a single color in the right-side image, for example the colors near blue such as dark blue, blue, light blue, and so on are grouped together into only one color which is blue in the right-side. Same as red, yellow, purple, green, etc. All the colors in the original image are grouped into 8 clusters, which are the 8 centroids found by K-Means.

Please note the white background is counted as a cluster, so there 7 colors on the right-side color wheel, plus white background, totally 8 colors.

 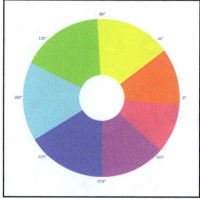

Figure 7-6 Color Quantization on Color Wheel

Here is the result of how many distinct colors in both images above:

```
Distinct colors in original image: 239
Distinct colors after color quantization: 8
```

Similarly, do the color quantization for k=6 and k=3, we can obtain the color wheels with fewer distinct colors, as Figure 7-7.

Note, the white background is counted as a distinct color.

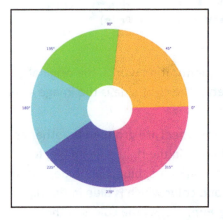 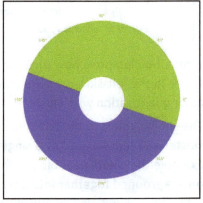

Figure 7-7 Color Quantization, k=6 and k=3

Here are the codes for color quantization:

```
1   def color_quantization(image, clusters):
2       X = image.reshape((-1,3))
3       X = np.float32(X)
4       criteria = (cv2.TERM_CRITERIA_EPS +
                cv2.TERM_CRITERIA_MAX_ITER,10,1.0)
5       ret,label,center=cv2.kmeans(X, clusters, None,
                    criteria, 10,
6                       cv2.KMEANS_RANDOM_CENTERS)
7       center = np.uint8(center)
8       result = center[label.flatten()]
9       result = result.reshape((img.shape))
10      return result
```

Explanations:

Line 1	*Define* `color_quantization()` *function.*
Line 2	*Reshape the image into a 2-dimensional array.*
Line 3	*Convert the datatype to* `float32`, *which is required by* `cv2.kmeans()` *function.*
Line 4	*Define the criteria of K-means, max iteration is set to 10 and the metrics is set to 1.0, which means the K-means calculation will stop either iteration reaches 10 or metrics is less than 1.0.*

210

Line 5 - 6	Call `cv2.kmeans()` function.
Line 7	The returned `center` is a list in `float32` datatype, convert it back to integer which is required by image display.
Line 8	Create a resulting image from `center` and `label`. If a pixel is labeled 0, then use `center[0]` to represent it; if a pixel is labeled 1, then use `center[1]`, and so on. Eventually the created image is consist of `center[0]` to `center[k-1]`, the number of color is k.
Line 9	Reshape the created image back to the original dimensions.
Line 10	Return the result of color quantization.

Let's take a look at a real picture and see the effects of color quantization, below images show the original, and the color quantized with 32, 16, 8 clusters.

The total distinct colors in each image:

```
Distinct colors in original: 154050
Distinct colors after color quantization(clusters=32): 32
Distinct colors after color quantization(clusters=16): 16
Distinct colors after color quantization(clusters=8): 8
```

Execute the codes in *K-MeansColorQuantization.py* to observe the above results, and feel free to modify the codes for your practices. With the techniques of color quantization, we can reduce the number of colors significantly while keeping the visual similarity as the original image.

7.1.3 Handwritten Digits Grouping

```
Source:        K-MeansHandWrittenDigits.py
```

This example will use K-means to group the handwritten digits. We use the MNIST (Modified National Institute of Standards and Technology) dataset, which is a commonly used dataset in the field of machine learning and computer vision, and it's the de facto "Hello World" dataset.

MNIST has 70,000 handwritten digits that have been preprocessed and normalized to fit into a fixed-size image of 28×28 pixels. The dataset contains 60,000 training images and 10,000 testing images, with each image representing a single digit from 0 to 9. The training set is normally used to train the model, and the testing set is used to evaluate the model, both are useful for machine learning processes. Now for this example, however, we only use the training set.

The dataset comes with `keras` package, it can be loaded by the following code:

```
1  from keras.datasets import mnist
2  (X_train, Y_train), (X_test, Y_test) =
                                mnist.load_data()
```

Line 1 is to import `mnist` dataset from `keras` package. Before the code is running make sure the `keras` is installed as the steps in section 2.3.2.

Line 2 is to load the dataset into (X_train, Y_train) as training set, and (X_test, Y_test) as testing set. There sizes are show as below:

```
X_train:  (60000, 28, 28)
Y_train:  (60000,)
X_test:   (10000, 28, 28)
Y_test:   (10000,)
```

X_train and X_test are the variables that contain the handwritten images, where Y_train and Y_test are the labels that tell us the images are 0, 1, 2, ..., 9. X_train has 60,000 images, each 28 × 28, this is indicated in the above results as (60000,28,28). And Y_train has 60,000 labels as (60000,)

In this example we do not use the labels in Y_train, because K-Means is an unsupervised algorithm which doesn't need the labels, it will find the similarity of the data and group the data by its own calculations. Figure 7-8 shows some random samples from MNIST dataset:

Figure 7-8 Random Samples from MNIST Dataset

Figure 7-8 is generated by show_random_digits() function in line 6 to 15 below.

In this example, K-means will be running against X_train, hopefully it can group the images based on their similarities, that is all 0's are grouped as one cluster, all 1's as another cluster, and so on.

Here are the source codes,

```
1   from keras.datasets import mnist
2   import numpy as np
3   import matplotlib.pyplot as plt
4   import cv2
5
6   def show_random_digits(X, Y, row, col):
7       _, axarr = plt.subplots(row, col, figsize=(6,
    6))
8       for i in range(row):
9           filter = np.where((Y == i))
10          X1, Y1 = X[filter], Y[filter]
11          for j in range(col):
12              index = np.random.randint(
                    X1.shape[0])
13              axarr[i, j].imshow(X1[index],
                    cmap="binary" )
14              axarr[i, j].axis('off')
15      plt.show()
16
17  def show_result(results):
18      fig, ax = plt.subplots(1, 10, figsize=(6, 1))
19      for axi, result in zip(ax.flat, results):
20          axi.imshow(result,
                    interpolation='nearest',
                    cmap="binary")
21          axi.axis('off')
22      plt.show()
23
24  if __name__ == "__main__":
25      print("Loading MINST dataset...")
26      (X_train, Y_train), (X_test, Y_test) =
                    mnist.load_data()
27      print('X_train: ' + str(X_train.shape))
28      print('Y_train: ' + str(Y_train.shape))
29      print('X_test:  ' + str(X_test.shape))
```

```
30          print('Y_test:    ' + str(Y_test.shape))
31          show_random_digits(X_train, Y_train, 10, 10)
32
33          print("Running K-Means...")
34          X = X_train.reshape(X_train.shape[0],
                        X_train.shape[1] * X_train.shape[2])
35          X = np.float32(X)
36          clusters = 10
37          criteria = (cv2.TERM_CRITERIA_MAX_ITER,10,1.0)
38          ret,label,center=cv2.kmeans(
                        X, clusters, None,
                        criteria, 10,
                        cv2.KMEANS_RANDOM_CENTERS)
39          center = np.uint8(center)
40          results = center.reshape(clusters,
                                X_train.shape[1],
                                X_train.shape[2])
41          show_result(results)
```

Explanations:

Line 1	Import `keras` package and import `mnist` from there. Make sure this package is installed.
Line 3	Import `matplotlib` package for data plotting. Make sure this package is installed.
Line 24	The starting point of the codes.
Line 26	Load `mnist` dataset into training and testing sets.
Line 27 - 30	Print out the size of each variable.
Line 31	Call `show_random_digits()` to display the sample handwritten images.
Line 34 - 35	Reshape `X_train` into a 2-dimensional array and convert the data into `float32` for K-Means purposes.
Line 36	Set clusters = 10.
Line 37	Set K-Means criteria.
Line 38	Run K-Means.

Line 39	The centroids returned from `kmeans ()` function is `float32` datatype, convert it to `uint8`.
Line 40	Reshape the center into 28 × 28 image.
Line 41	Show the results.

It could take several minutes to run K-Means because of the big dataset. The results look like Figure 7-9:

Figure 7-9 K-means Results on MNIST Dataset

As a conclusion, K-Means seems not a perfect method to deal with these handwritten images. We will introduce other algorithms in later sections and will revisit these handwritten images to see how other algorithms doing with this dataset.

7.2   K-Nearest Neighbors

7.2.1   What is K-Nearest Neighbors

```
Source:      K-NearestNeighbors.py
```

K-Nearest Neighbors (KNN) is a machine learning algorithm that works by finding the k closest data points in the training set to a new input data point and using the majority class of those k neighbors to make a prediction for the input data point.

It's a supervised machine learning algorithm, which is different from K-means in the previous section. It's supervised because it relies on labeled input data to learn and predict an appropriate output when given new unlabeled data. KNN is easy and simple, and can be used to solve classification problems as K-means does.

KNN is a *lazy* and *non-parametric* algorithm. Lazy means the dataset is not needed when fitting or training the models, instead it's used in the prediction phase. It only stores the dataset in the fitting or training phase, it does almost nothing until last minute when making predictions, that's why it's called *lazy* algorithm. This, however, makes predictions slower than fitting or training.

The opposite of lazy is *eager* algorithm, like the previous K-means algorithm, the training data is used to fit or train the model.

KNN is a *non-parametric* algorithm means it does not make any assumptions on the distribution of the dataset. In the case of parametric algorithm, like Support Vector Machine in the next section, it has to select appropriate kernel functions based on the distribution of the dataset, but it's not the case for KNN. This is sometimes helpful in the real-word projects where little knowledge about the datasets or the datasets do not follow any mathematical distributions.

How the KNN works? Let's take a look at the sample data, there are 2-dimensional data points grouped in two clusters, ● data points and × data points, as shown in Figure 7-10.

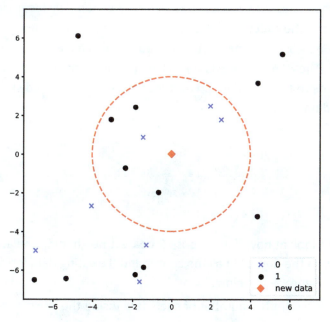

Figure 7-10 K-Nearest Neighbors, $k=7$

The • and × are labeled input data, the × is labeled as 0, and • as 1. Now there is a new data point ◆ in the center of Figure 7-10, we want to predict this new data belongs to × or •.

Draw a circle with the new data point as the center and 7 data points included, as shown in Figure 7-10. In another word, choose 7 nearest neighbors to the new data point which are within the circle.

Then count how many • and × data within the circle:

•: 4

×: 3

The number of • is more than that of ×, then the new data is predicted as •.

In reality, KNN will not draw any circles, it will calculate the distances from each point to the new point, and sort the distances from near to far, then take 7 data points with the nearest distances and count the number.

The source codes for KNN are in *K-NearestNeighbors.py* file, below is the result of the execution, the `result` is 1, which is •. The `neighbours` list the 7 nearest neighbours which have 4 ones (•) and 3 zeros (×). The `distance` lists the calculated distance from the 7 neighbours to the new data point, these are the 7 nearest distances from all data points.

```
result:   [[1]]
neighbours:   [[0 1 1 1 0 0 1]]
distance:   [[ 2.8350914   4.347414    6.090847
             9.372871    9.551281   10.086439
            12.6590185]]
```

Next, let's look at how if we choose 9 nearest neighbors, similarly draw a circle with the new data as the center and 9 existing data inside, as shown in Figure 7-11 below.

Then again, count the number of each data inside the circle:

•: 4

×: 5

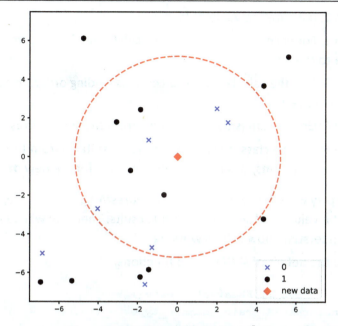

Figure 7-11 K-Nearest Neighbors, k=9

This time the new data is predicted as ×, because the number of × is more than •.

Below is the result of the execution, this time the `result` becomes 0. Similarly, the `neighbours` and the `distance` are listed in the results:

```
result: [[0]]
neighbours: [[0 1 1 1 0 0 1 0 0]]
distance: [[ 2.8350914    4.347414     6.090847
             9.372871     9.551281    10.086439
            12.6590185   23.584814    23.810982 ]]
```

In conclusion, the results of the K-Nearest Neighbors (KNN) algorithm can vary depending on the value of the k (the number of neighbors). If choose a very small value of k, say k=1, the algorithm will be highly sensitive to the noise in the data. On the other hand, if choose a very large value of k, the algorithm might not be able to correctly capture the data pattern.

Here is the summary of KNN, assume there are totally n data in the training set, and we want to predict a new data:

Step 1: Initialize the value of k.

Step 2: For each data from 1 to n, calculate the distance from the data to the new data.

Step 3: Sort the calculated distances in ascending order, this is an array of size n.

Step 4: Get the top (smallest) k items from the sorted array.

Step 5: Get the class (or label) with the most items from the top (smallest) k items, this is the predicted value for the new data.

You can play with the source code in *K-NearestNeighbors.py* file, select different k values and see the different results. Then you will be able to better understand how KNN is working.

Here are the details of *KNN* related functions:

```
1   knn = cv2.ml.KNearest_create()
2   knn.train(X_train, sample_type, y_train)
3   retval, results, neighbor, dist =
                     knn.findNearest(X_test, k)
```

Explanations:

Line 1	Initialize KNN classifier and return an empty model.

Line 2	Train the KNN model.
	`X_train`: *input data array, the datatype is* `float32`.
	`y_train`: *input label array.*
	`sample_type`: *either of the two values below,*
	  `cv2.ml.ROW_SAMPLE`: *training data in rows.*
	  `cv2.ml.COL_SAMPLE`: *training data in columns.*

Line 3	Finds the neighbors and predicts responses for the input array. `X_test`: *input data for prediction, the datatype is* `float32`. `k`: *number of nearest neighbors, k>1.* *Outputs:* `results`: *the prediction result array, same size as X_test,* *datatype is* `float32`. `neighbor`: *the corresponding neighbors.* `dist`: *the distance from the predicted data to the neighbors.*

7.2.2   KNN Evaluation

> Source: K-NNEvaluation.py

In the last section we understood that a different k value might cause a different predicted result. In this section we will evaluate the results of KNN and find out how to select the best k value.

7.2.2.1   How to Select K

Use functions in `sklearn` to generate data and split the data into training and testing sets,

```
1   from sklearn.datasets import make_blobs
2   from sklearn.model_selection import train_test_split
3
4   X, y = make_blobs(n_samples=800, centers=2,
                      cluster_std=6.8,
5                     random_state=2)
6   X_train, X_test, y_train, y_test =
7                     train_test_split(X, y,
                      test_size = 0.2, random_state = 1)
8   print('X_train: ' + str(X_train.shape))
9   print('Y_train: ' + str(y_train.shape))
10  print('X_test:  ' + str(X_test.shape))
11  print('Y_test:  ' + str(y_test.shape))
```

The sample data looks like Figure 7-12, there are a total of 800 data points as specified in line 4 above. The `train_test_split()` function separates 80% of the data into the training set and 20% into the testing set, as line 6 and 7 above. Here is the size of each data set:

```
X_train: (640, 2)
y_train: (640,)
X_test:  (160, 2)
y_test:  (160,)
```

`X_train` has 640 data points, it's a 2-dimensional array, its size is $(640, 2)$; `y_train` is the label of `X_train`, it tells each data in

`X_train` is labeled as 0 or 1, its size is `(640,)`. `X_test` and `y_test` are similar, their sizes are `(160,2)` and `(160,)` respectively.

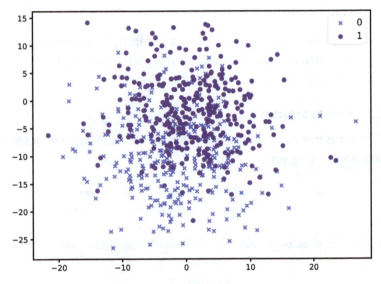

Figure 7-12 Sample Data for KNN

In machine learning it is a common practice to separate the data into training set and testing set, the former is used to train the model (in our case KNN), and the latter is used to verify the model to see how it is doing. We will follow this practice, let the KNN model learn from the training set, and the accuracy is evaluated from the testing set.

Below is the code to execute the KNN. Line 12 is to initialize a KNN model. Line 13 is to train the model with the training set. Line 14 is to use the trained model to predict results from the testing set with a given k.

```
12   knn = cv2.ml.KNearest_create()
13   knn.train(X_train, cv2.ml.ROW_SAMPLE, y_train)
14   ret, result, neighbour, dist =
15                       knn.findNearest(X_test, k)
```

The returned `result` is the predicted value, it is the same size as `X_test`; `neighbour` is an array of the nearest neighbours with size of k; `dist` is an array of the distances of k neighbours, its size is also k.

The `accuracy_score()` function in `sklearn` package will be used to evaluate the accuracy of the result. The returned `result` in line 14 will be compared with `y_test`, the label of the testing set, to obtain the accuracy. If the `result` is exactly the same as `y_test`, the accuracy is 100%, if some are missing the accuracy is less than 100%.

```
16   from sklearn.metrics import accuracy_score
17   accuracy = accuracy_score(y_test, result)
```

Now we will evaluate the accuracy for different k values. The `knn.findNearest()` will be run iteratively with k from 1 to 100, each time the accuracy is evaluated. Figure 7-13 shows the results.

First, look at the solid line in Figure 7-13, which shows the accuracy vs k value for the training set. When $k = 1$, 100% accuracy is achieved, but it drops significantly if k increases to around 10, eventually it reaches convergence at $k > 20$.

Next, look at the dashed line in Figure 7-13, which shows the accuracy vs k value for the testing set. The accuracy is at the lowest point at $k = 1$, but it increases when k increases, eventually it reaches convergence when k becomes larger.

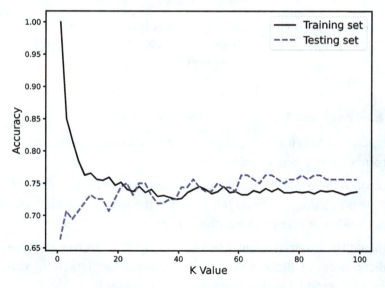

Figure 7-13 KNN Evaluation

Different data sets will have different accuracy curves, basically they all look similar to Figure 7-13. A best k value can be found from this kind of analysis. In this case selecting k=20 will make both training and testing sets achieve the accuracy near 0.75.

7.2.2.2 True Positive, False Positive, True Negative and False Negative

In order to evaluate the results of machine learning for classification problems, there are four important concepts, True Positive (TP), False Positive (FP), True Negative (TN) and False Negative (FN). They are explained in below table:

True Positives (TP)	Data is labeled as 1, and it's predicted as 1. (Correct). E.g., the color is predicted to be red, and it is actually red.
True Negatives (TN)	Data is labeled as 0, and it's predicted as 0. (Correct). E.g., the color is predicted not red, and it's actually not red.
False Positives (FP)	Data is labeled as 0, but it's predicted as 1. (Error). E.g. the color is predicted to be red, but it's actually not red.
False Negatives (FN)	Data is labeled as 1, but it is predicted as 0. (Error). E.g. the color is predicted not red, but it's actually red.

7.2.2.3 Precision, Recall and F_1 Score

Precision and Recall are two important metrics used to evaluate the performance of a classification model.

Precision is the proportion of true positive predictions out of all the positive predictions made by the model. It measures how accurate the model is when it predicts a positive outcome.

Recall, on the other hand, measures the proportion of true positive predictions out of all the actual positive cases in the data. It measures how well the model is able to detect positive cases in the data.

In other words, precision is about the accuracy of the positive predictions, while recall is about the completeness of the positive predictions. See Figure 7-14.

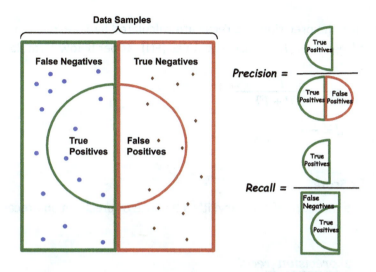

Figure 7-14 Precision and Recall

In Figure 7-14, the true positives (green half circle in the left) plus false negatives (green part in the left rectangle) are true labels in the dataset. The false positives (red half circle in the right) plus true negatives (red part in the right rectangle) are false labels in the dataset.

As shown in the right-side of Figure 7-14, the *precision* is defined as the percentage of true positives against all predicted positives. Simply put, precision is how many positives are real out of all predicted positives. Precision demonstrates the ability to distinguish the negatives, a high value of precision means it can effectively distinguish the positives from the negatives.

While the *recall* is defined as the percentage of true positives against all actual positives. Simply put, recall is how many positives are predicted out of all real positives. Recall demonstrates the ability to recognize the positives in the dataset, a high recall value means it can correctly recognize most of the positives.

For example, when diagnosing a disease, a high precision score means a smaller number of mistakes in the positive results, most positive results are real positives, only a small number of positive results are errors. A high recall score means most of the actual positives are diagnosed as positive, only a small number of actual positives are not correctly diagnosed.

As summary, the precision and recall are calculated by True Positives (TP), True Negatives (TN), False Negatives (FN), as per below formula:

$$precision = \frac{TP}{TP + FP}$$

$$recall = \frac{TP}{TP + FN}$$

What is F_1 Score

F_1 score is a measure of accuracy, it's a balance of precision and recall, it's defined as:

$$F_1 = \frac{2 \cdot precision \cdot recall}{precision + recall}$$

$$= \frac{TP}{TP + \frac{1}{2}(FP + FN)}$$

The highest F_1 score is 1.0, indicating perfect precision and recall. While the lowest possible value is 0, when either the precision or recall is zero.

Don't worry about the formula and calculations, `sklearn` provides functions to take care of all the calculations. The only thing we need to do is to pass the original label and predicted results to the functions, they do all the calculations and give us the results.

7.2.2.4   KNN Evaluation

Now let's go back to the above example, there are several metrics to measure the result of classification problems in `sklearn`. Line 1 to 3 below import three metrics,

```
1   from sklearn.metrics import confusion_matrix
2   from sklearn.metrics import accuracy_score
```

```
3   from sklearn.metrics import classification_report
4   print("Accuracy Score:",
                 accuracy_score(y_test, res_test))
5   print("Confusion Matrix:",
                 confusion_matrix(y_test, res_test))
6   print("Classification Report:",
                 classification_report(y_test, res_test))
```

Accuracy Score

`accuracy_score()` reports the accuracy of the predictions, it simply calculates the percentage of correct predictions over the whole samples. The parameters are the true labels and predicted results.

Say there are totally n data samples, y' is the predicted result, and y_i is the label of the sample data, then the accuracy is calculated as per the below formula:

$$accuracy(y, \ y') = \sum_{i=0}^{n-1} 1(y' = y_i)$$

Run the above codes with k = 20, the *Accuracy Score* is 75.6%, which means there are 75.6% of predicted values are correct compared with the true label.

```
Accuracy Score: 0.75625
```

Confusion Matrix

A confusion matrix is a table that summarizes the performance of a classification model on a dataset. It is a matrix that shows the number of true positive, true negative, false positive, and false negative predictions made by the model.

The confusion matrix provides a more detailed view of the performance of a classification model than the accuracy score. It can be used to calculate various metrics such as precision, recall, F1 score, and accuracy.

An example of a confusion matrix is shown as below table,

	Predicted Positive	Predicted Negative
Actual Positive	True Positive (TP)	False Negative (FN)
Actual Negative	False Positive (FP)	True Negative (TN)

Run the above codes with k = 20, the confusion matrix looks like:

```
Confusion Matrix:
 [[62 19]
  [20 59]]
```

The upper left value is the true positive which is 62, the lower right value is the true negative which is 59, they are the correct predictions. The upper right value is the false negative of 19, and the lower left value is the false positive of 20.

In summary, a good classification model will have a high number of true positives and true negatives, and a low number of false positives and false negatives. The confusion matrix provides a useful way to visualize the performance of the model and identify areas for improvement.

Classification Report

A classification report is a table that summarizes the performance of a classification model. It provides a comprehensive overview of the precision, recall, and F1-score for each class in the dataset. It is typically generated using the metrics calculated from the confusion matrix. And it is a commonly used tool in machine learning and data science to evaluate the performance of a model.

The classification report usually contains the following metrics for each class in the classification model:

- Precision: as described above, the proportion of true positives out of all positive predictions.
- Recall: as described above, the proportion of true positives out of all actual positive cases in the data.
- F1-score: as described above, a balance between the above two metrics.
- Support: the number of data points for each class.

Run the above codes with $k = 20$, the classification report looks like:

```
Classification Report:
          precision recall f1-score  support
    0        0.76     0.77    0.76       81
    1        0.76     0.75    0.75       79
accuracy                      0.76      160
macro avg    0.76     0.76    0.76      160
weighted avg 0.76     0.76    0.76      160
```

The classification report shows each class in one row, in this case there are two classes, 0 and 1, the classification report shows them in the first two rows. If there are 10 classes, there will be 10 rows displayed in the report. The `accuracy` is the same as the accuracy score discussed above. The `macro avg` is the mean or average of the metrics with equal weight on each class. The `weighted avg` is the average of the metrics in which the score of each class is weighted by its presence in the data sample.

The classification report provides a detailed breakdown of the performance of the model for each class, which is especially useful in cases where the data is imbalanced. It provides a detailed understanding of the model's performance for each class in the dataset, and it allows the model to be evaluated separately for each class, which can provide insights into areas where the model may need improvement.

The classification report is a useful tool for evaluating the performance of classification models and is often used in conjunction with other metrics such as the confusion matrix and accuracy score.

Feel free to play with the source codes in *K-NNEvaluation.py* file to better understand the KNN model and evaluation metrics.

7.2.3   Recognize Handwritten Digits with KNN

```
Source:      K-NNHandWrittenDigits.py
```

We have used the handwritten digit dataset in section 7.1.3 with K-means, this time will apply K-Nearest Neighbors to the same dataset.

7.2.3.1 Load MNIST Dataset

To recap, MNIST dataset has 70,000 handwritten digits with 28×28 pixels each, which can be loaded from `keras.datasets` package. The `load_data()` function will load the dataset and automatically separate it into a training set and a testing set, the training set of `[60000,28, 28]` has 60,000 data points; and the testing set of `[10000, 28, 28]` has 10,000 data items.

Here is the code to load MNIST dataset and show the random digits:

```python
def show_random_digits(X, Y, row, col):
    _, axarr = plt.subplots(row, col, figsize=(6, 6))
    for i in range(row):
        filter = np.where((Y == i))
        X1, Y1 = X[filter], Y[filter]
        for j in range(col):
            index = np.random.randint(X1.shape[0])
            axarr[i, j].imshow(X1[index], cmap="binary")
            axarr[i, j].axis('off')
            axarr[i, j].text(0.5, 1, str(Y1[index]),
                            fontsize=12, c='g')
    print("The true label is shown in green.")
    plt.show()

if __name__ == "__main__":
    print("Loading MINST dataset...")
    (X_train, y_train), (X_test, y_test) = mnist.load_data()
    print('X_train: ' + str(X_train.shape))
    print('y_train: ' + str(y_train.shape))
    print('X_test:  ' + str(X_test.shape))
    print('y_test:  ' + str(y_test.shape))
    show_random_digits(X_train, y_train, 10, 10)
```

Explanations:

Line 1 - 12	*Define function* `show_random_digits()` *to display the random images of the handwritten digits.*
Line 14	*Execution entrance.*
Line 16	*Load the MNIST dataset into the training and testing sets, each set has data in* `(X_train/X_test)` *and label in* `(y_train/y_test).`
Line 17 - 20	*(Optional) print out the size of each dataset.*
Line 21	*Show the random digits in 10 rows and 10 columns.*

Figure 7-15 shows 100 random samples from MNIST dataset with their labels:

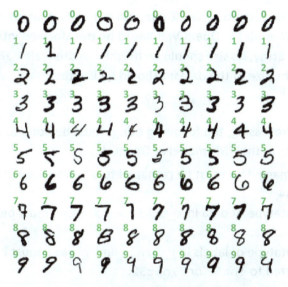

Figure 7-15 Random Samples from MNIST Dataset with Labels

In the previous section we displayed the random handwritten digits, but didn't show the labels that come with the digits because we didn't use them. This time Figure 7-15 shows the digits together with their labels, the labels are in green text at the upper-left corner of each digit. The labels are in `y_train` and `y_test`, we will use them later together with `X_train` to train the KNN model.

Line 17 to 20 in the above codes print out the size of each:

```
X_train:  (60000,  28,  28)
y_train:  (60000,)
X_test:   (10000,  28,  28)
y_test:   (10000,)
```

7.2.3.2 Pre-processing

The training dataset has 60,000 images, each has pixels of height=28 and width=28, so the size is like this,

```
X_train:  (60000,  28,  28)
```

Each image, or data point, is a 2-dimensional array, that doesn't work with the KNN model of OpenCV, it has to be transformed into a 1-dimensional array, its size should be height $\times$ width = 28 $\times$ 28 = 784. Therefore, the size of the dataset should be like this:

```
X_train:  (60000,  784)
```

As the pre-processing, the following things must be done to meet the requirements of the KNN model of OpenCV,

1. Each image data must be reshaped to a 1-dimensional array of size 784
2. The datatype of data in X_train and X_test must be converted to float32.
3. The datatype of labels in y_train and y_test must be converted to int32 or float32.

Below are the code snippets for pro-processing:

```
22  w, h = X_train[0, :, :].shape
23  X_train = X_train.reshape(X_train.shape[0],
                              w * h).astype(np.float32)
24  X_test = X_test.reshape(X_test.shape[0],
                            w * h).astype(np.float32)
25  y_train = np.int32(y_train)
26  y_test = np.int32(y_test)
```

232

Explanations:

Line 22	Get the width and height from the array.
Line 23 – 24	Reshape X_train and X_test array into the size of width × height. And convert their datatype to `float32`.
Line 25 – 26	Convert the datatype of y_train and y_test to `int32`.

7.2.3.3 Build and Train the KNN model

Now build the KNN model and train it with X_train data and y_train label. Then predict the result with $k = 7$.

```
27  knn = cv2.ml.KNearest_create()
28  knn.train(X_train, cv2.ml.ROW_SAMPLE, y_train)
29  k = 7
30  _, results, _, _ = knn.findNearest(X_test, k)
```

Explanations:

Line 27	Create a new KNN model.
Line 28	Train the KNN model with X_train and y_train. `cv2.ml.ROW_SAMPLE` means each training data is a row.
Line 29	Choose a k value
Line 30	Make a prediction with X_test data and k. "_" is used here to bypass other output values, this is a Python technique.

Line 30 in the above codes could take some time to run because of the amount of data, depending on the computer's performance it could take 5 minutes or more.

7.2.3.4 Post-processing

The results of the output of the KNN model should be re-formatted for evaluation purposes.

233

The results returned from `knn.findNearest()` function is in the format as a "vertical" array, which means the values are organized in one column and 10,000 rows, its size is as below,

```
results: (10000, 1)
```

In order to compare it with the original label in `y_test` which is formatted in a "horizontal" array, it must be converted to the same format as `(10000,)`. A `numpy` function, `np.hstack()`, can easily do this type of conversion.

We also need to do some reversal operations against pre-processing, here is what need to do as post-processing:

1. Re-format the results from the "vertical" array to "horizontal".
2. Reshaped `X_train, X_test` size from 784 to 28 × 28.
3. (Optional) Convert the datatype of `y_train, y_test` to `uint`.
4. (Optional) Convert the datatype of the result to `uint`.

Here are the codes:

```
31  results = np.hstack(results)
32  results = np.uint(results)
33  y_test = np.uint(y_test)
34  X_test = X_test.reshape(X_test.shape[0], w, h)
```

Since we are only interested in `X_test` and `y_test` in the following evaluation step, so we don't care about the `X_train` and `y_train`. However, if you want to use them later you have to convert them accordingly.

7.2.3.5   Evaluation

As explained in section 7.2.2.4, here is the code to evaluate the results.

```
35  from sklearn.metrics import accuracy_score
36  from sklearn.metrics import confusion_matrix
37  from sklearn.metrics import classification_report
38  print("K=", k)
39  print("Accuracy Score:",
```

```
                  accuracy_score(y_test, results))
40  print("Confusion Matrix:\n",
                  confusion_matrix(y_test, results))
41  print("Classification Report:\n",
                  classification_report(y_test, results))
```

Below are the reports, we got an *accuracy* of 96.94% which is pretty good. The size of the *confusion matrix* is much bigger than the one in section 7.2.2.4, because this time there are 10 classes, from 0 to 9, then the size of confusion matrix becomes 10 × 10 (which was 2 × 2 for two classes). The numbers in the diagonal of the matrix are true positives, such as 974, 1133, 988, ..., and so on. The majority of true positive indicates a good model.

```
K= 7

Accuracy Score: 0.9694

Confusion Matrix:
 [[ 974    1    1    0    0    1    2    1    0    0]
  [   0 1133    2    0    0    0    0    0    0    0]
  [  11    8  988    2    1    0    2   16    4    0]
  [   0    3    2  976    1   12    1    7    4    4]
  [   1    8    0    0  945    0    5    1    1   21]
  [   5    0    0    8    2  866    4    1    2    4]
  [   6    3    0    0    3    2  944    0    0    0]
  [   0   25    3    0    1    0    0  989    0   10]
  [   6    4    6   11    7   12    1    6  916    5]
  [   5    6    3    6    8    4    1   11    2  963]]
```

The *classification report* shows the *precision, recall* and *F1* score for each class. The *F1* score for every class is near 1.0 which is a good prediction.

```
Classification Report:
               precision    recall  f1-score   support
           0       0.97      0.99      0.98       980
           1       0.95      1.00      0.97      1135
           2       0.98      0.96      0.97      1032
           3       0.97      0.97      0.97      1010
           4       0.98      0.96      0.97       982
           5       0.97      0.97      0.97       892
           6       0.98      0.99      0.98       958
           7       0.96      0.96      0.96      1028
           8       0.99      0.94      0.96       974
```

9	0.96	0.95	0.96	1009
accuracy			0.97	10000
macro avg	0.97	0.97	0.97	10000
weighted avg	0.97	0.97	0.97	10000

7.2.3.6 (Optional) Show the Results

After the evaluation, we can display the results as Figure 7-16, similar to the previous Figure 7-15, this time it shows both the original labels in green at the upper-left of each digit, and the predicted value in red at the upper-right of each digit. For example, the top-left digit shows 3 3, which means its label is 3, and it is predicted as 3.

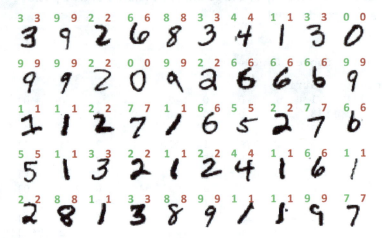

Figure 7-16 Results of KNN

Lastly, also as optional, if you are curious about what kind of digits are missed by the model, you can also display the erroneously predicted ones, here are the codes to pick them up and display them:

```
42      pred_err = np.where(y_test != results)
43      show_random_result(X_test[pred_err,:,:][0],
                           y_test[pred_err],
44                         10, 5,
                           results[pred_err])
```

Line 42 is to pick up those items that y_test!=results, meaning the mistakes in the predictions. np.where() function allows us to perform this kind of conditional operation. The results are shown as Figure 7-17, similar to the above result, the original label in green is at the upper-left of each digit, and the predicted value is shown in red at the upper-right. For example, the top-left digit shows **2 1**, which means its label is 2, but predicted as 1.

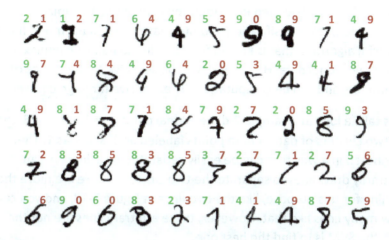

Figure 7-17 Errors in KNN Results

As shown in the evaluation reports of the confusion matrix and classification report, the majority of digits are correctly identified, and the accuracy is 96.94%. Figure 7-17 only represents a small portion of the missed ones.

7.3 Support Vector Machine

7.3.1 What is Support Vector Machine

> Source: SupportVectorMachine.py,
> common/gaussian.py

A Support Vector Machine (SVM) is one of the supervised machine learning algorithms, which means the learning or training is based on both the data and the labels. It is mostly used in resolving classification problems.

237

The basic idea behind SVM is to find the best possible decision boundary that separates the data into different classes. The decision boundary is chosen in such a way that it maximizes the margin, i.e., the distance between the decision boundary and the nearest data points from each class.

SVM has been widely used in various applications such as image classification, text classification, bioinformatics, and many more. It is a powerful algorithm that is known for its ability to handle complex and high-dimensional data. However, it can be sensitive to the choice of parameters and can be computationally expensive for large datasets.

Let's take a look at a sample 2-dimensional dataset as Figure 7-18, there are two clusters of data, • data points labeled as 0, and × as 1. They are distributed in a way that can be easily separated by a line; we can arbitrarily draw lines to separate the two clusters. There are more than one line for this purpose, like the two lines in Figure 7-18, and you can draw many lines like that. However, these arbitrary lines are not the best, the SVM is to find the best one.

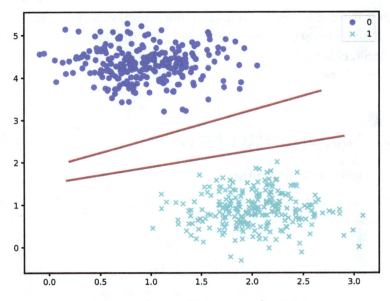

Figure 7-18 Sample 2-D Data for SVM

The objective of a Support Vector Machine is to find a line between the two clusters of the data that distinctly classifies the data points, and at the same time ensures the maximum margin, the margin is the distance between the line and the closest data points of each class. In other words, SVM seeks to find the line that is most robust to noise and other variations in the data.

As shown in Figure 7-19, the solid line in the middle is the best one that meets the requirements of SVM, it can separate the two clusters of the data, and it has the maximum margin between the two classes of data.

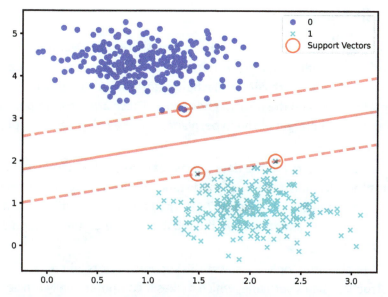

Figure 7-19 Decision Boundary and Support Vectors of SVM

What are Hyperplanes

Hyperplanes are also called *decision boundaries* that are used to classify the data points. Data points falling on one side of the hyperplane belong to one class; falling on the other side of the hyperplane belong to another class.

The solid line in the middle of Figure 7-19 is the *Hyperplane*, also called *Decision Boundary*. Any new data falling on either side of the decision boundary will be predicted as the corresponding cluster.

The two dashed lines parallel to the hyperplane are the separating lines which used to separate the two classes of data points, the hyperplane has the maximum margin to the two separating lines.

The dimension of the hyperplane depends on the number of features of the data (the dimension of the data or). If the number of features is 2 (or 2-dimensional data), then the *hyperplane* is just a line. If the number of features is 3 (or 3-dimensional data), then the *hyperplane* becomes a 2-dimensional plane. If the number of features is n (or n-dimensional data), then the hyperplane is a n-1 dimensional hyperplane.

What are Support Vectors

Support Vectors are data points that are closest to the *Decision Boundary* and influence the position and orientation of the *Decision Boundary*. The Support Vector Machine algorithm calculates these support vectors and the decision boundary. These are the data points that define the margin of the hyperplane, and they play a crucial role in the SVM algorithm.

The support vectors are the data points that are on the margin, which means that they have the smallest distance to the hyperplane, as the data points with circles in Figure 7-19. They are the most difficult data points to classify, and they have the most influence on the position of the hyperplane.

The SVM algorithm only considers the support vectors when constructing the hyperplane, which makes it computationally efficient and allows it to handle large datasets with many features. The other data points that are not support vectors are not used in the decision-making process of the SMV algorithm.

What are Kernels

The data might not be always as easy as the above example, sometimes the data is distributed in a way that is not able to separate by a line, as Figure 7-20. There are also two clusters of data, however it's not straightforward to find a line to separate them.

SVM algorithm applies a technique called *kernel* methods, kernels are mathematical functions used to transform the input data into a higher-dimensional space where it may be easier to separate the clusters. Kernels are used to handle non-linearly separable data, where the clusters cannot be separated by a linear hyperplane. The purpose of using a *kernel* is to enable SVM algorithm to find a non-linear decision boundary that can separate the data points into their respective classes.

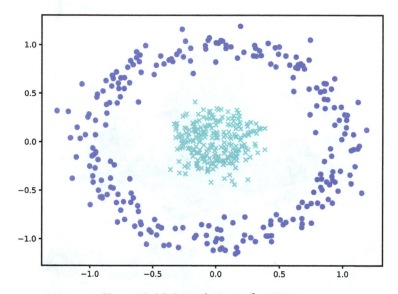

Figure 7-20 Sample Data for SVM

The idea behind using kernels in SVM is that in a higher-dimensional space, it may be possible to find a linear hyperplane that separates the clusters.

There are different types of kernels, the most commonly used are:

- Linear kernel is used when the data is linearly separable, as in the above example.
- Gaussian (Radial Basis Function) kernel is used when the data is not linearly separable, as in this example, and it transforms the data with the Gaussian function.
- Polynomial kernel is used when the data is not linearly separable, and it transforms the data with a polynomial function.
- And so on.

Then how the data is transformed by the kernel functions to a higher dimensional space? Let's look at the 2-dimensional Gaussian function as shown in Figure 7-21:

$\mu = [0, 0]$
$\Sigma = [[9, 0], [0, 9]]$

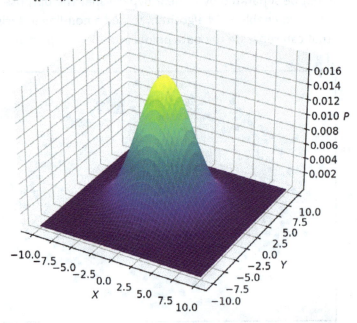

Figure 7-21 2-D Gaussian Function

generated by the code at common/gaussian.py

When the data is transformed by the Gaussian function from a 2-D space to 3-D, the data points near the center will be transformed to a higher position, while the data far from the center will be transformed to a lower position in the 3D space.

After applying the Gaussian function to the above data, it can be transformed into a 3D dimensional space as shown in Figure 7-22.

The × data were near the center area in the original 2-D space, now they are transformed to the top part in the 3-D space in Figure 7-22, the • data points were far from the center, and now in the lower part in the 3-D space.

Now image a 2-D plane is inserted between the × and • data points in the 3-D space, then we can successfully separate them. Same as the linear case, there could be many arbitrary 2-D planes to separate the data. The one with the maximum margin, meaning the maximum distance between data points of both clusters, is the *Decision Boundary*, and the data points that are closest to the decision boundary are *Support Vectors*.

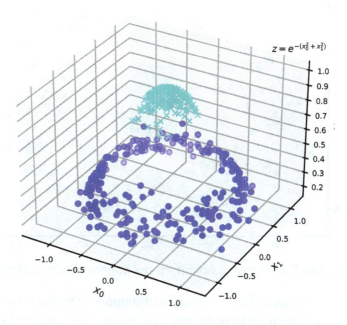

Figure 7-22 Data Transformed by Gaussian Function

Now, we have found the decision boundary and support vectors in the higher dimensional space, then transform them back to the original 2-D space, as shown in Figure 7-23. This time the decision boundary is a circle, instead of a line, because the data is distributed in a non-linear way. The circle in the solid line in the middle is the decision boundary, or hyperplane, the two dashed circles are the separating planes, and the data points on the separating planes, which are marked with circles, are support vectors.

Same as the previous linear case, the support vectors have the smallest distance to the decision boundary, and they have the most influence on the position of the decision boundary.

Any new data falling on either side of the decision boundary will be predicted as the corresponding classes, i.e. new data falling on the inner side of the decision boundary will be predicted as ×; and if on the outer side will be •.

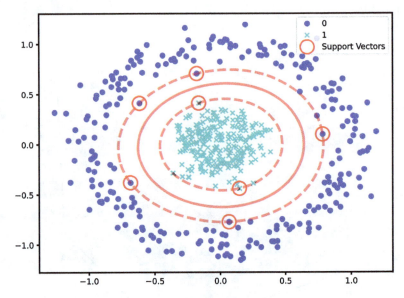

Figure 7-23 Decision Boundary and Support Vectors of SVM

OpenCV provides `cv2.ml.SVM` class to support SVM, the related functions can be used to build, train and predict the SVM models.

```
1  svm = cv2.ml.SVM_create()
2  svm.setKernel(cv2.ml.SVM_LINEAR)
3  svm.setTermCriteria((cv2.TERM_CRITERIA_MAX_ITER,
                        100, 1e-6))
4  svm.train(X_train, cv2.ml.ROW_SAMPLE, y_train)
5  predict = svm.predict(X_test)
```

Explanations:

Line 1	*Initialize an SVM model.*
Line 2	*Set a kernel for the SVM model, choose one of the predefined kernels from the below table of kernel list.*

244

Line 3	Set the algorithm termination criteria, that is, the iteration stops when the criteria are satisfied. This is the same as that introduced in K-means.
Line 4	Train the SVM model. `X_train` is the input data and `y_train` is the label. `cv2.ml.ROW_SAMPLE` means each data in a row; `cv2.ml.COL_SAMPLE` means each data in a column.
Line 5	Make a prediction using the trained SVM model. `X_test` is the input data for prediction, the datatype is `float32`.
	The output is a tuple, the first item of the tuple is the result for a single prediction when the `X_test` is a single data. The second is the array of the results for multiple prediction when the `X_test` is an array of multiple data.
	E.g. when `X_test` is an array of multiple data, the results are in `predict[1]`. It is formatted in a "vertical" matrix of shape `(m,1)`. It can be convert to a "horizontal" one by `np.hstack (predict[1])`.

OpenCV supports a number of SVM kernels, as shown in below table:

`cv2.ml.SVM_LINEAR`	Linear kernel, used when the data is linearly separable.
`cv2.ml.SVM_POLY`	Polynomial kernel, used when the data has a polynomial structure, and it maps the input data to a higher-dimensional space using a polynomial function.
`cv2.ml.SVM_RBF`	Radial basis function (RBF), or Gaussian kernel, used when the data has a non-linear structure, maps the input data to a higher-dimensional space using a Gaussian function. This kernel is particularly useful when the data has complex, non-linear relationships between features.
`cv2.ml.SVM_SIGMOID`	Sigmoid kernel, used when the data has a sigmoid structure, and it maps the input data to a higher-dimensional space using a sigmoid function.
`cv2.ml.SVM_CHI2`	Exponential Chi2 kernel, similar to the RBF kernel.

cv2.ml.SVM_INTER	*Histogram intersection kernel, used for measuring the similarity between two histograms to compute the intersection between the histograms of the two input samples.*

Please reference the OpenCV document for details at:
https://docs.opencv.org/4.7.0/d1/d2d/classcv_1_1ml_1_1SVM.html#aad7f1aa ccced3c33bb256640910a0e56

7.3.2 Recognize Handwritten Digits with SVM

Source: SVMHandWrittenDigits.py

In this section we will revisit the handwritten digits from MNIST (Modified National Institute of Standards and Technology) dataset. In sections 7.1.3 and 7.2.3, K-means and K-Nearest Neighbors are applied to it. In this section, the SVM will be applied to the same dataset to see how it is doing.

Loading the MNIST dataset and pre-processing are exactly the same as section 7.2.3, and will not repeat here.

7.3.2.1   Build, Train and Predict the SVM model

Now build the SVM model with linear kernel, and train it with X_train and y_train.

```
1  svm = cv2.ml.SVM_create()
2  svm.setKernel(cv2.ml.SVM_LINEAR)
3  svm.setTermCriteria((cv2.TERM_CRITERIA_MAX_ITER,
                         100, 1e-6))
4  svm.train(X_train, cv2.ml.ROW_SAMPLE, y_train)
5  predict = svm.predict(X_test)
```

Explanations:

Line 1	*Create an SVM model.*
Line 2	*Set the linear kernel to the SVM model.*

Line 3	Set the algorithm termination criteria.
Line 4	Train the SVM model with X_train and y_train.
Line 5	Make a prediction with the X_test.

It might take one or two minutes to train and predict the data.

7.3.2.2 Post-processing

The post-processing is similar to section 7.2.3.4 with only one difference. The svm.predict() function returns a tuple that has a single value and an array. If the prediction is for a single data, the result is in the first item of the returned tuple predict[0], if the prediction is for a dataset with multiple data items then the result is in the second item of the returned tuple result[1]. In this example we pass the testing set of X_test which has 10,000 data items, then take the results in predict[1].

```
6  results = np.uint8(predict[1])
7  results = np.hstack(results)
8  y_test = np.uint(y_test)
9  X_test = X_test.reshape(X_test.shape[0], w, h)
```

Explanations:

Line 1	Take predict[1] as the result, it has an array of prediction results.
Line 2	Re-format the results from the "vertical" array to "horizontal", see section 7.2.3.4.
Line 3	(Optional) Convert the datatype of y_test to uint.
Line 4	In pre-processing X_test is reshaped to an array of 784, now reshape it back to 28 x 28.

7.3.2.3 Evaluation

Same as section 7.2.3.5, print out the evaluation results as below, the accuracy is 68.15%.

```
Accuracy Score: 0.6815
Confusion Matrix:
[[ 898    0    3   12    4   44   18    1    0    0]
 [   0 1067    2   13    0    0    1    4   44    4]
 [  15  109  741   57   16    4   28   11   42    9]
 [  10   12   55  711    2  141    3   20   43   13]
 [   2    7   20   10  841    3   17   15    7   60]
 [  24   42   11  240   15  388   30   11  117   14]
 [  17    8  125   16   49   44  697    0    1    1]
 [   2   14   25   35   31    3    0  792    5  121]
 [  11   92   71  174   15   75   38   21  461   16]
 [   9    9    7   92  380   13    1  217   62   19]]
```

Classification Report:

	precision	recall	f1-score	support
0	0.91	0.92	0.91	980
1	0.78	0.94	0.86	1135
2	0.70	0.72	0.71	1032
3	0.52	0.70	0.60	1010
4	0.62	0.86	0.72	982
5	0.54	0.43	0.48	892
6	0.84	0.73	0.78	958
7	0.73	0.77	0.75	1028
8	0.59	0.47	0.53	974
9	0.48	0.22	0.30	1009
accuracy			0.68	10000
macro avg	0.67	0.68	0.66	10000
weighted avg	0.67	0.68	0.67	10000

7.3.2.4 (Optional) Show the Results

The random results and erroneously predicted results can be displayed optionally, the same as in section 7.2.3.6. Please execute the source codes at *SVMHandWrittenDigits.py* to observe the results.

7.3.3 IRIS Dataset Classification

> Source: SVMIrisClassification.py

7.3.3.1 About IRIS Dataset

IRIS dataset is another well-known and widely used multivariate dataset in machine learning and statistics, it's a collection of 150 samples of iris

248

flowers, with each sample containing four features: sepal length, sepal width, petal length, and petal width. It includes three species of iris flower -- Versicolour, Setosa and Virginica, 50 sample data for each species.

The Iris dataset has become a popular benchmark dataset in machine learning and statistics due to its simplicity, small size, and well-defined classification problem.

It's quite simple to load the IRIS dataset,

```
1  from sklearn import datasets
2  iris = datasets.load_iris()
3  print ("Data Structure:", dir(iris))
4  print ("Description:\n", iris.DESCR)
5  print ("Data (first 10):\n",iris.data[0:10])
6  print ("Label:\n", iris.target)
7  print ("Label Name:", iris.target_names)
8  print ("Unique Label:", np.unique(iris.target))
9  print ("Feature:", iris.feature_names)
```

Line 1 is to import `sklearn` library and line 2 is to load the IRIS dataset. There are several attributes that come with the dataset which include detailed information about the dataset. You can optionally print them out as line 3 to 9 in the above codes. The description of this dataset is in `iris.DESCR` attribute. The data itself is in `iris.data`; the label is encoded in `iris.target` with values of 0, 1 and 2, which corresponds to the three iris species. The names of the three species are in the `iris.target_names`. And the names of the features of this dataset are in `iris.feature_names`.

The IRIS dataset isn't a big dataset, it includes the following four features and one label:

1. sepal length in cm (feature)
2. sepal width in cm (feature)
3. petal length in cm (feature)
4. petal width in cm (feature)
5. species (label)

This dataset is about the measurements in centimeters of the sepal length, sepal width, petal length and petal width of the three iris species, 50 sample data for each, total 150 data items. It looks something like the below table,

Sepal.Length	Sepal.Width	Petal.Length	Petal.Width	Species
5.1	3.5	1.4	0.2	setosa
4.9	3	1.4	0.2	setosa
4.7	3.2	1.3	0.2	setosa
...	...	...	...	setosa
7	3.2	4.7	1.4	versicolor
6.4	3.2	4.5	1.5	versicolor
6.9	3.1	4.9	1.5	versicolor
...	...	...	...	versicolor
6.3	3.3	6	2.5	virginica
5.8	2.7	5.1	1.9	virginica
7.1	3	5.9	2.1	virginica
...	...	...	...	virginica

The dataset is often used for classification tasks, where the goal is to predict the species of the iris flower based on the four features.

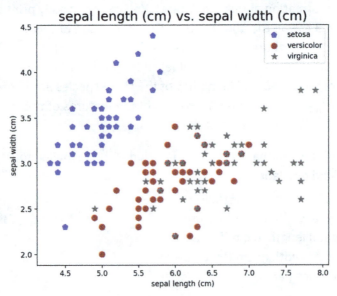

Figure 7-24 IRIS Dataset Sepal Length vs Width

After the IRIS dataset is loaded, it can be visualized as Figure 7-24 and Figure 7-25:

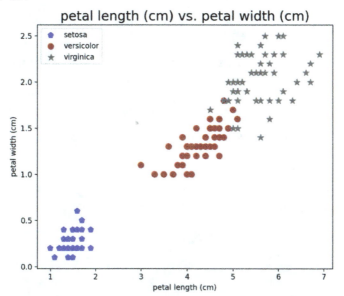

Figure 7-25 IRIS Dataset Petal Length vs Width

7.3.3.2 Pre-processing

After the data is loaded, it should be split into training and testing sets. The datatype must also be converted to `float32` as required by the OpenCV SVM model.

```
11  data = iris.data.astype(np.float32)
12  label = iris.target.astype(np.int32)
13  X_train, X_test, y_train, y_test =
14      model_selection.train_test_split(
                          data, label,
15                        test_size=0.2,
16                        random_state=2)
17  print('X_train: ' + str(X_train.shape))
18  print('y_train: ' + str(y_train.shape))
19  print('X_test:  ' + str(X_test.shape))
20  print('y_test:  ' + str(y_test.shape))
```

Explanations:

251

Line 11	Get the data from `iris.data` attribute and convert it into `float32` datatype.
Line 12	Get the label from `iris.target` attribute, and convert it into `int32`.
Line 13 – 16	Split the data and label into training and testing sets. Specify `test_size=0.2` meaning 80% training set and 20% testing set, and specify `random_state` as an integer to ensure the same splitting results for every execution.
Line 17 - 20	(Optional) print out the size of each data set.

The dataset is split as:

```
X_train:  (120, 4)
y_train:  (120,)
X_test:   (30, 4)
y_test:   (30,)
```

7.3.3.3   Build, Train and Predict the model

Same as previous section 7.3.2, a new SVM model is created, and trained with training set. The IRIS dataset is small, it will not take much time for the training.

After it is trained, the testing set is used to make predictions.

```
21  svm = cv2.ml.SVM_create()
22  svm.setKernel(cv2.ml.SVM_LINEAR)
23  svm.setTermCriteria(
                (cv2.TERM_CRITERIA_MAX_ITER, 100, 1e-6))
24  svm.train(X_train, cv2.ml.ROW_SAMPLE, y_train)
25  predict = svm.predict(X_test)
```

7.3.3.4   Post-processing and Evaluation

Same as in previous sections 7.3.2.3 and 7.3.2.4, the `predict` returned from `svm.predict()` function has the result data in a "vertical" array, it has to be converted to a "horizontal" one using `np.hstack()` function. And then print out the evaluation metrics:

```
26   results = np.uint(predict[1])
27   results = np.hstack(results)
28   print("Accuracy Score:",
                accuracy_score(y_test, results))
29   print("\nConfusion Matrix:\n",
                confusion_matrix(y_test, results))
30   print("\nClassification Report:\n",
                classification_report(y_test, results))
```

The results are shown as below, we get an accuracy of 100%:

```
Accuracy Score: 1.0

Confusion Matrix:
 [[14   0   0]
  [ 0  18   0]
  [ 0   0  13]]

Classification Report:
              precision    recall  f1-score   support
           0       1.00      1.00      1.00        14
           1       1.00      1.00      1.00        18
           2       1.00      1.00      1.00        13
    accuracy                           1.00        45
   macro avg       1.00      1.00      1.00        45
weighted avg       1.00      1.00      1.00        45
```

In conclusion, SVMs have several advantages over other machine learning algorithms. They are computationally efficient, particularly in high-dimensional feature spaces, and can handle large datasets. They are also robust to noisy data and outliers and have a strong theoretical foundation, which guarantees good generalization performance.

However, SVMs also have some limitations. They can be sensitive to the choice of kernel function and its parameters, which can affect the performance of the algorithm. Additionally, SVMs can be difficult to interpret and understand, particularly when using non-linear kernel functions.

7.4 Artificial Neural Network (ANN)

7.4.1 What is an Artificial Neural Network (ANN)?

Artificial Neural Network (ANN) is one of the algorithms for machine learning, which tries to learn things in the same or similar way as human. ANN is designed to mimic the structure and function of the human biological brain, specifically the way that neurons process and transmit information.

Neurons are the basic building blocks of the human brain and nervous system. They are specialized cells that are responsible for processing and transmitting information. The basic structure of a neuron consists of three parts: the *cell body*, *dendrites*, and an *axon*, as shown in Figure 7-26:

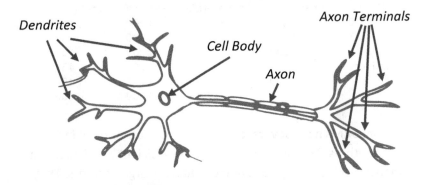

Figure 7-26 Neurons of Human Brain

Image by OpenClipart-Vectors from Pixabay

The transmission of information between neurons is accomplished through electrical and chemical signals. The dendrites receive input signals from other neurons or sensory receptors, the cell body processes the signals, and then the axon transmits output to other neurons or to muscles or glands via the axon terminals. There are billions of neurons in the human brain becoming neural networks to perform the functions.

Artificial Neural Networks (ANNs) are designed to mimic the biological structure and function of the human brain. Just like the human brain,

ANNs consist of interconnected artificial neurons that process and transmit information with simplified mathematical models.

One of the key features of the biological brain is its ability to learn and adapt through experiences. ANNs also have the ability to learn from data and improve their performance over time. This is achieved through the training process, in which the network is presented with a set of input data and corresponding output data, and adjusts its parameters to minimize the difference between its predicted output and the actual output.

The human brain is composed of multiple layers of interconnected neurons, and ANNs also consist of layers of interconnected *artificial neurons*. These layers can be designed to perform specific functions, such as processing visual information or processing sequential data.

Each artificial neuron receives input from other neurons and performs a set of mathematical calculations on the input. The output of the neuron is then transmitted to other neurons in the network.

An artificial neuron is a basic unit of computation in an Artificial Neural Network (ANN). Inspired by the biological neuron, an artificial neuron takes in one or more input values and produces a single output value. The inputs are multiplied by corresponding weights, which determine the importance of each input in the output calculation. The weighted inputs are then summed up, and an activation function is applied to the sum to produce the output value. The activation function determines whether the neuron should "fire" and produce an output signal. Figure 7-27 shows an artificial neuron.

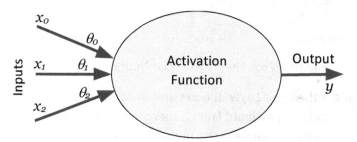

Figure 7-27 An Artificial Neuron

x_0, x_1 and x_2 are inputs of the artificial neuron, θ_0, θ_1 and θ_2 are the weights on the inputs, the inputs are multiplied by corresponding weights, then sum them up and send to the activation function for mathematical computations, and the result becomes the output y. The output of one artificial neuron can be connected to the input of another, forming a network of interconnected neurons. By adjusting the weights and activation functions of the artificial neurons through the training process, an artificial neural network can learn to perform complex tasks such as image recognition, natural language processing, and more.

Common activation functions include linear, sigmoid, relu (rectified linear unit), and tanh (hyperbolic tangent), which will be introduced in 7.4.2.

Many artificial neurons are put together to form an *Artificial Neural Network (ANN)*. Figure 7-28 shows a very simple artificial neural network, each artificial neuron is called a node in the network.

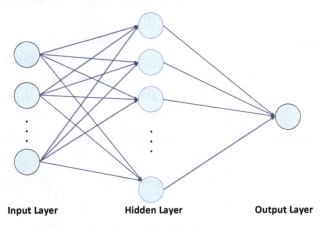

Input Layer　　　　Hidden Layer　　　　Output Layer

Figure 7-28 A Simple Artificial Neural Network

The left side is the *Input Layer*, it corresponds to the input data, there should be n nodes in the input layer if there are n features in the input data. There is a *Hidden Layer* in the middle, which takes the output of the input layer as input data. Then the *Output Layer* is at the right, there is only one node for the output in Figure 7-28, it could have multiple nodes depending on the needs.

An *Artificial Neural Network (ANN)* always has an *Input Layer* and an *Output Layer*, there could be multiple *Hidden Layers* depending on the needs, there could also be no *Hidden Layer* in which case the *Input Layer* directly connects to the *Output Layer*. The *Input Layer* should take the raw input data, so the number of nodes in the *Input Layer* should be the same as the dimension of the input data; the *Output Layer* is the one that makes the final prediction, so the number of nodes in the *Output Layer* should be same as the dimension of output data.

The number of layers and nodes of *Hidden Layers* depends on the needs, it doesn't mean the more the better, normally it is decided based on the evaluation of the accuracy, a trial and error process is often needed to determine how many hidden layers and how many nodes in each hidden layer. More hidden layers require more computation costs. See material #13 in the References section at the end of this book for artificial neural networks.

OpenCV supports the Multi-Layer Perceptron (MLP) of the *Artificial Neural Network*, which means it could have three or more layers in total. In other words, there could be one or more *Hidden Layers* apart from *Input* and *Output Layers*.

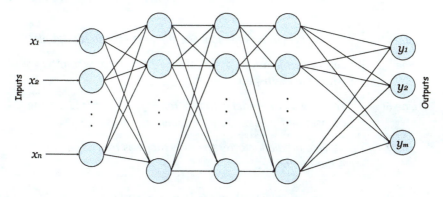

Figure 7-29 Multi-Layer Perceptron

Here are the code snippets to create an ANN model with OpenCV, train it and make predictions:

```
1  ann = cv2.ml.ANN_MLP_create()
2  ann.setLayerSizes(np.array([784, 64, 10]))
```

```
3  ann.setTrainMethod(cv2.ml.ANN_MLP_BACKPROP)
4  ann.setActivationFunction(
                    v2.ml.ANN_MLP_SIGMOID_SYM )
5  ann.setTermCriteria((cv2.TermCriteria_EPS |
                    cv2.TermCriteria_COUNT,
                    100, 0.0001))
6  ann.train(X_train, cv2.ml.ROW_SAMPLE, y_train)
7  result = ann.predict(X_test)
```

Explanations:

Line 1	*Initialize ANN_MLP and return an empty model.*
Line 2	*Set layers of the ANN. The parameter of* `[784,64,10]` *means a three-layer ANN that has 784 nodes in the input layer, 64 in hidden and 10 in output layers.*
Line 3	*Set the training methods. The BACKPROP is the most often used one.* `cv2.ml.ANN_MLP_BACKPROP`: *The back-propagation algorithm.* `cv2.ml.ANN_MLP_RPROP`: *The RPROP algorithm.* `cv2.ml.ANN_MLP_ANNEAL`: *The simulated annealing algorithm.*
Line 4	*Set the activation function. See the next section for details.*
Line 5	*Set the termination criteria, the iteration stops when the criteria are satisfied.*
Line 6	*Train the ANN model with the training set,* `X_train` *is the dataset and* `y_train` *is the label.*
Line 7	*Make a prediction after the ANN model is trained,* `X_test` *is the testing set.*

If you want to create an ANN with more layers, simply pass the parameter in above line 2 to specify the layers and nodes in each layer. For example, `[784,128,64,32,10]` will build an ANN with 784 nodes in the input layer, and three hidden layers with 128, 64 and 32 nodes respectively, then the output layer of 10 nodes.

258

In conclusion, with OpenCV we can create an artificial neural network model by specifying the number of layers and the number of neurons in each layer, and also customize the activation function used by the neurons.

Once we have defined the neural network model, we can train it using a variety of supervised learning techniques, such as backpropagation, finally we also use the trained network to make predictions on new data. OpenCV provides a powerful and flexible toolset for building and training artificial neural networks for a wide range of applications.

7.4.2   Activation Functions

> Source: common/ann_activation_functions.py

An *activation function* is a key component of artificial neural networks (ANNs) and is used to introduce non-linearity into the output of a neuron. In ANNs, activation functions are applied to the weighted sum of inputs to the neuron in order to produce an output.

An activation function must be defined for each node, it is responsible for transforming the input data into the output for the node.

As Figure 7-27, the inputs are multiplied by corresponding weights and sum them up:

$$z = x_0\theta_0 + x_1\theta_1 + x_2\theta_2 + \dots$$

then z is sent to the activation function for calculations, the activation function is represented as:

$$g(z) = g(x_0\theta_0 + x_1\theta_1 + x_2\theta_2 + \dots)$$

There are numerous activation functions that can be divided into the following two categories:

1.   Linear activation functions
2.   Nonlinear activation functions

OpenCV supports the following activation functions:

`cv2.ml.ANN_MLP_IDENTITY`	Identity, or Linear function
`cv2.ml.ANN_MLP_SIGMOID_SYM`	Symmetrical sigmoid function
`cv2.ml.ANN_MLP_GAUSSIAN`	Gaussian function
`cv2.ml.ANN_MLP_RELU`	ReLU, or Rectified Linear Unit, function
`cv2.ml.ANN_MLP_LEAKYRELU`	Leaky ReLU function

What are Derivatives

Derivatives are used extensively in machine learning to train models that can make accurate predictions or decisions. In particular, derivatives are used in the optimization of model parameters through the process of *gradient descent*.

In calculus, the derivative of a function is a measure of how that function changes as its input changes. Geometrically, the derivative corresponds to the slope of the tangent line to the function at a particular point on its graph.

If a function is denoted as

$g(z)$

Then its derivative is denoted as:

$g'(z)$

In this book we do not deep dive into the mathematical details of these topics, although we will introduce both the functions and derivatives of the most widely used active functions of artificial neural networks.

7.4.2.1 Identity (or Linear) Function

The identity function, also called the linear function, is a simple function that returns the same value of input as the output value, which means that it does not modify the input in any way.

The Identity function is defined as:

$g(z) = z$

Its derivative function is defined as:

$$g'(z) = 1$$

As shown in Figure 7-30, the left side is the Identity function, the right side is the derivative of it.

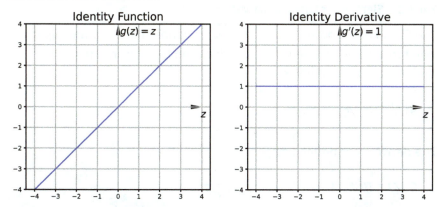

Figure 7-30 Identify or Linear Function

Generated by source code at common/ann_activation_functions.py

One advantage of using the identity function is that it does not introduce non-linearity into the network, which can be useful when the problem being solved does not require complex non-linear transformations. Another advantage is that it preserves the gradient of the output with respect to the input, which can make the training process more stable.

However, in many cases, it is limited in its capacity to learn complex functional mappings and solve complex problems. The reason is that no matter how many layers a neural network has, it behaves just like a single layer because summing up all the layers will give another linear function, which is exactly the same as a single layer.

Another problem of the identity function is its derivative is a constant, it has no relation to the input data z. The training will use its derivative to perform a process called *back-propagation*, the constant value loses the information of the input data, and then not able to provide a better prediction.

In most cases, the non-linear activation functions which are introduced in the following sections are used to learn and solve complex data and provide accurate predictions.

7.4.2.2 Sigmoid or Logistic Activation Function

The Sigmoid, or Logistic, is a non-linear function that maps any input value to a value between 0 and 1, which can be interpreted as a probability. It's defined as:

$$g(z) = \frac{1}{(1 + e^{-z})}$$

The derivative is defined as:

$$g'(z) = g(z)(1 - g(z)) = \frac{e^{-z}}{(1 + e^{-z})^2}$$

As shown in Figure 7-31, the left side is the Sigmoid function, the right is its derivative.

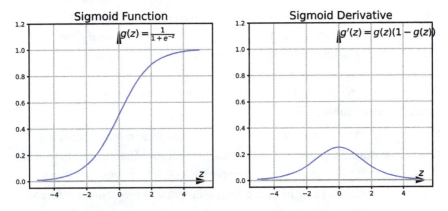

Figure 7-31 Sigmoid Function and Derivative

Generated by source code at common/ann_activation_functions.py

The Sigmoid function gives an "S" shaped curve between 0 and 1. It's one of the most widely used non-linear activation functions. It transforms the input values into the range between 0 and 1. As the input value z increases, the output of the function approaches 1, while as z decreases, the output approaches 0.

In ANNs, the sigmoid function is often used as the activation function in the hidden layers. This is because it introduces non-linearity into the network, allowing it to learn more complex patterns and relationships in the data. The derivative of the sigmoid function can also be easily calculated, which is important for back-propagation and the optimization of the network parameters.

However, the sigmoid function can suffer from the vanishing gradient problem, meaning the gradients of the function become very small as the input values become very large or very small. This can make the training process of deep networks slower and more difficult. Therefore, other activation functions, such as the ReLU function, have become more popular in recent years.

7.4.2.3   Tanh Function

The tanh function, short for hyperbolic tangent function, is also a non-linear function that maps any input value to a value between -1 and 1. Like the sigmoid function, the tanh function also has an S-shaped curve, but its output ranges between -1 and 1 instead of 0 and 1. As z increases, the output of the function approaches 1, while as z decreases, the output approaches -1.

It's defined as:

$$g(z) = \frac{e^z - e^{-z}}{e^z + e^{-z}}$$

The derivative function is defined as:

$$g'(z) = 1 - g(z)^2$$

It is often used as the activation function in the hidden layers of ANNs. It introduces non-linearity into the network, allowing it to learn more complex patterns and relationships in the data. The derivative of the tanh function can also be easily calculated, which is important for backpropagation and the optimization of the network parameters.

As shown in Figure 7-32, the left side is the Tanh function, the right is the derivative of it.

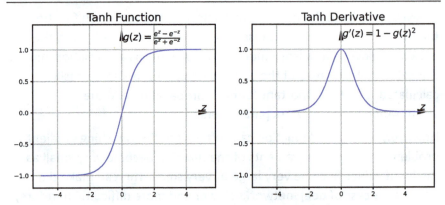

Figure 7-32 Tanh Function and Derivative

Generated by source code at common/ann_activation_functions.py

Compared to the sigmoid, the tanh function has a steeper derivative around the origin, which means it can be more effective in capturing the nuances of data. Sometimes Tanh works better than the sigmoid function when negative output values are needed.

However, like the sigmoid, the tanh function can also suffer from the vanishing gradient problem, where the gradients of the function become very small as the input values become very large or very small.

7.4.2.4   ReLU (Rectified Linear Unit) Function

ReLU, or Rectified Linear Unit, is a partial linear function, it's the same as the identity function when input is positive, otherwise it will output zero. ReLU function is simple and computationally efficient, it's very quick to converge. However, it's not good for negative input data because it always returns 0 when input data is negative.

It is defined as:

$$g\ (z) = max(0,\ z)$$

The derivative function is defined as:

$$g'(z) = 1, \ when\ z > 0$$
$$= 0, when\ z < 0$$

The ReLU function and derivative are shown in Figure 7-33:

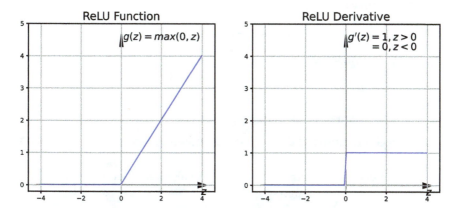

Figure 7-33 ReLU Function and Derivative

Generated by source code at common/ann_activation_functions.py

The advantage of the ReLU function over other activation functions, such as the sigmoid and tanh functions, is that it avoids the vanishing gradient problem, which occurs when the gradients of the activation function become very small for very large or very small input values, making the training process of the neural networks slower and more difficult.

However, it's not appropriate for all types of data, as it can suffer from the "dying ReLU" problem, where some neurons may become permanently inactive due to the large negative input values, resulting in a dead neuron that does not contribute to the output of the network, because it always output 0 when input is negative, and its derivative is also 0 for negative inputs. To address this issue, various modifications to the ReLU function have been proposed, such as the leaky ReLU.

7.4.2.5   Leaky ReLU Function

Leaky ReLU function is a modified version of the ReLU function, which is another popular activation function used in ANNs and other machine learning models. It is a non-linear function that maps any negative input value to a small negative output, and any positive input value to the same input value.

It is defined as:

$$g(z) = max(\varepsilon z, z)$$

The derivative function is defined as:

$$g'(z) = 1, \ when \ z > 0$$
$$= \varepsilon, \ when \ z < 0$$

Normally ε is a small value something like 0.1, or 0.01 and so on.

Leaky ReLU function and derivative are shown in Figure 7-34.

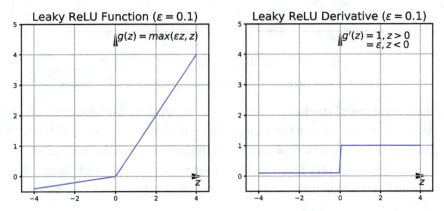

Figure 7-34 Leaky ReLU Function and Derivative

Generated by source code at common/ann_activation_functions.py

The Leaky ReLU function is similar to the ReLU function, but it addresses the "dying ReLU" problem. By introducing a small negative slope for negative input values, the Leaky ReLU function can prevent neurons from dying, and improve the performance of the network.

It has been shown to outperform the ReLU function in some cases, particularly in neural networks. However, the choice of activation function depends on the specific task and data at hand, and it is often a matter of trial and error to determine the optimal activation function for a particular problem.

7.4.2.6   Gaussian Function

Gaussian functions are widely used in many areas, as we have introduced in Gaussian blur in section 5.8.2 and the kernel function of support vector machine in section 7.3.1.

Gaussian function is defined as:

$$g\,(z) = exp\,(-z^2\,)$$

The derivative function is defined as:

$$g'(z) = -2z\,exp(-z^2\,)$$

It is also a non-linear function, as shown in Figure 7-35,

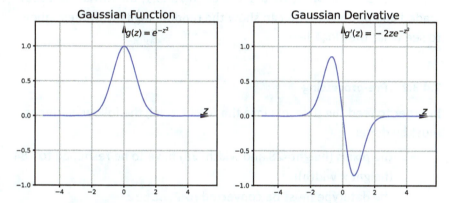

Figure 7-35 Gaussian Function and Derivative

Generated by source code at common/ann_activation_functions.py

This is a one-dimensional Gaussian function, Figure 7-21 in section 7.3.1 shows a two-dimensional Gaussian function.

OpenCV supports Gaussian function as an activation function for ANNs, it is also widely used in many fields, including physics, chemistry, engineering, and finance, because it accurately models many natural phenomena and processes that exhibit a bell-shaped distribution.

In conclusion, activation functions are an essential component of artificial neural networks (ANNs). The choice of activation function should be made with consideration for the specific problem being solved and the architecture of the network.

7.4.3 Recognize Handwritten Digits with ANN

> Source: ANNHandWrittenDigits.py

We have applied several machine learning models to the handwritten digits from MNIST (Modified National Institute of Standards and Technology) dataset in previous sections, like K-Means, KNN and SVM. Now we apply the ANN to the same dataset and see how it works.

7.4.3.1 Load the MNIST dataset

Exactly the same as what we did in section 7.2.3.1, the MNIST dataset is loaded and optionally you can show the random digits with their labels to see what they look like.

7.4.3.2 Pre-processing

In order to feed the datasets into the ANN model, the following things must be done:

- the pixels (height=28 and width=28) have to be reshaped to 784 (height × width)
- the datatype must be converted to `float32`
- the input data values must be converted between 0 to 1
- the label must be transformed into categorical data using One-hot Encoding

What is One-hot Encoding

One-hot encoding is a technique used to represent categorical data in a numerical format. Each category is converted into a binary vector with a length equal to the total number of categories. The vector contains 0s for all categories except for the one corresponding to the category being encoded, which is assigned a value of 1.

This technique is useful for machine learning algorithms that expect input data to be in a numerical format, as it allows the algorithm to process categorical data as numerical features.

See material #14 in the References section at the end of this book for one-hot encoding.

In this example, the label of the training set in `y_train` is an array of numbers from 0 to 9, which looks like below,

```
[0, 1, 2, 3, 4, 5, 6, 7, 8, 9]
```

One-hot encoding is basically used for categorical data that have no relationship to each other, the above 1, 2, 3, and so on do not relate to each other, they just indicate different clusters, and don't mean 3 is in a better position than 1. Machine learning algorithms treat the numbers as an attribute of significance, meaning a higher number is better or more important than a lower number.

As the comparison, consider an example of the quantitative data, say the number of bedrooms of a house, there are 0, 1, 2 and 3 bedrooms and so on. A house with 3 bedrooms is significantly better than that with 1 bedroom, so in this case 3 has more value than 1 when doing the calculation in the model.

One-hot encoding is to convert the categorical data of 0 to 9 to the vectors that have only 0 and 1, for example 2 becomes [0 0 1 0 0 0 0 0 0 0]. The function `keras.utils.to_categorical()` will do the job, it converts 0 to 9 to the below vectors, and also change the datatype to float:

```
0 => [1. 0. 0. 0. 0. 0. 0. 0. 0. 0.]
1 => [0. 1. 0. 0. 0. 0. 0. 0. 0. 0.]
2 => [0. 0. 1. 0. 0. 0. 0. 0. 0. 0.]
3 => [0. 0. 0. 1. 0. 0. 0. 0. 0. 0.]
4 => [0. 0. 0. 0. 1. 0. 0. 0. 0. 0.]
5 => [0. 0. 0. 0. 0. 1. 0. 0. 0. 0.]
6 => [0. 0. 0. 0. 0. 0. 1. 0. 0. 0.]
7 => [0. 0. 0. 0. 0. 0. 0. 1. 0. 0.]
8 => [0. 0. 0. 0. 0. 0. 0. 0. 1. 0.]
9 => [0. 0. 0. 0. 0. 0. 0. 0. 0. 1.]
```

Below are the code snippets for the pro-processing for the ANN in this example:

```
1    from keras import utils
2    w, h = X_test[0,:,:].shape
3    X_train = X_train.reshape(X_train.shape[0],
                                w * h).astype(np.float32)
4    X_test  = X_test.reshape(  X_test.shape[0],
                                w * h).astype(np.float32)
5    X_train = X_train / 255
6    X_test  = X_test / 255
7    y_train_onehot = to_categorical(y_train)
8    print('X_train:' + str(X_train.shape))
9    print('y_train:' + str(y_train.shape))
10   print('X_test:' + str(X_test.shape))
11   print('y_test:' + str(y_test.shape))
12   print('y_train_onehot:'+str(y_train_onehot.shape))
```

Explanations:

Line 1	*Import* `keras.utils` *package, it's used for converting the label into one-hot categorical data.*
Line 2	*Get the width and height of each image.*
Line 3 - 4	*Reshape the image pixels into a flat array of width × height = 28 × 28 = 784. And convert the datatype to float32.*
Line 5 - 6	*Divide the data by 255 to convert the data between 0 and 1.*
Line 7	*Transform the label into one-hot categorical data.*
Line 8 - 12	*(Optional) print out the size of each dataset.*

Then print out the pre-processed data as following:

```
X_train: (60000, 784)
y_train: (60000,)
X_test:  (10000, 784)
y_test:  (10000,)
y_train_onehot:  (60000, 10)
```

7.4.3.3   Build and Train the ANN model

Figure 7-36 is the ANN topology we are going to build. Since we have already made each digit image data into 784 elements in the pre-processing step, the *Input Layer* of the ANN model will have 784 nodes.

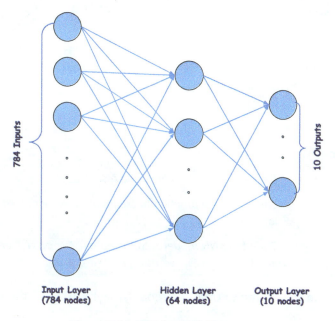

Figure 7-36 ANN for MNIST Dataset

And we have converted the label to ten categorical elements with one-hot encoding, those labels are corresponding to the output of the ANN model, therefore there are 10 nodes in the *Output Layer*.

The *Hidden Layer* has 64 nodes for now, we can change it later to see how the accuracy is affected by the number of nodes in this layer.

The execution time is affected by the number of nodes in the *Hidden Layer*, the more nodes we have, the longer it takes to complete the training process.

Here are the code snippets to create and train an ANN model:

```
13   def create_ANN(layers):
14       ann=cv2.ml.ANN_MLP_create()
15       ann.setLayerSizes(np.array(layers))
```

```
16      ann.setTrainMethod(cv2.ml.ANN_MLP_BACKPROP)
17      ann.setActivationFunction(
                    cv2.ml.ANN_MLP_SIGMOID_SYM)
18      ann.setTermCriteria((cv2.TermCriteria_EPS|
                        cv2.TermCriteria_COUNT,
                    100, 0.0001))
19      return ann
20
21   ann = create_ANN([784,64,10])
22   ann.train(X_train,
                cv2.ml.ROW_SAMPLE,
                y_train_onehot)
```

Explanations:

Line 13 - 19	Define a function to build the ANN model.
Line 21	Call the above function to create an ANN model with the layers of [784,64,10].
Line 22	Train the ANN model with the data (X_train) and label (y_train_onehot).

It could take some time to train the model, maybe 10 to 15 minutes or so.

7.4.3.4   Save and Load the Trained ANN Model

We can save the model into an XML file after the model is trained, and load it later to save the time of training.

```
23   def save_model(model, filename):
24        model.save(filename)
25   def load_model(filename):
26        ann=cv2.ml.ANN_MLP_load(filename)
27        return ann
28   save_model( ann, '../res/mnist_ann_784_64_10.xml')
29   ann = load_model('../res/mnist_ann_784_64_10.xml')
```

If you load a trained model, then no need to build and train it again, but still need to load dataset and pre-processing.

7.4.3.5   Prediction

After the ANN model is trained, or loaded from an XML file, predictions can be made with the testing set. We don't pre-process the testing label `y_test` because we don't need it for prediction, only testing data is needed here for prediction, `X_test` is pre-processed in line 4 and 6 in the above codes.

```
30   result = ann.predict(X_test)
31   predict = result[1]
```

The `ann.predict()` function returns a tuple that has a single value and an array. If the prediction is for a single data the result is in the first item of the tuple `result[0]`; if the prediction is for a dataset with multiple data items then the result is in the second item of the tuple `result[1]`. In our case we pass the testing set of `X_test` which has 10,000 data items, then we should use the second item in `result[1]`.

7.4.3.6   Post-processing

The output of the ANN model is in the categorical data format, which is the same as the label data we pre-processed.

An output data item looks something like the below:

```
[0.10 0.08 0.15 0.12 0.11 0.11 0.10 0.97 0.10 0.09]
```

The data will be treated as 1 if it's near 1, and 0 if near 0. So, the above data will be converted to:

```
[0 0 0 0 0 0 0 1 0 0]
```

As a reversal of the one-hot encoding, the above item is converted back to `[7]`.

The numpy array has a function `argmax()` that can do the reversal of one-hot, it returns the indices of the maximum values in the array.

```
32   predict = predict.argmax(axis=1)
33   X_test = X_test * 255
34   X_test   = np.uint(X_test)
35   X_test = X_test.reshape(X_test.shape[0], w, h)
```

Explanations:

Line 32	*Convert the categorical data into the number from 0 to 9.*
Line 33 - 34	*In pre-processing* X_test *is converted to* `float32` *and then divided by 255 to make it between 0 and 1. Now reverse the operation, and then convert it back to* `uint`.
Line 35	*In pre-processing* X_test *is reshaped to the array of 784, now reshape it back to 28 × 28.*

7.4.3.7   Evaluation

Same as what we did for SVM and KNN in previous sections, the same metrics are applied to the prediction results against the original label data:

```
36   print("Accuracy Score:",
                  accuracy_score(y_test, predict))
37   print("\nConfusion Matrix:\n",
                  confusion_matrix(y_test, predict))
38   print("\nClassification Report:\n",
                  classification_report(y_test, predict))
```

We get an accuracy of 93.87% for this ANN model:

```
Accuracy Score: 0.9387
Confusion Matrix:
 [[965    0    1    2    1    2    6    1    2    0]
 [   1 1119    5    2    0    1    3    0    4    0]
 [  22    1  948   12   10    4   12    9   14    0]
 [  12    2   14  936    0   17    5   10    9    5]
 [   4    1    2    0  940    0   12    6    3   14]
 [  20    4    2   18    7  814    7    3   12    5]
 [  13    4    4    1    4   11  918    1    2    0]
 [   4   14   18    4   10    3    1  961    1   12]
 [  22    4    7   13   12   21    6    8  873    8]
 [  16    6    1    9   34    6    1   16    7  913]]

Classification Report:
               precision    recall  f1-score   support

           0       0.89      0.98      0.94       980
           1       0.97      0.99      0.98      1135
           2       0.95      0.92      0.93      1032
```

3	0.94	0.93	0.93	1010
4	0.92	0.96	0.94	982
5	0.93	0.91	0.92	892
6	0.95	0.96	0.95	958
7	0.95	0.93	0.94	1028
8	0.94	0.90	0.92	974
9	0.95	0.90	0.93	1009
accuracy			0.94	10000
macro avg	0.94	0.94	0.94	10000
weighted avg	0.94	0.94	0.94	10000

Optionally, we can display the image of digits with predicted values, as well as the erroneously predicted digits, which are the same as what we have done in previous sections.

You can execute the source codes and play with the ANN model to see different nodes in *Hidden Layer* will produce different accuracy. For example, try the model with [784,10] which does not have a *Hidden Layer*, and also try [784,16,10] and [784,32,10] and so on to see the differences. Please note that more nodes in *Hidden Layer* will require more time for training, for example the model with [784, 256,10] could take an hour or so, of course it depends on the hardware resources and the power of the computer.

Here are the results of executing *ANNHandWrittenDigits.py* in my environments for different models:

ANN Model	Approx. Execution Time	Accuracy
[784, 10]	2 minutes	0.8924
[784, 16, 10]	3 minutes	0.8705
[784, 32, 10]	5 minutes	0.8503
[784, 64, 10]	13 minutes	0.9376
[784, 128, 10]	11 minutes	0.9195
[784, 256, 10]	56 minutes	0.9023

From the above table, more nodes in the *Hidden Layer* do not mean higher accuracy, but for sure require more computation resources and more time.

The pre-trained model of `[784,64,10]` is saved in the Github repository under *res* folder, the file name is *mnist_ann_784_64_10.xml*. It can be loaded by the following code:

```
39  ann = load_model('../res/mnist_ann_784_64_10.xml')
```

In conclusion, compared with traditional machine learning algorithms like K-means, KNN and SVM, ANNs have a number of advantages, including the ability to learn non-linear relationships between input and output variables, and the ability to handle large and complex datasets. ANNs also allow parallel processing, meaning many pieces of information can be processed at the same time, making them highly efficient for tasks such as image processing and object detection.

ANNs have a wide range of applications in various fields, including image recognition such as object detection, facial recognition, and autonomous driving. As well as many other fields like financial, energy, marketing forecasts, and so on.

However, ANNs are computationally intensive that need significant computational resources, and require significant amounts of data to train which can be costly and time-consuming to collect.

Due to their complex nature, ANNs are lack of transparency and often considered as a "black box" because it can be difficult to understand how they arrive at their decisions. This can make it challenging to explain their results, which can limit their usefulness in certain fields, such as healthcare, where transparency and interpretability are crucial.

7.5 Convolutional Neural Network (CNN)

7.5.1 What is a Convolutional Neural Network

A Convolutional Neural Network (CNN) is a type of deep learning neural network that is commonly used for analyzing images and pictures. CNN is designed to automatically detect patterns and features in images, making them well-suited for tasks such as image recognition, object detection such as faces and eyes, and image segmentation such as separating the foregrounds from the backgrounds.

In the previous section of an artificial neural network (ANN), the handwritten digits dataset has images of 28 × 28 pixels, which means there are 784 pixels for each image, in order to feed the data into an ANN, the input layer has 784 nodes to take the input data.

Now consider a high-resolution 4K color picture that has 3840 × 2160 pixels, meaning 8 million pixels, and each pixel has three color channels, it's not realistic to build a neural network to correspond so many input data for each picture, let alone tens of thousands of pictures are needed to process.

When human look at a picture we do not scan the pixels one by one from top-left towards bottom-right, instead we look at the features or objects in the picture. For example, in a picture of a dog, we look at things like eyes, nose, mouth, ears, head, body and tails, then we know it's a dog. And in most cases, we ignore the background or colors to identify the dog. CNNs do it in a similar way to find "features" from the images, the features are things like eyes, nose, mouth etc. Then send these features to a neural network to learn.

The basic building block of a CNN is the convolutional layer, which performs a mathematical operation called *convolution* on the input image. This operation involves sliding a small filter, also called a *kernel* or a *feature detector*, across the image and computing the dot product between the filter weights and the corresponding pixel values in the image. The output of this operation is a *feature map* that highlights the areas of the image that match the filter's pattern.

CNN typically also includes other types of layers known as pooling layers, and fully connected layers. Pooling layers down-sample the feature maps by reducing their size, and fully connected layers connect the output to an ANN, allowing the CNN to learn complex relationships between features.

See materials #15 and #16 in References at the end of this book for some detailed descriptions of CNN.

7.5.2   Convolution Layer

> Source: `ConvolutionalNeuralNetwork.py`

Convolution is a mathematical operation that is commonly used in signal and image processing. In CNNs, convolution is used in the convolutional layers to extract features from input images.

In mathematics convolution is an operation on two functions, f and g, to produce a third function $(f * g)$, that represents how the shape of one is modified by the other. It's defined as:

$$(f * g)(t) = \int_{-\infty}^{\infty} f(\tau)\, g\,(t - \tau)\, d\tau$$

We are not going to deep-dive into the mathematical details here, the basic idea is to consider one function as the original image, and the other function as a feature, the convolution operation is to identify or extract the features from the original image.

For example, there is a 1D array:

$$f = [\,1, 2, 1\,]$$

And there is another 1D array:

$$g = [\,3, 0, 2, 4, 2, 1\,]$$

The convolution of $f * g$ is defined as the integral of one array sweeping over the second and multiplied at each position of overlapping. Say, we want to detect a pattern of $[2,4,2]$ from g, then choose a feature $f = [1,2,1]$, and do a convolution operation.

The convolution is to use f to sweep over g from left to right, and perform the dot product on the covered items, the dot product means the sum of the products of the corresponding items under the covered items. So the first item of the result is calculated as:

$$1 \times 3 + 2 \times 0 + 1 \times 2 = 5$$

$f = $

1	2	1

The result:

$g = $

3	0	2	4	2	1

$\Rightarrow$

5			

Then f is shifted towards right by one item and calculate the sum of products for the second item:

$1 \times 0 + 2 \times 2 + 1 \times 4 = 8$

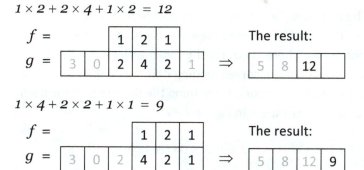

And then f is shifted again towards right one item by one item, and calculate the rest items,

$1 \times 2 + 2 \times 4 + 1 \times 2 = 12$

$1 \times 4 + 2 \times 2 + 1 \times 1 = 9$

From the result of the convolution, the third item is the largest one, meaning the pattern of $[2, 4, 2]$ is found at the third item of g. Considering g is a very long array, which might represent a series of signals, we can use convolution to identify a specific pattern from it.

Python `numpy.convolve()` function can do the convolution for 1D array,

```
1   def convolution1d():
2       f = np.array([1, 2, 1])
3       g = np.array([3, 0, 2, 4, 2, 1])
4       conv = np.convolve(f, g, mode = 'valid')
5       print("f =", f)
6       print("g =", g)
7       print("f*g =", conv)
```

The result is:

```
f = [1 2 1]
g = [3 0 2 4 2 1]
f*g = [5 8 12 9]
```

See material #17 in References for more details on convolution, and also Wikipedia at *https://en.wikipedia.org/wiki/Convolution*.

The above example is the convolution on a 1-dimensional array which is mostly used for signal processing. The images are 2-dimensional arrays, let's look at how the convolution works in this case.

Say there is an image g, we want to identify a pattern of Π from it. Create a feature f that represents the shape Π, and perform the convolution operation of $f * g$. The first item of the convolution result is calculated as the dot product for the covered items.

Note, it could be confusing by saying dot product here, the feature f appears as 2D matrix, and its covered area of g is also a matrix, however the dot product here is not for the two matrices, it is simply the sum of the products of the corresponding items, as if the two matrices are flattened into vectors, then doing the dot product for both vectors. The calculation is shown in Figure 7-37:

$$1 \times 1 + 1 \times 3 + 1 \times 1 + 1 \times 1 + 0 \times 1 + 1 \times 1 + 1 \times 2 + 0 \times 1 + 1 \times 9 \ = 18$$

$g =$

1	3	1	0	2	1	0
1	1	1	2	1	2	1
2	1	9	9	8	2	0
0	2	9	1	9	0	1
1	0	9	0	8	2	1
3	1	1	2	0	2	2
1	3	1	3	3	2	0

$f =$

1	1	1
1	0	1
1	0	1

$f * g =$

18				

Image   *Feature*   *Convolution*

Figure 7-37 Convolution on Images

Then the feature f is shifted towards right by one item, and the second item is calculated as:

$$1 \times 3 + 1 \times 1 + 1 \times 0 + 1 \times 1 + 0 \times 1 + 1 \times 2 + 1 \times 1 + 0 \times 9 + 1 \times 9 \ = 17$$

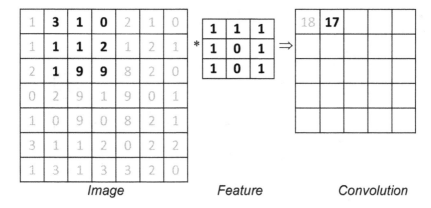

Image		Feature		Convolution

Figure 7-38 Convolution on Images, Continue

The feature *f* is continuously shifting towards right, and then towards down, and calculates the items one by one. Finally, it reaches the bottom-right corner of the original image, as shown in Figure 7-39:

$$1×8 + 1×2 + 1×1 + 1×0 + 0×2 + 1×2 + 1×3 + 0×2 + 1×0 = 16$$

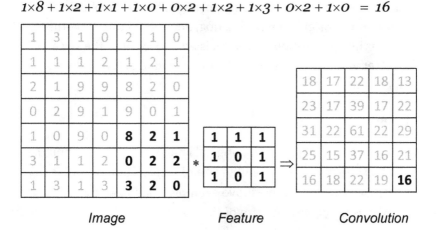

Image   Feature   Convolution

Figure 7-39 Convolution on Images

The purpose of convolution is to identify a specific object from the image. The feature, or kernel, in this example is the shape of Π, it's sweeping over the whole image to identify the shape. As Figure 7-40 the Π shape appears in the middle of the original image, and the value of 61 in the convolution result also appears in the middle, the value is significantly larger than all other values, meaning the shape is identified in the middle of the image.

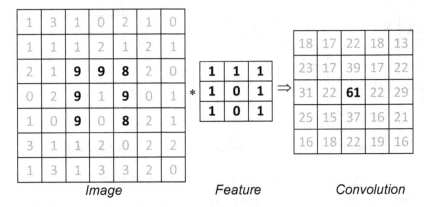

| | | Image | | | | | | | | Feature | | | | | Convolution | | |

Image *   Feature   ⇒   Convolution

Figure 7-40 Convolution to Identify an Object on Images

If the shape appears in a different part of the original image, the largest value will appear in the corresponding position of the convolution result. Consider the original image is a dog, and the feature or kernel is its nose, then the convolution operation is able to identify the nose. It doesn't matter where the nose is in the original image, it will always identify its location.

Padding and Stride

In the above example, suppose the original image size is $i_h \times i_w$, and the feature/kernel size is $k_h \times k_w$, then the size of convolution output is $(i_h - k_h + 1) \times (i_w - k_w + 1)$. In the above example, the image size is 7×7, the kernel size is 3×3, and the size of the output is:

$$(7 - 3 + 1) \times (7 - 3 + 1) = 5 \times 5$$

Padding and stride are techniques of convolution to control the size of the outputs. The convolution might lose some information if the features appear at the boundary or corners of the image, although it depends on the kernel size, a larger kernel might lose more information.

Padding is used to resolve this kind of problem by adding some rows to the top and bottom of the image, and adding some columns to the left and right as well. In general, add p_h rows to the image, half on the top and half on bottom; and add p_w columns half on left and half on right, all padding rows and columns have value of 0. As shown in Figure 7-41:

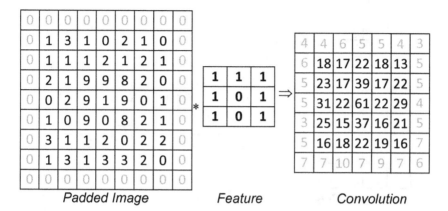

Padded Image   Feature   Convolution

Figure 7-41 Padding for Convolution

Then the convolution is performed on the padded matrix, and the size of the output will be:

$$(i_h + p_h - k_h + 1) \times (i_w + p_w - k_w + 1)$$

In most cases, choose $p_h = k_h - 1$ and $p_w = k_w - 1$, and the kernel size is an odd number, like 3, 5, 7, 9 and so on. Then the same number of paddings will be added to the top and bottom, and same for left and right. In the above example, kernel size is 3×3, the padding size is 2×2 meaning one on top, one on bottom, one on left and one on right.

As a result, the convolution output is in the size of 7×7, which is the same as the original image size.

Stride is another technique of convolution. When the feature/kernel slides over the input image in the above example, it starts from the upper-left corner and moves to the right by one element at a time by default, and after it reaches the very right, it moves down by one element by default. The stride is the number of elements the feature/kernel traverses on each move, in this case the stride is 1 by default.

Sometimes the feature/kernel will traverse more than one element, for example, two or three elements on each move, then the stride is 2 or 3. Figure 7-42 shows the convolution with stride=2.

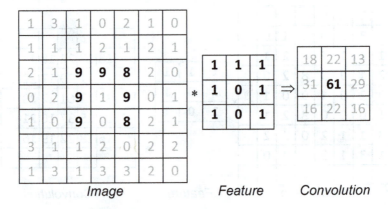

Image   Feature   Convolution

Figure 7-42 Convolution with Stride=2

In general, if the stride is s_w in the horizontal direction, and s_h in the vertical direction, then the convolution output size is:

$$(i_h + p_h - k_h + s_h) / s_h \times (i_w + p_w - k_w + s_w) / s_w$$

In most cases, the padding is selected as $p_h = k_h - 1$ and $p_w = k_w - 1$, then the output size is:

$$(i_h + s_h - 1) / s_h \times (i_w + s_w - 1) / s_w$$

The purpose of stride is to reduce the size of the original image for computational efficiency while keeping the features of the original image. In Figure 7-42 the Π shape can also be captured in the convolution result, the value of *61* is still in the middle of the result, which is significantly larger than other values. Most often it is used when the feature/kernel is large because it captures a large area of the original image.

Python Implementation of the Convolution

In Python, the convolution is implemented by below code snippets:

```
1    import numpy as np
```

```
2   def convolution2d(image, kernel,
3                           stride=[1,1], padding=[0,0]):
4       p_h, p_w = padding
5       s_h, s_w = stride
6       image = np.pad(image,
7                           [(p_h, p_h), (p_w, p_w)],
8                           mode='constant',
9                           constant_values=0)
10      k_h, k_w = kernel.shape
11      i_h, i_w = image.shape
12      output_h = (i_h - k_h) // s_h + 1
13      output_w = (i_w - k_w) // s_w + 1
14      output = np.zeros((output_h, output_w))
15      for y in range(0, output_h):
16        for x in range(0, output_w):
17          c = image[y*s_h : y*s_h+k_h,
18                    x*s_w : x*s_w+k_w]
19          c = np.multiply(c, kernel)
20          output[y][x] = np.sum(c)
21      return output
```

The above example of no padding can be calculated:

```
22  image = np.array([[1, 3, 1, 0, 2, 1 ,0],
23                    [1, 1, 1, 2, 1, 2 ,1],
24                    [2, 1, 9, 9, 8, 2 ,0],
25                    [0, 2, 9, 1, 9, 0 ,1],
26                    [1, 0, 9, 0, 8, 2 ,1],
27                    [3, 1, 1, 2, 0, 2 ,2],
28                    [1, 3, 1, 3, 3, 2 ,0]])
29  kernel = np.array([[1, 1, 1],
30                     [1, 0, 1],
31                     [1, 0, 1]])
32  conv2d = convolution2d(image, kernel)
33  print(conv2d)
```

The convolution results are:

```
[[18. 17. 22. 18. 13.]
 [23. 17. 39. 17. 22.]
 [31. 22. 61. 22. 29.]
 [25. 15. 37. 16. 21.]
 [16. 18. 22. 19. 16.]]
```

The above example of padding=2 can be calculated:

285

```
34    conv2d = convolution2d(image, kernel,
35                            padding=[1,1])
36    print(conv2d)
```

The results are:

```
[[ 4.   4.   6.   5.   5.   4.   3.]
 [ 6.  18.  17.  22.  18.  13.   5.]
 [ 5.  23.  17.  39.  17.  22.   5.]
 [ 5.  31.  22.  61.  22.  29.   4.]
 [ 3.  25.  15.  37.  16.  21.   5.]
 [ 5.  16.  18.  22.  19.  16.   7.]
 [ 7.   7.  10.   7.   9.   7.   6.]]
```

The above example of stride=2 and no padding can be calculated:

```
37    conv2d = convolution2d(image, kernel,
38                            stride=[2,2] )
39    print(conv2d)
```

The results are:

```
[[18. 22. 13.]
 [31. 61. 29.]
 [16. 22. 16.]]
```

Convolution for a Picture

Then how the convolution works on a picture? Consider a picture of a dog, when human look at the picture we look at the features or objects in the picture instead of pixel by pixel, like eyes, nose, mouth, ears, head, body and tails, then based on the experiences we know it's a dog.

First, we want to identify, for example, the eyes of the dog. Create a feature or kernel matrix for the eye, the convolution operation is performed by sweeping the feature over the whole image, in the convolution results there will be two eyes identified in the corresponding location. If the two eyes of the dog appear at the left part of the image, there will also be the two largest values at the left part of the convolution results.

The convolution results are called *feature maps* in the terminology of convolutional neural network (CNN), because they contain the features identified from the image.

286

Then we will detect other features from the image in the same way, like nose, mouth, ears, head, body, tails and so on. As the results, there are multiple *feature maps* generated in this convolution layer.

A color picture has three color channels for blue, green and red. The convolution is performed on each color channel, and then the results are summed up by channels, and become the output of the convolution.

Alternatively, the color picture can be converted to a grayscale one in the pre-processing step, as described in earlier sections. Then do the convolution on the grayscale image.

In conclusion, the convolution layer will output n channels of feature maps in 2D matrices. Each feature map might have the same size as the original image or might reduce the size to some extent depending on the stride as introduced earlier. The important thing is that the convolution layer is not to reduce the size but identify the features.

The features are part of the learning process of the convolutional neural network (CNN), meaning the model will learn by itself during the training, in other words, we don't have to specify the contents of the features, like eyes, nose, ears etc., they will be learned by the CNN model.

7.5.3   Pooling Layer

The purpose of the pooling layer is to down-sample, or reduce the size while keeping the identified features. It is normally applied after the convolution layer. There are different types of pooling methods, the most widely used are *max pooling* and *average pooling*.

Similar to the convolution operation, pooling also uses a kernel matrix to sweep over the feature maps, instead of doing a dot product, the pooling takes the maximum value of the covered area in the feature maps, which is the *max pooling*. In the case of *average pooling*, take the average value of the covered area.

As Figure 7-43, this is a 3 × 3 kernel for max pooling, take the maximum value from the 3 × 3 area covered by the kernel in the upper-left, which is 23, this is the first value in the max pooling result.

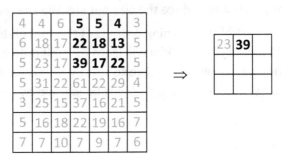

4	4	6	5	5	4	3
6	18	17	22	18	13	5
5	23	17	39	17	22	5
5	31	22	61	22	29	4
3	25	15	37	16	21	5
5	16	18	22	19	16	7
7	7	10	7	9	7	6

23		

Figure 7-43 Max Pooling

In the case of *average pooling*, take the average value of the area covered by the kernel as the first value of the result, which is 11.

Then slide the kernel to the next position, and find the maximum, or average of the covered area. Different from convolution, it will not overlap the already covered elements.

4	4	6	5	5	4	3
6	18	17	22	18	13	5
5	23	17	39	17	22	5
5	31	22	61	22	29	4
3	25	15	37	16	21	5
5	16	18	22	19	16	7
7	7	10	7	9	7	6

23	39	

Figure 7-44 Max Pooling, Continue

Finally, the kernel will traverse the entire matrix of the feature map and get the result in Figure 7-45.

The result of the pooling layer significantly reduces the size of the input while keeping the features. In Figure 7-45 of the max pooling result, the value in the middle is 61, which is the same as that identified by the convolution layer. Say this is identified as the nose of the dog, it is kept in the max pooling result.

Same as convolution, the *Padding* and *Stride* still apply to the pooling layer in the same way.

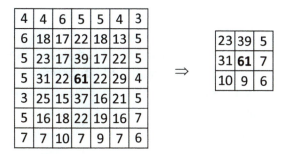

Figure 7-45 Max Pooling Result

Here is the python implementation of max pooling:

```
41   import numpy as np
42   def maxpooling2d(image, kernel=[3,3],
43                    stride=[0,0], padding=[0,0]):
44     p_h, p_w = padding
45     s_h, s_w = stride
46     k_h, k_w = kernel
47     image = np.pad(image,
48                    [(p_h, p_h), (p_w, p_w)],
49                    mode='constant',
50                    constant_values=0)
51     i_h, i_w = image.shape
52     output_h = -(-i_h // (k_h + s_h))
53     output_w = -(-i_w // (k_w + s_w))
54     output = np.zeros((output_h, output_w))
55     for y in range(0, output_h):
56       for x in range(0, output_w):
57         y_, x_ = y*(s_h+k_h), x*(s_w+k_w)
58         c = image[y_: y_+k_h, x_ : x_+k_w]
59         output[y][x] = np.amax(c)
60     return output
```

Then run `maxpooling2d()` after `convolution2d()`,

```
61   conv2d = convolution2d(image, kernel,
62                          padding=[1,1])
63   maxp2d = maxpooling2d(conv2d, kernel=[3,3])
64   print(maxp2d)
```

The max pooling result is:

```
[[23. 39.  5.]
```

```
[31.  61.   7.]
[10.   9.   6.]]
```

In conclusion, the purpose of this layer is to reduce the size of data, or down-sampling. It takes the n channels of feature maps from the convolution layer, and performs pooling operations on every channel, then outputs n channels of pooling results, each as 2D matrix.

The above codes are available at *ConvolutionalNeuralNetwork.py* in the Github repository.

7.5.4 Fully Connected Layer

The fully connected layer is basically an artificial neural network (ANN) introduced in section 7.4.

The output of the pooling layer consists of n channels of 2D matrices, they are flattened into a 1D array and then connected to the input of a fully connected layer in Figure 7-46:

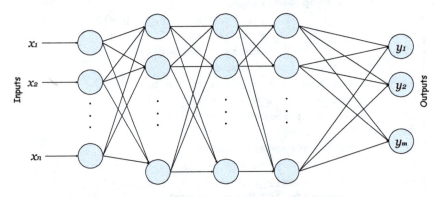

Figure 7-46 Fully Connected Layer of CNN

Although there are several hidden layers shown in Figure 7-46, it depends on the needs, it could be only one hidden layer, or even no hidden layers. Some adjustments and fine-tunes are normally needed at this layer for the best results.

7.5.5   CNN Architecture

A CNN is made of the convolution layers, the pooling layers and a fully connected layer. Now put them together, the architecture of the CNN is shown as Figure 7-47.

Picture

The original pictures are the input of the CNN model. A number of features are applied to the picture in the first convolution layer, it generates n_1 feature maps. And then goes to the pooling layer, max pooling is performed on the feature maps and generates n_1 channels of pooling output.

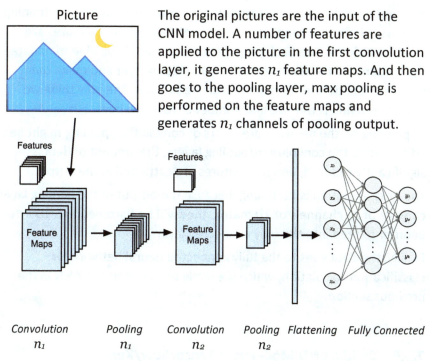

| Convolution | Pooling | Convolution | Pooling | Flattening | Fully Connected |
| n_1 | n_1 | n_2 | n_2 | | |

Figure 7-47 CNN Architecture

There are two layers of convolution/pooling in the above architecture, depending on the needs it could be one or multiple layers of convolution/pooling.

Consider the first convolution/pooling layer to identify some features in the first level like edges, eyes, nose, mouth, ears, paws etc. The output of this layer becomes the input of the second convolution/pooling layer.

In the second convolution layer, again, a number of features are applied, and this layer generates n_2 channels of feature maps, the pooling operations will be performed on these feature maps.

Consider the second convolution/pooling layer to identify the next level of features like the head, body and legs of the dog, this is a higher level of features because the head includes the eyes, nose, mouth, ears, and the legs include paws, and so on.

In CNN models, we do not need to provide the contents of the features, the model will learn by itself from the input pictures during the training process, where thousands or even tens of thousands of pictures are used for training. The back-propagation process will be able to update the contents of the features in the convolution layer and make them best fit to the dataset during the training process. The only thing we need to provide is the size and number of features in each layer.

Depending on the needs, more layers of convolution/pooling might be added. After the convolution/pooling layers, the amount of data is significantly reduced, and the features are extracted in the output.

The next operation is flattening, because the output of the pooling layer consists of n_2 channels of 2D matrix, they will be flattened to a 1D array in order to feed into the fully connected layer.

Finally, the data goes to the fully connected neural network for classification calculation, which is exactly the same as the ANN in the previous section.

7.5.6   Build a CNN Model with Tensorflow/Keras

```
Source:  CNNonCIFAR10.py
```

`tensorflow` and `keras` are libraries for deep learning, they will be used to build the CNN model in this section. If the libraries are not installed, follow section 2.3.2 to install them.

Developed by Google, `tensorflow` is a low-level library that allows complex numerical computations to be performed efficiently, especially for training large neural networks. It provides a wide range of tools for building and deploying machine learning models. `keras`, on the other hand, is a high-level neural networks APIs that are built on top of `tensorflow` to simplify the process of building and training deep learning models. The versions of both libraries used for this book are depicted in section 1.4.

CIFAR-10 Dataset

CIFAR-10 dataset will be used in this section as the example, it's a collection of images that are widely used for machine learning or computer vision purposes. It contains 60,000 color images in ten different clusters, each has 32 × 32 pixels. And each cluster has 6,000 random images.

Although this dataset is not real-world pictures and is in very low resolution (32 × 32), it's ideal for learning purposes, because it does not cost high computation resources, users can quickly try different algorithms without a long time (many hours) of training process.

The dataset comes with `keras` library and is divided randomly into a training set of 50,000 and a testing set of 10,000. The ten clusters are evenly and randomly divided into both training and testing sets, meaning each cluster has 5,000 in the training set and 1,000 in the testing set. The ten clusters are airplane, automobile, bird, cat, deer, dog, frog, horse, ship and truck.

See details of CIFAR-10 dataset at:
https://www.cs.toronto.edu/~kriz/cifar.html

Now load the CIFAR-10 dataset,

```
1  import keras
2  from keras.datasets import cifar10
3  (X_train, y_train), (X_test, y_test) =
4                           cifar10.load_data()
5  print("X_train", X_train.shape)
6  print("y_train", y_train.shape)
7  print("X_test", X_test.shape)
8  print("y_test", y_test.shape)
```

The size of the training and testing sets:

```
X_train (50000, 32, 32, 3)
y_train (50000, 1)
X_test (10000, 32, 32, 3)
y_test (10000, 1)
```

The cluster labels are in `y_train` and `y_test`, they look something like:

```
[6, 9, 2, 3, 4, 5, 0, 3 ... ]
```

Each cluster is represented by a number from 0 to 9.

The source codes at *CNNonCIFAR10.py* show 100 random sample images with their labels from the dataset, reference it to see what the images look like.

Build a CNN Model

`keras` defines models in a sequence of layers. First, create a Sequential model, which will make the output of a layer as the input to the next layer:

```
9   cnn_model = Sequential()
```

Add the first convolution and max pooling layers to the `cnn_model`:

```
10   input_shape = X_train.shape[1:]
11   cnn_model.add(Conv2D(128, kernel_size=(3, 3),
12                        input_shape = input_shape,
13                        strides = (1, 1),
14                        padding = "same",
15                        activation = "relu"))
16   cnn_model.add(MaxPooling2D(pool_size = (2, 2)))
```

The convolution layer is added by `Conv2D()` function to the model, the first parameter is the number of features, it's a best practice that the number should be the power of 2, like 4, 8, 16, 32, 64, 128, etc., although this is not required. The second parameter is the size of the features, it's common to use odd numbers, like 1×1, 3×3, 5×5 or 7×7, and so on. As mentioned earlier, only the number and size of the features need to be specified, the contents will be learned by themselves during the training process.

The third parameter is the size of the input image, the fourth and fifth parameters are the stride and padding, which are optional. As explained earlier, `strides = (1, 1)` specifies strides for horizontal and vertical are 1 and 1, meaning the kernel moves one by one in both directions. `padding="same"` specifies the paddings will be added accordingly to make the output the same size as the input. The padding can also be specified as `"valid"`, meaning no padding. Therefore, in this case `strides = (1,1)` and `padding= "same"` will make the output the same size as the input.

The last parameter of `Conv2D()` is the activation function, ReLU function is specified here, see section 7.4.2.4, it will convert all negative values to 0, and linear for positive values.

The input data is color images, so each image has RGB three color channels, as explained earlier, the convolution will be performed on each color channel, and then the result values of the three channels will be summed up to generate the convolution results.

The pooling layer is added to `cnn_model` by `MaxPooling2D()` function in line 16, it performs the max pooling operation on the convolution outputs, and the pool size is specified as 2×2 here.

Then add two more convolution/pooling layers following the first one:

```
17    cnn_model.add(Conv2D(64,
18                              kernel_size=(3, 3),
19                              strides = (1, 1),
20                              padding = "same",
21                              activation = 'relu'))
22    cnn_model.add(MaxPooling2D(pool_size = (2, 2)))
23    cnn_model.add(Dropout(0.25))
24
25    cnn_model.add(Conv2D(32,
26                              kernel_size=(3, 3),
27                              strides = (1, 1),
28                              padding = "same",
29                              activation = 'relu'))
30    cnn_model.add(MaxPooling2D(pool_size = (2, 2)))
31    cnn_model.add(Dropout(0.25))
```

The second layer has 64 features, and the third has 32. The feature size, activation function and pool size are the same as the previous one.

In line 23 and 31, `Dropout()` is added to the model, dropout is a technique used in deep neural networks to prevent overfitting. *Overfitting* occurs when a model is too complex, and it starts to fit to noise in the training data rather than the underlying pattern. Dropout helps prevent this by randomly dropping out some of the neurons in a layer during training, which forces the remaining neurons to learn more robust features that generalize better to new data. Please see materials #18 and #19 in References section at the end of this book for more details about overfitting.

The parameter of `Dropout()` is the percentage of neuron nodes to drop temporarily. Here `0.25` is specified, meaning 25% of nodes will be dropped during the training process.

Now there are three layers of convolution/pooling in `cnn_model`, the first layer has 128 features, the second has 64 and the third has 32. Next is to flatten the output into a 1D array in order to feed into the fully connected neural network.

```
32   cnn_model.add(Flatten())
```

The last one is the fully connected layer, it's basically an artificial neural network, and its input is the output of the flattened data.

```
33   cnn_model.add(Dense(units=256, activation='relu'))
34   cnn_model.add(Dropout(0.5))
35   cnn_model.add(Dense(units=128, activation='relu'))
36   cnn_model.add(Dropout(0.5))
37   cnn_model.add(Dense(units=10, activation='softmax'))
```

`Dense()` function is to specify the fully connected layer. As introduced earlier, an artificial neural network has an input layer, an output layer, and the hidden layer(s). In this case the input layer is the output from the `Flatten()` in line 32, then line 33 and 35 specify two hidden layers with nodes of 256 and 128 respectively, the activation function is ReLU. The output layer has 10 nodes corresponding to the ten clusters of the dataset, the activation function is `softmax`, which is commonly used in the output layer of neural networks for multi-cluster classification problems, where the goal is to predict the probability of each cluster.

Two `Dropout()` layers are added in between to prevent overfitting, in line 34 and 36.

Finally compile the model,

```
38   cnn_model.compile(optimizer='adam',
```

```
39                            loss='categorical_crossentropy',
40                            metrics=['accuracy'])
```

When compiling a `keras` model, we need to specify three key components: the optimizer, the loss function, and the evaluation metrics, these components are specified in the compile method in line 38 to 40.

The *optimizer* determines the algorithm used for optimizing the weights of the neural network during training.

The *loss function* measures how well the model performs during training. The loss function calculates the differences between the predicted output and the actual output for a given input.

The *metrics* evaluate the performance of the model after training. They are similar to the loss function, but they are used for monitoring specific metrics during training, such as accuracy or precision.

`keras` provides a variety of predefined optimizers, loss functions and metrics, the choice of them depends on the specific problems and the characteristics of the data. In this example we choose `adam` as the optimizer, `categorical_crossentropy` as the loss function and `accuracy` as the metrics. See *https://keras.io/api/optimizers/* for details.

The structure of `cnn_model` can be displayed by `summary()` function:

```
41   cnn_model.summary()
```

It's displayed like below:

```
Model: "sequential"
Layer (type)                    Output Shape              Param #
=================================================================
conv2d (Conv2D)                 (None, 32, 32, 128)         3584
max_pooling2d (MaxPooling2D)    (None, 16, 16, 128)            0
conv2d_1 (Conv2D)               (None, 16, 16, 64)         73792
max_pooling2d_1 (MaxPooling2D)  (None, 8, 8, 64)               0
dropout (Dropout)               (None, 8, 8, 64)               0
conv2d_2 (Conv2D)               (None, 8, 8, 32)           18464
max_pooling2d_2 (MaxPooling2D)  (None, 4, 4, 32)               0
dropout_1 (Dropout)             (None, 4, 4, 32)               0
flatten (Flatten)               (None, 512)                    0
dense (Dense)                   (None, 256)               131328
dropout_2 (Dropout)             (None, 256)                    0
```

```
dense_1 (Dense)              (None, 128)              32896
dropout_3 (Dropout)          (None, 128)                  0
dense_2 (Dense)              (None, 10)                1290
============================================================
Total params: 261,354
Trainable params: 261,354
Non-trainable params: 0
```

Each layer is shown in one line in the summary above. The first line is the convolution layer with the name of `conv2d` and the type of `Conv2D`, where the name is unique in the model. The output size of this layer is $(32, 32, 128)$, because the number of kernels is specified as 128, and each image size is 32×32.

The next is the max pooling layer, the kernel size was specified as $(2, 2)$, so the output of this layer becomes $(16, 16, 128)$, which is reduced from the previous layer.

And the same things happen in the next two convolution and max-pooling layers. The dropout layers do not change the size from inputs to outputs.

The flatten layer converts the previous output of $(4, 4, 32)$ into 1D array of size (512), and it becomes the input to the fully connected neural network layer.

The fully connected neural network has two hidden layers of 256 and 128, then the final output is 10, which corresponds to the ten clusters of the dataset.

Before starting the training process, it's necessary to normalize the input data, we use the `StandardScaler()` from `sklearn` library for this purpose:

```
42  from sklearn import preprocessing
43  scaler = preprocessing.StandardScaler()
44  X_train = scaler.fit_transform(
45              X_train.reshape(-1, X_train.shape[-1]))
46              .reshape(X_train.shape)
47  X_test = scaler.transform(
48              X_test.reshape(-1, X_test.shape[-1]))
49              .reshape(X_test.shape)
```

The standard scaler is a data preprocessing technique commonly used to normalize the data before training so that it has a mean of 0 and a standard deviation of 1. By scaling the data to have a common scale, the algorithm can converge faster and perform better, it helps to prevent data with larger scales from dominating the model and allows for easier comparison of data between different features.

Then the training process:

```
50   history = cnn_model.fit(
51           X_train,
52           to_categorical(y_train),
53           batch_size = 128,
54           epochs = 100,
55           verbose = 1,
56           validation_data=(X_test,
57                           to_categorical(y_test)))
```

The one-hot encoding is performed by `to_categorical()` function on `y_train` and `y_test` at line 52 and 57.

This training process could take some time due to the amount of data and the complexity of the model. Depending on the hardware resources, e.g. CPUs vs GUPs, it could take from minutes to hours. Sometimes, if the hardware is not powerful enough, you might get errors in `fit()` process, in this case try to use a subset of the input data, say `X_train[0:5000]` and `y_train[0:5000]`. However, it might eliminate the errors but not do a good job for the training. A powerful machine is needed to perform the training of deep learning projects.

The `fit()` function accepts a validation dataset to evaluate the performance of the training process, we use the testing set for the validation purpose as line 56 and 57 above. The results of the training and validation are shown in Figure 7-48 and Figure 7-49.

The solid lines in both figures are the accuracy and loss of the training set; the dotted lines in both figures are for the validation of the model. And both the solid and dotted lines are moving close when the epoch is increasing, which means the model is appropriately built and trained, without significant overfitting and underfitting.

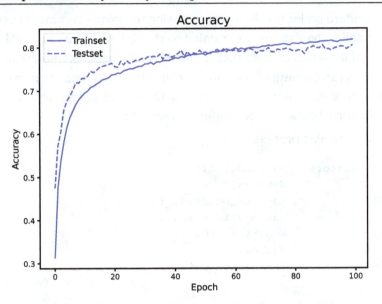

Figure 7-48 Accuracy of Training and Testing Sets

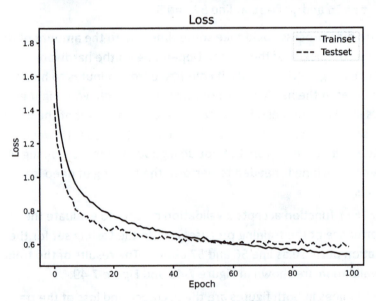

Figure 7-49 Loss of Training and Testing Sets

In most cases the model of this complexity will not get a good result on the first try, it's usually necessary to fine-tune and adjust parameters and try back and forth until reaching a better result, this is a trial-and-error process.

The factors to adjust in the fine-tune process include number of layers, number of features in `conv2d` layer, feature sizes, number of hidden layers in fully connected layer, number of nodes of each layer, etc.

Once the model is trained, it can be saved to a file, and can be loaded later to avoid the long training process next time.

```
58   from tensorflow.keras.models import load_model
59   # Save the model
60   cnn_model.save('cnn_on_cifar-10.h5')
61   # Load the model
62   cnn_model = load_model('cnn_on_cifar-10.h5')
63   cnn_model.summary()
```

There are two ways to evaluate the model. One is to use the `evaluate()` function of the model:

```
64   score = cnn_model.evaluate(X_test,
65                              to_categorical(y_test))
66   print('Test loss:', score[0])
67   print('Test accuracy:', score[1])
```

The result is:

```
Test loss: 0.6104579567909241
Test accuracy: 0.794700026512146
```

Another way to evaluate is to use the metrics as we did in previous sections:

```
68   from sklearn import metrics
69   y_pred = cnn_model.predict(X_test)
70   y_pred = np.argmax(y_pred, axis=1)
71   a_score = metrics.accuracy_score(y_test,y_pred)
72   c_matrix = metrics.confusion_matrix(y_test,y_pred)
73   c_report = metrics.classification_report
74                              (y_test,y_pred)
75   print("Accuracy Score:\n", a_score)
76   print("Confusion matrix:\n", c_matrix)
77   print("Classification Report:\n", c_report)
```

The results are:

```
Accuracy Score:
 0.7947
Confusion matrix:
 [[825  18  32   3  14   2   5   5  73  23]
  [ 11 917   2   3   2   0   5   0  16  44]
  [ 62   0 700  21  86  22  71  23   9   6]
  [ 37   9  71 580  57  96  82  39  16  13]
  [ 18   3  41  21 830   8  34  38   7   0]
  [ 16   3  53 191  50 584  27  63   5   8]
  [  6   6  33  35  24   3 881   5   6   1]
  [ 17   0  42  21  39  20   6 848   2   5]
  [ 38  15   7   5   4   0   4   2 909  16]
  [ 20  59   7   7   0   2   3  11  18 873]]
```

Classification Report:

	precision	recall	f1-score	support
0	0.79	0.82	0.80	1000
1	0.89	0.92	0.90	1000
2	0.71	0.70	0.70	1000
3	0.65	0.58	0.61	1000
4	0.75	0.83	0.79	1000
5	0.79	0.58	0.67	1000
6	0.79	0.88	0.83	1000
7	0.82	0.85	0.83	1000
8	0.86	0.91	0.88	1000
9	0.88	0.87	0.88	1000
accuracy			0.79	10000
macro avg	0.79	0.79	0.79	10000
weighted avg	0.79	0.79	0.79	10000

7.5.7 Popular CNN Architectures

Instead of building them from scratch, there are some popular CNN architectures that can provide a good starting point for developing an effective model for image recognition tasks, and can offer several benefits in terms of accuracy, efficiency, and community support.

The popular CNN architectures have been developed and refined over many years and have shown to be effective in achieving high accuracy. This is especially true for large datasets such as ImageNet, where the top-performing models are typically based on popular CNN architectures. They normally have a large community of users, developers, and researchers who are constantly improving and optimizing the architectures, developing new variants, and sharing best practices. This can provide valuable resources for troubleshooting, optimizing performance, and staying up-to-date with the latest developments.

However, it's important to note that while the popular CNN architectures can be a good starting point, they may not always be the best fit for every application. Depending on the specific task and data, it may be necessary to customize or develop a new architecture to achieve optimal performance.

Here are some of the popular CNN architectures:

- **LeNet-5**: Developed in the 1990s by Yann LeCun, it's one of the earliest CNN architectures and designed for handwritten digit recognition. It consists of seven layers, including three convolutional layers and two fully connected layers.
- **AlexNet**: Developed by Alex Krizhevsky, Ilya Sutskever, and Geoffrey Hinton, this architecture won the 2012 ImageNet competition by a large margin. It has eight layers, including five convolutional layers and three fully connected layers.
- **VGGNet**: Developed by the Visual Geometry Group at the University of Oxford, VGGNet has multiple variants (VGG16, VGG19, etc.) that differ in the number of layers. VGGNet has a very simple architecture, with many small filters in each convolutional layer.
- **Inception**: Developed by Google researchers, this architecture won the 2014 ImageNet competition. It has a unique "Inception" module that allows for parallel processing at different scales.
- **ResNet**: Also developed by Microsoft researchers, ResNet (short for Residual Network) has a very deep architecture, with up to 152 layers. It uses residual connections to address the vanishing gradient problem that can occur in very deep networks.
- **MobileNet**: Developed by Google researchers, MobileNet is designed to be lightweight and efficient, making it well-suited for mobile devices. It uses depth wise separable convolutions to reduce the number of parameters in the network.

In this section we are not going to introduce them one by one, instead, we include a code example for LeNet-5 with MNIST dataset in the Github repository, the source code is in *CNN_LeNet_5.py*.

LeNet was introduced in 1990's by Yann LeCun, it starts the era of Convolutional Neural Networks (CNN), see the original paper called "Gradient-Based Learning Applied to Document Recognition" at material #20 in References section.

The architecture is straightforward and simple, it consists of seven layers which can be summarized as follows:

1. Input layer: The input is designed as grayscale image of size 32×32 pixels, however we use 28×28 from MNIST dataset.
2. Convolutional layer 1: The first convolutional layer has 6 filters of size 3×3 and stride of 1. Each filter produces a 26×26 output feature map.
3. Average pooling layer 1: The output feature maps from the first convolutional layer are fed into an average pooling layer of size 2×2, which reduces the size of the feature maps to 13×13.
4. Convolutional layer 2: The second convolutional layer has 16 filters of size 3×3 and stride of 1. Each filter produces a 11×11 feature map as the output.
5. Average pooling layer 2: The output feature maps from the second convolutional layer are fed into another average pooling layer of size 2×2, which reduces the size of the feature maps to 5×5.
6. Fully connected layer 1: The output feature maps from the second pooling layer are flattened into a vector of size 400 and fed into a fully connected layer with 120 neurons.
7. Fully connected layer 2: The output from the first fully connected layer is fed into another fully connected layer with 84 neurons.
8. Output layer: The output from the second fully connected layer is fed into the final output layer, which has 10 nodes corresponding to the 10 clusters of digits in the MNIST dataset.

LeNet-5 is a reliable and efficient CNN architecture that can be used as a baseline for many image recognition tasks, especially those involving small datasets. If interested, please reference the related resources for other popular CNN architectures.

Index

A

Accuracy, 227

Activation Function, 255, 259

Activation Functions, 259

ANN, 254

Area, 134

Artificial Neural Network, 254

Artificial Neuron, 255

Average Pooling, 287

Axon, 254

B

Background, 170

Back-propagation, 261

BGR, 36, 72, 87

Bitwise Operation, 94

Blend Image, 91

Blur Background, 189

Brightness, 83

C

Callback Function, 54

Canny Edge Detection, 122

Canvas, 43

Cell Body, 254

Centroids, 201

Color Detection, 139

Color Quantization, 208

Contour, 175

Contours, 133

Contrast, 83

Convolutional Layer, 277

Convolutional Neural Network, 276

Crop, 77

Crop Image, 62

D

Decision Boundary, 239, 240

Dendrites, 254

Derivatives, 260

Dilation, 125

Draw Circles, 46, 56

Draw Ellipses, 46

Draw Polygon, 60

Draw Polylines, 46

Draw Rectangles, 46

Draw Shapes, 42

Draw Texts, 48

References

1. *https://docs.opencv.org/4.7.0/index.html*
2. *https://scirp.org/reference/referencespapers.aspx?referenceid=18 34431*
3. *https://lear.inrialpes.fr/people/triggs/pubs/Dalal-cvpr05.pdf*
4. *https://www.merl.com/publications/docs/TR94-03.pdf*
5. *https://learnopencv.com/histogram-of-oriented-gradients/*
6. *https://www.cs.cmu.edu/~efros/courses/LBMV07/Papers/viola-cvpr-01.pdf*
7. *https://www.analyticsvidhya.com/blog/2022/04/object-detection-using-haar-cascade-opencv/*
8. *https://medium.com/analytics-vidhya/haar-cascades-explained-38210e57970d*
9. *https://github.com/tensorflow/models/tree/master/research/dee plab*
10. *http://host.robots.ox.ac.uk/pascal/VOC/*
11. *https://github.com/ayoolaolafenwa/PixelLib*
12. *https://www.researchgate.net/publication/221621494_Support_V ector_Machines_Theory_and_Applications*
13. *https://ieeexplore.ieee.org/document/483329*
14. *https://www.researchgate.net/publication/320465713_A_Compar ative_Study_of_Categorical_Variable_Encoding_Techniques_for_ Neural_Network_Classifiers*
15. *https://arxiv.org/abs/1511.08458*
16. *https://insightsimaging.springeropen.com/articles/10.1007/s1324 4-018-0639-9*

17. *https://arxiv.org/abs/1603.07285*
18. *https://jmlr.org/papers/volume15/srivastava14a/srivastava14a.pdf*
19. *https://www.researchgate.net/publication/331677125_An_Overview_of_Overfitting_and_its_Solutions*
20. *http://yann.lecun.com/exdb/publis/pdf/lecun-01a.pdf*

About the Author

James Chen, a highly accomplished IT professional with a solid academic background, holds a degree from Tsinghua University, one of China's most prestigious universities, and has developed a deep understanding of computer science theory and practices. With his extensive technical background, James has played key roles in designing and developing cutting-edge software solutions for a variety of industries including technology, financial, healthcare, e-commerce, etc. He has been working with all aspects of system design and development and actively contributed as the lead implementer of complex multi-clients and multi-tiered systems such as web systems, traditional n-tiered systems, mobile applications, and mixed software/hardware systems. He has a talent for identifying key business problems and designing customized solutions that are both efficient and effective.

His wide-ranging technical interests led him to the emerging fields of computer vision and machine learning since 2016, James has a passion for artificial intelligence and has honed his skills in this area through a combination of academic study and practical experiences. He has developed an in-depth understanding of the latest tools and techniques in computer vision and machine learning and is always looking for new ways to apply this knowledge to real-world problems.

www.ingramcontent.com/pod-product-compliance
Lightning Source LLC
Chambersburg PA
CBHW071232050326
40690CB00011B/2090